MILLER'S

collecting
vinyl

John Stanley

French mime artist Marcel Marceau, who made an album with 19 minutes of silence on each side, plus two minutes of clapping!

Miller's Collecting Vinyl
John Stanley

To my wife Janis for her unfailing support

First published in Great Britain in 2002 by Miller's, an imprint of Octopus Publishing Group Ltd, 2–4 Heron Quays, London, E14 4JP

Miller's is a registered trademark of Octopus Publishing Group Ltd

© 2002 Octopus Publishing Group Ltd
Reprinted 2003

ISBN 1 84000 511 4

Commissioning Editor	Anna Sanderson
Executive Art Editor	Rhonda Fisher
Project Editor	Emily Anderson
Page Design	Victoria Bevan, Colin Goody
Jacket Design	Colin Goody
Editor	Claire Musters
Proofreader	Miranda Stonor
Indexer	Sue Farr
Production	Angela Couchman
Special Photography	Steve Tanner

A CIP catalogue record for this book is available from the British Library

Set in Trade Gothic & Antique Olive East
Printed and bound by Mladinska knjiga tiskarna d.d., Slovenia

Half-Title: Old Grey Whistle Test badge, given only to performers on the TV show

collecting
vinyl

John Stanley

CONTENTS

Boxed sets with booklets and artists' images on the label are nothing new but, despite its age, this important 1937 Mahler recording is worth just a sixth of the 1969 L.S.O. *Tommy* set.

INTRODUCTION TO VINYL

Music is the landscape to our lives. For me, Beach Boys songs mean long 1960s journeys to the Scottish Isles in my black Cooper S, while Fleetwood Mac conjures up memories of sun-drenched drives back from studios through Californian canyons. It is definitely true that good music can return you to a time, person, or situation quicker than any novel or movie can. Among your box of neglected records is an artist and/or music style that once spoke for you, revealing how you felt, and what you stood for. Most potential record collectors aren't even aware they qualify as such. For example, at a major London record fair I was once pushed aside by two well-groomed ladies in pursuit of Queen material. One explained that they weren't record collectors but Freddie Mercury fans, yet the knowledge they exchanged with the stallholder was possibly more detailed than some EMI staff could muster.

A Growing Market

You may not be curious about whether your box of old discs is worth anything, and certainly don't wish to don the metaphoric anorak to become an obsessive collector, yet you know all the words to key songs in your heart and the career details of those you followed as a teenager. With so many people in the same position this has caused a stunning explosion in collecting vinyl. Thanks to sophisticated collectors' magazines, websites, and even fairs, thousands of people are now finding it easy to revisit their golden eras of music, and to discover other recordings by similar artists that they had no idea existed at the time. The fact that there are monetary values attached is often largely irrelevant. These are people who love music, and now turn the pages of *Record Collector* or *Goldmine* spotting record after record they have, or always meant to buy. When the records in most people's collections were new there was very little information available apart from the publication of a chart. In Rock & Roll's time that meant ordering and waiting perhaps weeks for any record outside chart status, without a chance to hear it first. Even as late as the 1970s and '80s tapping into a simple website to capture a full biography, discography, and method of obtaining the music would have seemed nothing more than a pipe dream. Record collecting is currently booming because there is now the means to shop globally from your home, to explore the music you once loved, and search out its influences and imitators, foreign pressings, and limited editions.

This book aims to introduce some of the collecting possibilities from every strand of vinyl. Within the artists and prices mentioned we make no pretences at representing the breadth available (indeed the prices that are given are generally for the more eye-catching examples), but over the course of these pages you will discover that stardom does not automatically mean value – frequently quite the reverse. Almost every page is filled with fresh ideas for collecting – there are just so many themes beyond the recorded material of a single star, such as the output of a particular record company dealing in your kind of music, the work of a particular composer, or record producer, or the soundtracks of a movie director, Television's Sci-Fi output, or the fumbling singles of stars before they were famous. There are the complex daisy chains of collectable styles that represent Reggae, Punk, and Jazz, which are all touched on in this book to give you insight into their credentials, representative artists, values, and the ones to watch. The hunt for chosen target records is the essence of a collector's pursuit but, unlike other forms of collecting, records also bring secondary excitement through their music. Not only do you build up a fascinating, and perhaps very valuable, collection but you also dramatically widen your knowledge of the artist, the music, the songwriters, the producers, and the musical roots too.

I have been lucky enough to have worked with, or alongside, a great many leading figures in this book, watching while their mighty records have been born, staged, filmed, and just like in any other industry the mystique is missing when on the inside. Yet backstage, on aircraft, in clubs, or hotel rooms, even the superstar's unguarded conversations are never far from favourite records and musical discoveries. For example, during most of a bleak Ford Transit journey from London to North Wales for a gig with Long John Baldrey, the keyboard player huddled in the back with a scarf wrapped around his face drafting lists of his record collection in the tiniest of handwritings. His name changed to Elton John, and his fortunes also improved, but the enthusiasm of his record collecting continued for decades until it was finally auctioned for charity in the 1990s.

A Brief History

So when did it all start? A few people in Britain were collecting American Dixie and Swing Band 78's during the 1940s, following their war-time exposure, and, as you'll discover later, the rapid demise of Big Bands led to many ex-band singers becoming soloists. This extended collectors' interest to the likes of Sinatra and Crosby, and other, more Blues-influenced, figures such as Jimmy Rushing. In the USA Jazz turned modern, and frustrated UK fans eager to own the new sounds of John Coltrane and Charlie Parker began a modest trade in specialist shops. However, the real impetus occurred during the 1950s with a sequence of three events. First the industry began transferring its single format from bulky and vulnerable 78's to 45's. Then Rock & Roll exploded, fanning the demand – British charts witnessed Elvis and others, but critics were fierce and neither stores nor radio serviced more than the big chart singles. In the USA Presley returned from military duty to a 1960s initially awash with lightweight US Pop, followed by the invasion of The Beatles. All this left UK Rock & Roll fans with no new product reaching them, which led fans to order from emerging specialist record shops, meet weekly at city market stalls, and place personal adverts in the uninspired music papers.

Throughout the 1960s and '70s the groundswell grew, first with R&B in fashion, and then British Beat music. In 1979 an unlikely hero crystallized UK record collecting – Johnny Dean. He had started publishing monthly reprints of the early '60s Beatles fan magazine, in which he slipped additional free sheets of small adverts. Within six months the demand for record adverts, not just from The Beatles, was so great that it became an independent publication in March 1980 and *Record Collector* was born. *Record Mart*, *Record Mirror*, and, to a lesser extent, *Melody Maker*, had provided a partial mail-order route, but suddenly the general public and dealers had a complete means of communication, and specialist stores took to promoting themselves in the same magazine. This took record collecting from an underground movement to a national, and then international, pastime. The magazine has grown sevenfold and, as each year passes, so more and more target artists are fazed into the collectors' circle. The Beatles are far and away the world's most collectable band, with extraordinary prices for their rarer items, such as a particular pressing with a distinct logo, credit, sleeve construction, or photo. Being the most collectable act in the world naturally heightens all their values disproportionately, but the crazy figure paid for a cardboard flap on the sleeve, or a tiny music publishing credit change, is in fact a physical clue to the specific generation of a record pressing.

Everyone understands what a book with "First Edition" on it means, but with records no such definition is printed so packaging or credit detailing are the only benchmarks. After The Beatles, Elvis Presley is the global collectors' number two, with a wide range of values to match his career diversity. His landmark Rock & Roll records are clearly important, as are many of his film soundtracks – which were actually an embarrassment for many true Rock fans. This is where the subjectivity of record collecting clashes head-on with your personal valuation of the music itself. Not only can a terrible record go for crazy money if two fans are fighting over it at an auction, scarcity is another valuation criterion that bears great influence. For example, a global smash from Michael Jackson, such as *Thriller*, is currently £8, while the relatively unknown single *Baby I've Got News for You*, by Miller, is £250. The reason for this is that *Thriller* rightly sold so many copies that there is absolutely no shortage of copies available, while lesser-known bands with unsuccessful records actually have scarcity value built in by their very failure. This makes the occasional forgotten and failed record worth a lot of money.

Another factor to grasp is the relationship between the two principle trading partners of recorded music – the United States and the UK. The Michael Jackson situation of "smash hit = no value" may apply in one country and yet utterly fail in the other, conversely raising the same title's worth in that one nation. Unfortunately small packaging details will identify the origin of each pressing, so you can't just buy up armfuls in the country of surplus and sell them in the other! National tastes also deeply affect some records. Humour – which at one time in the US virtually relied on vinyl while broadcasters were suppressing modern comedians – found very few fans in the UK. With the exceptions of Peter Sellers (thanks to movies), certain stage performers like Flanders and Swann (thanks to Broadway exposure), and David Frost (thanks to a US TV series), UK comedy had a similar problem when trying to appeal to collectors in the USA.

Curiously, three of America's music forms have actually been granted more reverence in foreign lands than on home soil. Modern Jazz players' missions were understood much more readily in Europe than in the USA, and these

The centres of 7" singles changed towards the end of the 1950s from triangular to circular, which makes the triangles more desirable today. Both were designed to be popped out for jukebox use and some have been replaced by temporary centres; these records still work but are worth less without the original centre.

appreciative fans helped ignite and confirm many bands' crusades for something new in the Jazz world to replace the tired and predictable crowd-pleasing ways of the Big Bands. Both New Age and, to a lesser extent, Country were also beneficiaries of European enthusiasm – Britain, and particularly Germany, were keen to hear, even replicate, American Country while New Age music sat very comfortably beside existing European chamber performances as well as the more ethereal strands of Celtic Pop like Clannad, Enya, or Iona. In fact, the German ECM label was itself responsible for commissioning many excellent New Age-style albums.

Getting Started

The sheer density of issues over what's valuable or worthless should not overwhelm you as they really only exist in guidebooks, or perhaps for general vinyl traders where all aspects of the music are being embraced at once. For anyone just entering the world of vinyl collecting, the only market conditions that count are those for your chosen style of music, so you can ignore everything else.

Your most valuable aide to successful collecting is knowledge – something you will already have in part just from enjoying your favoured brand of music. Let's take as an example Reggae music – you've danced to it many times without knowing the record details, and Bob Marley is perhaps your one frame of reference, but otherwise you don't know where to start. Well, begin with the music that you do know and log onto a good music reference website, such as www.allmusic.com, and call up "Bob Marley". This will give you a biography, the eras in which he was active, what he played, links to any movies he was associated with, pages of record details, other people's discs he's appeared on, and some individual track highlights. There are over 300 recordings listed here (each with full production/track details), a great many of which are much later CD compilations – now you are beginning to get to know more about the type of Reggae he produced. For a wider search, below his name are search fields for each style of Reggae he performed – Roots Reggae, Jamaica, Rocksteady, Ska, Caribbean, and Political Reggae. Click on one, such as Political Reggae, and you are presented with a definition, its two closest musical relations (here, Rocksteady and Ska), a list of important political LPs, and the key artists in this field. If you want a clearer understanding of who falls under Ska, Reggae, Rocksteady, Dub, and Lovers' Rock styles you can go back to the Marley site and click on "Music Map" to get a timeline of which movement flowed into what – again including the key artists for each. Within maybe half an hour you will actually know some of the pivotal artists and records. Such websites are not specifically aimed at record collectors, but rather to direct-selling of currently available CDs. However, they are great places to start, to get the basic information that you can then build on. A single, quality reference book on Reggae, such as the excellent *Rough Guide* by Steve Barrows and Peter Dalton (*see* page 226), will then be invaluable and, with the knowledge that you have picked up, you will be able to read it with confidence. For example, if you have found out that your main interest lies in Ska, you can go straight to the clearly marked sections on that subject and drink in all the fascinating detail, such as which records prompted the style, the producers' significance, and, for instance, if your chosen style was politically motivated what was the grievance.

Hunting Out Vinyl Records

Once you have read around the subject and decided what type of music you want to collect, you will then need to start looking for specific records. The nuances concerning values may alarm you, but a current copy of the *Record Collector* magazine will give you their master reference index of all back issues and their subjects. Pick and order the one(s) within your chosen area and you'll learn which are the dominant collectables, names, records, and significant packaging details.

There is, of course, the matter of where to look for the records themselves, which, as a result of the surge in vinyl collecting, has become more of a challenge. In earlier times junk shops and car boot sales were awash with neglected vinyl that few even knew how to price, but things have now changed. Finds can still be achieved using this route but it depends on the type of music you are hunting, and record condition always remains vital. Both sides of the Atlantic are strewn with specialist dealers that are usually experts in a very specific field – such as a particular strand of Jazz, Christian music, very precise aspects of Punk, or Doo Wop, and once you strike up contact with one compatible to your interest then you will have acquired an invaluable human search engine. Two ways of

Until the end of the 1960s record sleeves were generally covered with a thin protective lamination and the front secured with a folded flap, as shown above; all later records were flapped internally.

encountering specialist dealers are either through the local telephone book, or via the growing circuit of record fairs, which are great gatherings of individual dealers. For example there is an annual Music Fair at London's Olympia, with the largest selection of vinyl and memorabilia on sale in the UK, and traders from all around the world. Until the mid-1980s these were relatively rare but today organizations like VIP-24 (www.vip-24.com) are continuously arranging regional fairs. Such events in the UK or USA are regularly advertised within the collectors' magazines. Less energetic ways to hunt are through the extensive classified advertisements in the record collector magazines, which boast pages of dealer lists, or through the thousands of individual websites. Auction houses also offer some opportunities, with the massive US website version, www.ebay.com, perhaps the most substantial.

This release has no particular value, and no chart history, but collectors do specialize in the output of single labels and this one is clearly marked "001, Jive Records", which means it is the very first release of a now massive organization.

This 1986 recording came with a press release from a leading PR company stating: "Although Chase has only been with us since January 8th, at 6:34pm, we expect his career to take off quickly, and can guarantee a Number One single by the year 2000. We welcome him to LA ... and the World. A commemoration of the PR's newborn son."

Collecting Areas

There is a general perception that certain elements of The Beatles' and Elvis Presley's catalogues are veritable gold mines, and early Jazz and Rock & Roll are also desirable, but what else is revered? Many Blues recordings are important and constantly high in value – another case of research seriously enriching the collector – plus R&B, Soul, and Hit Paraders (an infectious, innocent era of charts stars that fell between the Jazz times and Rock & Roll – see pages 39–43). However, sometimes the delights of collecting are not about investments and gains but simply the hunting down and enjoyment of owning collections. How about gathering together all the winners of the Eurovision Song Contest or the huge assortment of individuals with recorded obsessions about Sci-Fi? I've discovered a personal favourite in the *Best of Marcel Marceao* (sic) – an album celebrating the awesome skills of the legendary French mime artist, which naturally features 19 minutes of recorded silence on each side plus two minutes of audience appreciation! Some collectors feature all the releases from a particular label, which could be an extremely expensive collection to create, so why not begin a collection with a younger label like Jive? Serious collectors dream of gathering in all the releases from London Records – the UK outlet for many of the significant '50s and '60s singles, and Jazz aficionados compete to own the stunning material and packaging of the Blue Note label. Again a good list of artists from any specific label can easily be found on the www.allmusic.com website.

A very cheap form of collecting, which gives you vast choices and introduces you to a wide range of artists, is gathering together compilations. These are currently unloved across most countries so the prices are nice and low. Start by gathering together all the available compilations on the type of music you are interested in and you'll soon be able to decide in which artist. or specific area, you wish to specialize.

Sometimes albums that were initially treated as virtual background music, such as Lounge or Exotica, grow in status and value because of cover artwork, or due to genuine shifts in public taste. For art gallery-quality sleeve graphics certain Jazz periods are in a league of their own as rivals hired serious design talent in order to outstrip one another. (Blue Note records are again among the most respected.) Beyond these options and criteria there is another world, in which the music doesn't really matter but the period covers do. Plenty

Officially a promo-only record, this 1964 interview disc provides firsthand material from The Beatles and is valued at around $10. The same record, but with white labels and blue print, commands $10,000.

After a five year lay-off Peter Hammill's Prog Rock band Van der Graaf Generator issued VIP guests at their Paris premiere with these press packs. They feature press cuttings, history, and photos, along with handwritten white-label copies. These are valuable only to fans of the group.

of Easy Listening covers with 1950s American lifestyle images are highly collectable, as are celebrity recordings for the same reason. The British *Top of the Pops* budget LPs, featuring cover recordings of hits of the day, are highly sought after purely because of the model girls dressed in nostalgic floppy hats, bikinis, and hot pants – the records themselves were never considered quality items.

There are similar appeals for television-related records, with a surprising number of collecting options. Popular and quite valuable are the LPs surrounding adventure series like *The Avengers*, *Danger Man*, and *The Prisoner*, and many of the much-loved westerns such as *Bonanza* and *Maverick*, while Sci-Fi cults like *Star Trek*, *Dr. Who*, and *Thunderbirds* have committed followers. When you consider the enormous fan base Cliff Richard enjoys – and you add in the army of *Thunderbird* fanatics – it's not hard to understand why the EP *Thunderbirds Are Go* by Cliff Richard and The Shadows is so sought after that it has recently doubled in value. Just a single TV series can present a collectors' theme – apart from Cliff's EP, *Thunderbirds* stories were the subject of 7 LPs and 37 EP releases in just three years, and four different bands produced themed song records. For those with less critical ears almost every TV soap star and entertainer managed to make records, as indeed did a high proportion of radio DJs.

For many the act of collecting is simply fun, and frequently the temptation is to select a really offbeat theme. At its most extreme there is a very active world collecting what one website refers to as "Crap Records". Obviously no one makes a deliberately bad record but certainly they do exist – and often they are accidentally very funny. Two gloriously bizarre yet fascinating books embracing this genre are *Incredibly Strange Music Vols. I & II*, within which are detailed out-of-tune sitars playing the *Sound of Music*, a psychopath's *Born to Trouble*, and a spoken LP homage to Chicago's O'Hare airport. If you want to create both an unusual and quirky collection, there is definitely a lot out there to choose from!

Collecting as a Journey

Jazz was not only the initial impetus for record collecting, it is probably the most absorbing, which is why it is being used here as an example of how collecting vinyl records can take you on a fascinating journey. If you have a hunger to tackle a real challenge – within a full century of changing musical styles – then Jazz would be perfect. By the end you will have not only discovered the work of a distinguished list of talent, but also have been drawn into the constantly changing social conditions that the differing strands of Jazz highlight.

Like Blues, Folk, and some Country, Jazz mirrored real feelings and attitudes, and many parallels exist with the art and Classical music worlds. Schoenberg and the Atonal School deliberately moved the Classical gateposts as an extreme reaction to so much sugar-coated Romanticism, intending to clear out audiences that were not prepared to face something new. In art, following the soft lines of the Impressionist Movement, some painters chose to look at

In the 1950s it was not strange to have more than one version of a song in the charts simultaneously but it was rare in the 1970s. Here is a nearly complete set of chart-making versions of the song *Since You've Been Gone* (the missing one is by Head East), together with the extremely rare original songwriter's Abbey Road Studios acetate of the same tune.

the world through the more angular and fractured viewpoint of Cubism. And so it was with Jazz in the 1940s, following the over-exposure of sweet Big Band Jazz – the backbone of escapist entertainment and nationalism throughout World War II. Increasingly arranged and choreographed, the essence of spontaneity and expression was being drained from Jazz, so the intellectual heart of Jazz reacted and Experimental Jazz was born.

Initially so extreme some challenged if it actually qualified as "music", Jazz is a bewildering genre to the outsider. Yet if you start a Jazz collection and research from this point then the extreme forays into Free Jazz will make perfect sense, as you'll see them for what they were intended to be. You can then also embrace the subtle but important changes that were put into the less hostile Avant-Garde – a short journey similarly made by many of the key Free Jazz recording artists – and you will also inadvertently absorb a prodigy of Bebop. At this point you'll be standing on the threshold of what was an irresistible temptation for many Jazz musicians who were envious of the 1970s Rock elite. Rock stars wanted to flaunt "musical credentials" for credibility, while Jazz musicians dreamed of a stadium audience of 50,000 and a Rock Star pay cheque – Jazz Fusion was the inevitable outcome.

The main point to make is that once you have chosen the starting point for your vinyl collection – and by necessity embarked on some basic research – you will have begun a truly rewarding adventure that offers you challenges, music, and modern history. Whether you are driven by a passion for a style of music, the distinctive talents of a particular group, individual, composer, or movie director, building a related vinyl collection will place you much closer to your area of interest.

HOW TO USE THIS BOOK

With such a diversity of subject matter, values, and even reasons to collect, a single guidebook inevitably cannot do more than introduce you to this fascinating world. Over the following pages the types of music are divided up into suitable family clusters to offer you examples of the various collectable themes. However, to cover such a huge range of material the following conventions have been used:

Suggested Strands

These represent illustrations of the kind of collecting themes possible for each type of music, but, ultimately, you are only limited by your imagination. Under Pop Groups, for instance, you will find Instrumentals – particularly popular in the late '50s with the likes of Duane Eddy and UK domestic stars like The Shadows and Bert Weedon, and Bubblegum – which includes The Monkees, The Osmonds, and a host of teen Pop idols. Status bands like The Rolling Stones, The Kinks, ABBA, and Queen are grouped together, and there is also a catch-all "General Groups" to give you a feel for the prospects of The Hollies, Dave Clark Five, The Spencer Davis Group, and The Tremeloes. The heading "Hidden Talents" encompasses very collectable failed records by unfamiliar bands who, in time, became hugely famous, and the huge jump in value for unknown groups' singles that never hit the spotlight but featured a famous session player, like Jimmy Page.

Rising Stars

These are our tips on artists that are showing signs of growth in value. There may be a dependence on one nation for that status (rather than worldwide), but if your interest in collecting is towards that particular category of music then it is worth taking a closer look at the acts listed here. Remember that sometimes it is only LPs – or maybe just singles – that are pushing prices upwards. You should certainly never assume that everything by any one artist is a good investment, as even the biggest of names can list rock-bottom prices for some records.

Average Record Cost

The scale of prices you are likely to meet within each genre of music has been indicated using a star rating system. Naturally the more extreme collectables are often mentioned in these sections, which superficially points to permanently high group costs. However, for every high figure there are thousands of records that are available for literally loose change. This therefore ridicules any attempts at fixed price categories. So this star system is a personal judgement, due in part to the discs featured, and covers the more conspicuously expensive as well as a wider spread of those of more average prices. Thus ✰ represents anything under around £15 ($20), ✰✰ is roughly £15–50 ($20–70), ✰✰✰ £50–100 ($70–140), ✰✰✰✰ £100–150 ($140–200), and the rare ✰✰✰✰✰ stars are worth the big money. To try and indicate the big value records we have placed a ★ wherever a record is currently listed at three figures or more in value. This may be US dollars or pounds sterling, depending on the territory in which it is prized.

Listings and Record Types

Within each subsection we also provide listings to give you a flavour of the records available. Any guide to a technology-based product spanning decades inevitably traverses a number of formats, and we have used the following simple terms within the listings: LP incorporates standard 12" albums, 10" LPs, and, where appropriate, broadcast programme discs. Singles embrace the conventional 45's, 12" singles, and older 78' products. EPs (Extended Play), which were introduced in the 1950s and '60s, are simply as stated.

Other Points

- There are infrequent references to matrix numbers, which are the designated identity for a record. These occasionally have a differing prefix to denote a slight change (such as when a record is a re-release).

- With such a truly international subject there are inevitably going to be some name duplications – there are, for instance, multiple subsections named "First Class". However, the nature of the music being discussed should clarify any duplication issues.

- A variety of specialized pressings are mentioned – all of which are defined in the glossary on page 224.

- The Index at the back of the book can be used to locate a particular artist or group if you are unsure to which musical genre they belong.

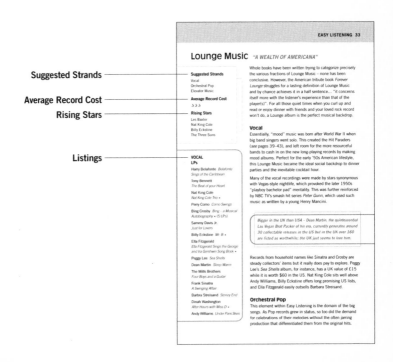

Suggested Strands ——

Average Record Cost ——

Rising Stars ——

Listings ——

EASY LISTENING 33

Lounge Music *"A WEALTH OF AMERICANA"*

Suggested Strands
Vocal
Orchestral Pop
Elevator Music

Average Record Cost
♪ ♪ ♪

Rising Stars
Les Baxter
Nat King Cole
Billy Eckstine
The Three Suns

VOCAL
LPs
Harry Belafonte *Belafonte Sings of the Caribbean*
Tony Bennett *The Beat of your Heart*
Nat King Cole *Nat King Cole Trio* ◆
Perry Como *Como Swings*
Bing Crosby *Bing . . a Musical Autobiography* ◆ (5 LPs)
Sammy Davis Jr. *Just for Lovers*
Billy Eckstine *Mr. B* ◆
Ella Fitzgerald *Ella Fitzgerald Sings the George and Ira Gershwin Song Book* ◆
Peggy Lee *Sea Shells*
Dean Martin *Sleep Warm*
The Mills Brothers *Four Boys and a Guitar*
Frank Sinatra *A Swinging Affair*
Barbra Streisand *Stoney End*
Dinah Washington *After Hours with Miss D* ◆
Andy Williams *Under Paris Skies*

Whole books have been written trying to categorize precisely the various fractions of Lounge Music – none has been conclusive. However, the American tribute book *Forever Lounge* struggles for a lasting definition of Lounge Music and by chance achieves it in a half sentence... "it concerns itself more with the listener's experience than that of the player(s)". For all those quiet times when you curl up and read or enjoy dinner with friends and your loved rock record won't do, a Lounge album is the perfect musical backdrop.

Vocal
Essentially, "mood" music was born after World War II when big band singers went solo. This created the Hit Paraders (see pages 39–43), and left room for the more resourceful bands to cash in on the new long-playing records by making mood albums. Perfect for the early '50s American lifestyle, this Lounge Music became the ideal social backdrop to dinner parties and the inevitable cocktail hour.

Many of the vocal recordings were made by stars synonymous with Vegas-style nightlife, which provoked the later 1950s "playboy bachelor pad" mentality. This was further reinforced by NBC TV's smash hit series *Peter Gunn*, which used such music as written by a young Henry Mancini.

Bigger in the UK than USA – Dean Martin, the quintessential Las Vegas Brat Packer of his era, currently generates around 30 collectable releases in the US but in the UK over 160 are listed as worthwhile; the UK just seems to love him.

Records from household names like Sinatra and Crosby are steady collectors' items but it really does pay to explore. Peggy Lee's *Sea Shells* album, for instance, has a UK value of £15 while it is worth $60 in the US. Nat King Cole sits well above Andy Williams, Billy Eckstine offers long promising US lists, and Ella Fitzgerald easily outsells Barbara Streisand.

Orchestral Pop
This element within Easy Listening is the domain of the big songs. As Pop records grew in status, so too did the demand for celebrations of their melodies without the often jarring production that differentiated them from the original hits.

PRICES AND CONDITION

Record Prices

The various price guidebooks listed in the bibliography (*see* pages 226–227) represent the only formalized massed price structures but, as each reminds you, they are purely indicators. Values of any collectable are related to two or more people seeking the same item – a situation governed by chance, an artist's death, an anniversary, or simply fashion. Some published lists deliberately undervalue rather than exaggerate, and all are inevitably out-of-date by the very nature of publication processes. However, they are all ideal barometers of fashions and trends, and comparisons between UK and US volumes provide fascinating insight.

The major cautions are that the headline prices are for absolutely perfect examples – which are very rare. You should never, never get carried away with apparent matches of a title in your hand and some dream price tag – there will be a particular reason for the high value and your version of the same record will probably not boast the same feature. As with most collectable trading, a dealer's selling price is very different from what they will buy in for, and an interesting experiment by a vinyl collectors' magazine underlines this point: they took four relatively modest records with a combined "list" value of £115 to well-known dealers, offering them for sale. The best offer amounted to £41.50, which is why direct-selling from collector to collector via the magazines or through Internet auctions is rising in popularity, allowing collectors to bypass dealers.

Record Grading

With such a high proportion of vinyl-collecting linked to remote purchases – be it classified advertising, calls to dealers, or website purchases – it is critical to understand fully the generally accepted shorthand for the condition of a record. The UK and American grading systems run fairly parallel, except that the UK grants additional lower category status. Before parting with any money make sure there is a money-back fail-safe against your discovering the record is not the exact grade it claims to be. You should be aware that dealers frequently grade discs and sleeves independently, and their adverts may often use abbreviations for the terms below:

Mint These must be absolutely perfect, maybe even unplayed, and are therefore in reality quite rare. LPs in this category might still be sealed up. However, a word of warning – sometimes unofficially retro-sealed records aren't quite what they appear, so be careful if you are suddenly asked to pay big money for a rare "unopened" recording. Inevitably most of the recognition clues are concealed inside.

Near-Mint For all practical purposes this is what dealers use as their top grade category. There should be no, or only very slight, signs of play and none that affects the sound reproduction. Sleeves should not be marked or damaged in any way – effectively, it should be as if you had just bought the record new and unwrapped it for the first time.

Very Good+ or Excellent There should only be very superficial marks on these, and absolutely none that affects performance. Slight blemishes on the label are passable but there should be no warping. Covers should again only have superficial markings – no splits or punched holes (these denote a discontinued record). The price of such records is usually 50 per cent of near-mint examples. This category is the prime candidate for descriptive abuse as it represents the most plausible high prices.

Very Good Within this category surface scratches begin to be heard during quiet passages on the record. Sleeves or labels may have a handwritten name or sticker on them. You might just be able to feel the worst surface scratches with your fingernails.

Good These will still play without jumping but surface noises affect reproduction and the record sleeves might have amateur repairs with tape or discolouring. Only buy at this level if you really need an example for your collection and plan to upgrade as soon as you are able to find a better copy. Approximately fetching 10–15 per cent of near-mint prices, this is roughly the condition-level found in most careful households.

Fair These are just playable but may very well jump or stick through surface damage. The record covers will have tears or marks on them.

Poor These records barely play because of the levels of, inevitably noisy, damage and parts of the packaging are often damaged or simply missing. Buy only if a particular example is super-rare or particularly desired.

Bad Records in this category will be cracked or unplayable and will also have a defaced or split sleeve that is barely able to house the disc. It is really not worth buying records in this state.

Britain's *Record Collector* magazine publishes a "Grading Ready Reckoner" table that lays out the relative values of records from £2 to £1,000 (in Mint condition) and then reveals their proportionate values in each of the other gradings. As a single example: a £50 Mint disc would be worth £40 in Excellent, £25 in Very Good, £15 in Good, £8 in Fair, £4 in Poor, and just £1 for plain Bad.

TYPES OF RECORDS

It is the casualties of technology that fuel collecting, whether in the form of classic cars, sewing machines, clocks, or, in this case, records. If every piece of music released had appeared on exactly the same device then there simply wouldn't be need for a record-collecting world. Though smash hits, stars, and powerful memories are strong collecting motivations, it's definitely the format and age of the carrier that provides the status and value of an item.

Used as production references, just a few acetate discs are cut by studios using soft lacquer. Some gems contain material that doesn't make it to final releases, and are worth considerably more as a result. The decade between these two examples reveals how EMI Studios switched to the name Abbey Road.

Sound Reproduction

Before describing the individual formats it's worth discussing briefly the types of sound reproduction. For the first 50 years or so mono was the only option, and it offered the complete audio image from a single speaker. With nothing to compare it with, its limitations were accepted, and for touring big bands it allowed their concerts to appear even more powerful. The crossover period towards stereo has brought the last-ever monos a certain collectors' elitism. The 7" single remained in mono well into the 1960s as teenagers' home equipment was still mono-orientated. Stereo had been evolving before World War II, but it didn't catch on until the advent of vinyl LPs, and was first exhibited publicly in 1957. It quickly became the norm for albums, and later singles, and remains to this day an industry standard. For an initial period from the mid-'60s companies rummaged through their mono bestsellers, crudely attempting phoney stereo by remixing masters, but the results pleased no one. The only other challenge to the stereo format was quadrophonic, which was fanned by hopeful hi-fi manufacturers in the 1970s looking for another lucrative hardware wave. It coincided with the indulgences of Prog Rock concept LPs, filled with colour and effects, such as Pink Floyd's *Dark Side of the Moon*. Expensive kit, and finding room space for four speakers, made sure the fashion was very shortlived.

Re-issues and Pressings

Another element of an innocent-looking disc that preoccupies collectors is whether it's an original or a re-issue. Essentially, originals are perfectly straightforward record releases, but record companies are basically traders and from time to time make commercial decisions on old master tapes. Perhaps an old signing becomes a big name with a rival company – so they may decide to re-issue their material to cash in on this. Or maybe a recent record launch was inconclusive so they re-release to try again. In either case first releases, the "originals", will be of higher value than "re-releases", even though they are ostensibly identical products. This is where the printing, logo positioning, and small print matter becomes critical. Quite separately, record companies also began licensing their material to third parties, which meant that a lot of rare and desirable music reappeared that often looked superficially like the originals.

Another nuance that affects value and frequently causes disappointments is the number of pressings. Important records that sell and sell are sometimes re-pressed many times to meet the demands, and again it's the first ones that rise the most in value. This can be a source of frustration to new collectors who believe they own the genuine article but eventually find out that they actually have a later pressing that is worthless. As is discussed later, The Beatles' products best highlight this, as there are so many generations of "pressings" involved. Detailed research on the packaging provides the clues, although sometimes it is a more obvious, radical shade change in the sleeve colours, or missing first pressing luxuries such as lyric sheets or free posters,which will act as the tell-tale signs.

In a show-business world excessive promotional efforts are inevitable, and the record industry never wasted any moment to use records in fresh ways. Limited editions were obvious, coloured vinyl stemmed right back to early 45's, picture discs could be conventional or fabricated in an appropriate shape, and there were also transparent discs and flexi-discs (often magazine freebies). Interview or performance LPs for radio use and advance DJ pressings were also packaged in various ways to look exclusive and just-off-the-press. All these generate keen collectors' interest.

The Formats

78rpm Single Everyone's vision of an "old record" is a 78'. These were mostly 10" discs, usually manufactured in a quite brittle substance called shellac, and they were universally used until the emergence of the vinyl 45'. Equivalents to an album were stoutly constructed sets of 78's. Despite their appearance very few are actually worth collecting – other than for their music's worth – with the only exception being late '50s Jazz and Rock & Roll records, which represent the last examples released simultaneously with modern vinyl 45's. Certain countries like Germany have pockets of devoted 78' collectors.

45rpm Single This is definitely the modern classic – 7" vinyl was first introduced in the USA in 1949, then to the UK in the early '50s, and had completely replaced the 78' format by 1961. Much more durable than the shellac 78's, 45's quickly became everyone's favourites until record companies forcefed CD equivalents from the late 1980s. However, there are still a number of UK independent record companies that produce vinyl 45's today. Coloured vinyl added to the 45's repertoire and picture bags brought extra glamour – and frequently value. The discerning collector's appetite is for the more desirable early 45's, which are clearly distinguished by triangular

A variety of temporary labelled pressings enjoy the catch-all term "White Labels", but they can actually be promotion discs or even factory Test Pressings; frequently artist information is missing.

centres – designed to be pushed out for play on jukeboxes. Later ones have a circular or solid centre, and records missing their centres lose value.

12" singles A product of the '70s, largely for promotional use, the 12" single came into its own in the 1980s when Dance music was fashionable. Offering extra playing time and much stronger audio dynamics, the 12" quickly became the format of choice for alternative-mix releases, alongside the standard singles. Picture disc versions became plentiful, and so many derivatives of a single song started appearing that chart-gathering rules had to be tightened. As with much of business in the 1980s, greed caused its production to go into overdrive and the craze for such singles then died away – though 12" vinyl is still the main format used for Dance music releases.

EP Much loved by collectors, the EP (which stands for Extended Play) was ostensibly a 7" single that had extra tracks squeezed onto rather more vulnerable grooves – this makes top-condition EPs harder to find. However, they looked and felt good, and often had laminated picture sleeves, just like miniature LPs. During the '50s and '60s they offered an alternative way to buy Rock & Roll and Jazz, as key LPs were often also offered as two or three volumes of EP. Sometimes soundtrack EPs appeared where there was insufficient material for an album, and despite eventually losing ground to the more affordable LP competition, this format was adopted by Punk, and later Independent-label bands.

10" album Used extensively in the pre-vinyl era by Jazz and Classical artists, 10" albums are often found in bound shellac sets. From 1948 onwards many early vinyl LPs appeared in 10" form, ranging from Jazz to chart music. As 10" vinyl LPs are inevitably from an early period, they are popular with collectors.

12" album The huge limitations placed on artists over the decades by recording limits of just three or four minutes had artistically stunted the public's knowledge of the power of some music styles. Only a broadcast or live concert gave musicians an opportunity to display improvisation, or a conductor the impact of multiple changes in tempo. With the birth of vinyl LPs everything changed – the public and performers both discovered more choice and the record companies discovered gold. Columbia alone posted 3.5 million sales for a single year. Some bands, like Pink Floyd (*Dark Side of the Moon*) or The Beatles (*Sgt Pepper's Lonely Hearts Club Band*), created projects to fit the LP length. Famously, Led Zeppelin's powerful manager, knowing that the best profits lay within albums, simply instructed their record company that they could only release LPs, not singles. During major tours the group often had every LP that they had released sitting in the US charts.

Other Formats There have been a number of other sound carriers over recent years that are not strictly within this book's mandate but nevertheless successfully sell the music. As the first LP-length material began emerging companies released boxed spools of tape featuring major LPs for playing back at home on bulky tape recorders; few of these have survived or have any value now. Cassette albums offered a convenience factor for in-car or Walkman usage but virtually no one collects them now. Tape's predecessor, the bulky 8-track cartridge, was designed by William Lear of Lear Jet fame, and was used primarily in cars in the '60s and '70s. The sound quality on these broader tapes was very good indeed, but the machines gave little freedom to control selection. Log onto www.8trackheaven.com for a fascinating website dedicated to this carrier.

Pirates, Counterfeits, and Bootlegs Before getting too engaged in searching out and buying vinyl it is advisable to understand something of the unofficial side of record releases. An industry generating such vast profits is bound to attract what might best be described as "opportunists". Illegal records are a complex subject for collectors who are drawn to anything scarce, yet are naturally cautious about what they are buying.

Record industry campaigns about pirate copies has tended to polarize matters because although all might be illegally generated, there are differing strands of records. Strict pirate material is very bad news for everyone, including the purchaser who is destined for poor quality and little packaging or information. Counterfeits are dangerous as they deliberately attempt perfect copies of rare and valuable records – actually disturbing the original's worth if detection is uncertain. Bootlegs, on the other hand, can hold a certain illegal charm – some are very collectable indeed and represent part of a key artist's musical archive. John Lennon actively collected every Beatles bootleg record, while The Grateful Dead encouraged their fans to record the gig they were attending rather than be ripped off by third parties.

Essentially, bootlegs are the unofficial releases of material that has not been featured on any official products. This means that bootlegs vary enormously in quality and significance. Many were very crude recordings from a member of the audience with a non-directional microphone recording as much crowd activity as that on the stage. At the other end, professional sound mixing desks sweetening a live concert sound output usually recorded each concert for later reference or band analysis and these sometimes mysteriously turn into reasonable-quality live bootleg LPs. There are also bootlegs that feature studio recordings, rejected tracks, try-outs, or sometimes more modest demos, and all naturally appeal to the collector. Many of the higher-profile bootleg LPs were once openly sold, and even prompted record companies to compete with their own official products, but concerted efforts by the record industry have driven this trade underground. You will not find such records advertised in the record collector magazines, and clearly the nature of the product makes the quality of what you might be offered uncertain – in the case of a bootleg cassette it might even be blank.

Demos, Promos, "A" labels, and Samplers – some types of limited-circulation media discs are worth less than regular versions, while others can fetch a great deal more. This discrepancy is evident within early Rock & Roll, where the real thing is considered more collectable; in other cases the free distribution to media may represent a larger number than retail sales, making regular versions more valuable.

COVERS AND SLEEVES

Hollywood apart, no other entertainment industry is so dependent upon its imagery than the record world. Movies naturally self-promote their status with excesses on the big screens, but an album is restricted to a square of coloured cardboard and real cover excellence traditionally has been within the world of modern Jazz. Heavily self-promoted Rock designs from Roger Dean and Hipnosis deserve a mention too, although their breadth of styling is small in comparison to Jazz's Reid Miles, of Blue Note, or David Stone Martin of Clef. More often it's the design of a single LP that lingers, such as Pink Floyd's prism idea, or Peter Blake's *Sgt Pepper* crowd for The Beatles. Compact discs deliver quality audio, but there is a universal mourning for the loss of a vinyl album's packaging and its visual sense of what the record will offer.

A Growing Area

One of the more extraordinary aspects of record packaging is the growing number of avid collectors who are not actually interested in the records themselves. Perhaps the surge in vinyl collecting has coincided with swings in general nostalgia towards '50s, '60s, and '70s culture – or maybe the generations that lived through those decades have simply turned reflective. Either way, if you have a cupboard full of over-the-top 1960s LPs, the covers might be more envied than the discs themselves.

Records that celebrate the clothes, hairstyles, and colours of an evocative era quite literally have a value as pieces of kitsch art. The magnificent cover art on Jazz records is generally matched by important vinyl recordings. Other musical genres contributed: Easy Listening, for example, includes hundreds of Lounge and Exotica albums with evocative '50s "cocktail hour" images and styling that make wonderful framed prints; and the chart stars of the same era created a wealth of EPs and LPs, with "period" portraits of stars like Doris Day, Pat Boone, Connie Francis, and Frank Sinatra. These are genuinely collectable as pictures, and if a good cover houses an unplayable record then why not treat the cover as art and frame it?

There were three basic forms of packaging for a standard 12" vinyl album:

The Boxed Set This was the most sophisticated format, and probably the most common examples are to be found at record fairs in the form of multi-LP compilations from companies like Reader's Digest, which lack any style or collector's value but contain huge musical selections for the money. Increasingly, record companies use this format for anthologies of long-standing, or lost, artists. However, original albums such as George Harrison's *All Things Must Pass* were sometimes boxed if the items included were more than two LPs – this one includes two LPs plus a third LP of "extra" material (you will discover that such material often includes additional posters, photos, or other freebies).

The Gatefold Sleeve This was a more prestigious double-album package with a central fold, which allowed it to open out like a book. Used by both supergroups and relative unknowns, it frequently housed a single LP but always contained a feast of images and printed information. Island Records' Quintessence gatefold LP actually evolved as a meditation triptych due to its stunning artwork (*see* page 167).

Conventional Album The standard 10" and 12" album cover changed very little over the years, housing everything from Comedy through to Rock, and Showtunes to Anarchy with equal ease. Many included insert sheets, while others had elaborate inner sleeves full of images. The one important package detail was that early albums had a thin laminated cover film, and the front cover folded over onto the back area with a glued flap. These are generally viewed as being more valuable than later examples.

The packaging of singles is slightly more varied:

Die-cut Sleeves 78's and, more especially, 45's were normally housed in paper or thin cardboard sleeves, which were either completely plain or corporately marked in order to allow their use with any artist's work. The company sleeves are surprisingly interesting, and so many variations exist that these sleeves are themselves a collectable item (*see* page 65). Companies frequently updated their logos, graphics, and colours to try and stay on the crest of the current fashion, and the serious collector will know which precise sleeve edition belongs to his or her cherished discs. An excellent source for replacement corporate sleeves is www.bigboppa.co.uk. You may see references that specifically mention die-cut sleeves – most corporate examples are die-cut, which simply means that the central hole is big enough to view the entire record label.

Poster Sleeves These were simple but clever packages that became popular during the 1980s. The idea behind them was that the record cover could literally be unfolded to transform into a poster. Virgin Records' band XTC offered a novel version in the form of a foldout board game complete with playing pieces. These are naturally more vulnerable than standard sleeves so copies still in good condition are getting rarer.

Picture Sleeves This is the favoured ground for most collectors and, to some extent, it is the French market that bred the love affair. While the UK had to be content for the most part with corporate die-cut sleeves, the French were presented with singles in glamorous picture sleeves. Both France and the USA had operated this way from the 1950s, but only the EP package gave the UK record industry any style until the mid-'70s. Therefore a collector's groundswell already naturally existed for desirable imports and the few 1950s and '60s picture-bagged singles. As you will discover, a picture-sleeve edition will always command higher prices than conventional die-cut corporate versions, and collectors concentrating on purely picture-bagged products will often sub-categorize them as Art Sleeves, Picture Sleeves, Text Sleeves, and even Movie sleeves. One picture-sleeve collector has so far logged over 17,000 examples in his database – all American and not including EPs!

THE CHARTS

If a one-legged man chose a walking stick riddled with dry rot, it would be no more a mistake than the music industry's decision to depend commercially on an arbitrary chart. Conditioning the market to respond only to a vulnerable and ill-defined partial sales list has brought much confusion and ill repute, and has also caused disillusioned talent to walk over the years. The inflammation of corporate and artists' egos, the criminal transactions to assist positions, and the ostracizing of talent that didn't comply with "chart styles" does not reflect well on a supposedly nurturing industry. For instance, the American publisher of the US charts was very reluctant to provide any details of their publication without written evidence of this guidebook's credibility, which seems bizarre as the charts are an official and public record of the success of their nation's musicians. However, there is a lot of easily discovered information about the birth of the modern British Pop chart. The *New Musical Express* was first published in April 1952, having taken over *Musical Express*, which ceased in February of that year. Song charts (which were calculated from things such as the sales of sheet music) were at that time published by various parties, including *Musical Express*, with *Melody Maker* being the first in 1946. In the USA John G. Peatman's *Weekly Survey* had begun the same process back in 1942 – but again these were calculated from things like sheet music. The current American record sales charts started in 1946.

In 1952 the *New Musical Express* was still a paper of its time, as it included headlines like "What I expect of a rhythm section" by a dance band leader, but Percy Dickins (who was responsible for *NME* advertising, layout, and printing) also found time to plan the UK's shift from using sheet music to actual record sales to compile the charts. He personally contacted the record stores to gather data, and the very first UK Singles Record Chart was published in the *NME* on 14th November 1952. Dickins remained with *NME* until 1982 and sadly recently passed away, aged 80. That first chart was topped by ex-American bricklayer Al Martino with *Here in My Heart*, his one and only million-seller, which held the US No.1 spot for two weeks, and the UK No.1 for a staggering nine weeks. At No.2 was Jo Stafford with *You Belong to Me*, and other established figures including Nat King Cole, Bing Crosby, Mario Lanza, and Vera Lynn also appeared. The latter had two chart singles including *Auf Wiedersehen* at No.10, which came complete with a chorus of soldiers, sailors, and airmen of Her Majesty's forces, and was the first UK single to top both British and American charts, selling two million copies. The young blood of the day included Rosemary Clooney (*Half As Much*, at No.6, was her third million-seller in that one year), and Johnnie Ray with *Walking My Baby Back Home*. Frankie Laine was at No.7 with *High Noon* (which won an Academy Award for film music), and again at No.8 duetting with Doris Day on *Sugarbush*. The following year saw his single *I Believe* enjoy nine weeks at the UK No.1 spot. This first 1952 chart was a Top 12, as opposed to the more familiar Top Ten, with 15 entries because of ties between records (*see* over the page for a full listing of the chart).

The First British Singles Chart (14 November 1952)

1   Al Martino   *Here in My Heart*

2   Jo Stafford   *You Belong to Me*

3   Nat King Cole   *Somewhere Along the Way*

4   Bing Crosby   *Isle of Innisfree*

5   Guy Mitchell   *Feet Up*

6   Rosemary Clooney   *Half as Much*

7=   Vera Lynn   *Forget Me Not*

7=   Frankie Laine   *High Noon*

8=   Doris Day and Frankie Laine   *Sugarbush*

8=   Ray Martin   *Blue Tango*

9   Vera Lynn   *Homing Waltz*

10   Vera Lynn   *Auf Wiedersehen*

11=   Max Bygraves *Cowpuncher's Cantata*

11=   Mario Lanza   *Because You're Mine*

12   Johnnie Ray   *Walking My Baby Back Home*

So with that first British singles charts 50 years ago a self-judgement process began, augmented by the first UK LP chart in the *NME* in November 1958, which had the classic movie soundtrack of *South Pacific* at No.1. Then 1964 witnessed the first broadcast of BBC Television's *Top of the Pops* chart show, hosted by Jimmy Savile, which was opened by The Rolling Stones singing *I Wanna be Your Man* (at No.13), and The Beatles who were No.1 with *I Want to Hold Your Hand*. (The Fab Four had a total of six singles in that week's chart!) In the 1950s and '60s charts may have been rather amateur, and indeed not well-policed, but at least they reflected the recorded output of the stars of the day. In more recent times artists and bands have been cast and groomed specifically to suit a TV chart-show appearance.

From the record collectors' point of view, finding all the No.1s of a year, or a particular era, is a perfectly legitimate target, but overexposed records usually have little value or kudos. Ironically, it is perhaps because record companies and the media have become excessive chart statisticians, rather than being talent biased, that many of the truly inspiring records have been allowed to escape without reaching the centre spotlight. It is these unnoticed gems that are the very essence of record collecting.

EASY LISTENING

If you've never thought of collecting records and consider it to be a whole different world, full of eccentrics clutching vinyl, then step into this particular corner. Prepare to smile from ear to ear with original pop, be entertained by virtually every movie star and public figure that walked, be washed with lush romanticism, transported to exotic islands, even space itself, or perhaps stunned by the truly weird and wonderful. Exploring Easy Listening is like signing up to satellite television and scrolling through the choices for the first time. Before introducing the various sections on offer let's deal with its one great enemy – its name. In essence it is the correct definition – Easy Listening is a broad-based phrase defining any form of music that is comfortably played in support of what you are doing, rather than demanding your direct attention. Strictly speaking, it embraces much of Classical music, originally written for just this purpose, hundreds of Jazz recordings, great slices of Pop, and even Rock, but clearly lines have to be drawn and for the purposes of this guide the softer side of these genres are dealt with in their own sections.

Easy Listening's identity crisis is actually rooted in its very appeal. It was home territory for the parents of the rock generations and to them it was considered highly fashionable to take cocktails with neighbours to a backdrop of lush string arrangements, Moog synthesizers, or Pacific Island rhythms.

Family Failure – Murry Wilson, the infamous father of the Beach Boys (he initially managed them), actually put out his own LP, which states that it was "conceived and produced by Murry Wilson". The cover was awash with trendy young girls and yet the back revealed a middle-aged dad with glasses and a pipe. A musical zenith, the single was called The Plumber's Song!

Pop music then became dominant, but within its arsenal were the more melodic records identified as M.O.R. – Middle of the Road. They were scorned by the rock fans who, despite jeans and trendy shades, failed to remain young and increasingly were drawn to their version – A.O.R. (Adult-Orientated Rock). Shrewdly, the American charts spotted that the name Easy Listening sounded dated and, in 1979, re-christened Easy Listening as A.C. – Adult Contemporary. Depending on your taste, one of these categories may be enjoyable, the others passé. This extending musical pathway causes some strange anomalies – Elvis Presley savagely wounded Easy Listening by leading the Rock "n" Roll crusade, yet statistically he is now Easy's top artist – we pick up his work in another chapter.

The truth is that Easy Listening probably has the widest appeal of any single form of music and this demand generates an enormous landscape for the potential collector.

Because of the divergence of material, values naturally vary but in general these are highly affordable records to collect. In many cases they can be found languishing in car boot sales and junk shops, but times are changing and some of the Easy Listening categories are now more sought after, thanks in part to the powerful nostalgia of the record covers. A 1950s star in all his/her youthful glory now makes a natural postcard or wall poster, but add the powerful echo of once-loved music and you can begin to understand the desire to own a copy, and even frame it, for your wall. For this reason, collecting Easy Listening doesn't require deep knowledge of the artist or music – you can start by simply using your own reactions to the artwork.

For the sake of this guide Easy Listening has been subdivided into six categories, each with its own character, artists, and collecting themes:

Lounge
This area is quite complex. Surprisingly, some of its roots are found in the military, as the music was sometimes tuned to revitalize human performance. Until you look into its history you have no idea of its importance – one expert adjudged over 90 million people listen to this type of music each day. It is a good idea to study one of the excellent books on the subject before focusing on a theme (see pages 226–227). It's an area that is largely made up of album collecting, and the period artwork is much valued, but key orchestras/arrangers matter too. Beyond the obvious Nelson Riddle, Henry Mancini, Percy Faith, and Ray Conniff are other key names like the 101 Strings, the Mystic Moods Orchestra, Hugo Montenegro, and the Melanchrino Orchestra.

Essentially Lounge is cocktail hour, with its roots in vintage "good-life Americana", but beyond the core material are acres of extraordinary one-offs tuned to your Martini or indeed your subsequent intentions for the evening – though for some of these unusual examples you will need to hunt through websites. These albums were being thrown away but now collectors are agog at £25–50/$40–75 prime prices, so expect records and prices to move quickly.

Nat King Cole *Night of the Quarter Moon*
Nat triumphed over white Anglo-American fashion by crooning like an Italian.

Exotica
This is a parallel strand to Lounge but its roots rest more within adventure. These were the Eisenhower and Kennedy years, when middle America was flourishing and there was real status in the size of your TV and the quality of your hi-fi. Stereo was a buzzword, as was foreign travel, and Exotica skilfully catered to both desires. Most of it was lightweight orchestral material cleverly arranged to incorporate clichéd musical colour from glamorous parts of the world, but often embracing exaggerated stereo mixes to underline the new world of hi-fi stereo. Ethnic percussion,

jungle sounds, and highly evocative covers were the USA's interpretations of other countries' releases. As an extension of this same escapism, there were space travel versions with strange covers and modern keyboard work. When new, these were all considered quite lightweight but the '90s fashion for Alternative music swung Exotica into vogue. As with Lounge, most of the key material is Stateside, and it has roughly matching prices too.

Hit Paraders

This section focuses on single artists rather than orchestras and groups. Such artists cut individual songs in the 1950s and '60s, so collecting this genre primarily means you will be hunting out singles. An album only occurred after hits, and so their relative scarcity makes them desirable. Aficionados base collections on specifics like the output of a single producer or label. However, single-artist collections are simple, highly affordable themes.

Another option would be to collect the gems from an era. This is the cheapest way to start, as inevitably big hits push vast numbers into circulation. Perry Como sold over 100 million copies and had 322 weeks on the charts with *Magic Moments*; its current value is just £6. Or take a particular week's chart – maybe the week you were born – and try collecting the entries.

UK Hit Paraders differ from those in the American marketplace – not over songs, as they were usually hits in both countries, but with artists. It was common practice to spot a promising new release and copy it with a domestic star across the Atlantic. Focus on these to create a fascinating theme.

The Unexpected

This is collector's heaven if you love the truly offbeat. It stretches the definition of Easy but most of the records are too earnest to belong in Comedy. The more inventive among you might evolve specific collection themes, but in reality it's the utterly mad cross-section of material that is this category's charm. Quite a lot of it is American, but collectors' magazines and websites open the way once you've discovered that the records exist. Maybe you'd start with a singing wrestler's LP *Pencil Neck Geek*, or *Where there Walks a Logger there Walks a Man* from a singing forester. There are singing witches in long boots, singing psychics, New York taxi drivers, Marcella: The Chicken that Sang Opera, a guide to surviving the atom bomb, music to make automobiles by, 12 songs for Canary Training, and even US Air force Firepower Sound Effects. Anything and everything goes – stupid, crazy, and very addictive, the Unexpected records are enormous fun to collect and not at all expensive.

First UK No.1 – A casual BBC Radio 2 broadcast of a golden oldie in 1973 led to requests, a crossover to pop stations, and put the 1965 record Spanish Eyes *high into the charts again, where it remained for months. Coincidentally, the artist on the record, Al Martino, held the very first UK No.1 in the* NME *Singles Charts with* Here In My Heart. *A copy of the original 1960s release of* Spanish Eyes *is now worth just £5.*

Celebrities

This is an excellent first collection through which you can discover more about the routes to finding records. Although there are thousands of eligible American recordings, the UK has a substantial number of celebrities on vinyl too. Records such as Barbara Cartland singing *Love Songs* through to author J.R. Tolkien singing in "Elvish" are hidden around the country. Comedians, TV cops, movie stars, even Sir Winston Churchill's speeches – you just simply select a nominal theme and gather them together. Virtually all of them can be picked up for rock-bottom prices, although some exceptions exist: Peter Wyngarde (TV's Jason King) commands £200–400 for his one eponymous LP, while the original Musketeer on the American Mickey Mouse Club, Annette Funicello, enjoys 117 records valued between $10 and $600/£6.50 and £400. Exceptional numbers of sports figures offer an easy option for collectors – one or two are unlikely to win trophies for their vocal efforts, although John McEnroe shrewdly played guitar on his disc and invited lead singer of The Who, Roger Daltrey, to sing instead.

Glamorous

The 1950s and '60s unlocked a range of perceptions over sexuality. Hollywood airbrushed its stars and starlets into perfected form, while Europe began to unleash a freer spirit with the likes of Brigitte Bardot and Sophia Loren. In print, *Playboy* brought fantasies into the public domain. The record world reflected this diversity too, with glamorous movie stars rushing to record albums, Vegas strippers taking you through their workout steps, and even Truck Drivin' albums to offend the most half-hearted of feminists.

This strand of collecting is almost exclusively based around LPs, although some picture discs are eagerly pursued. The mainstream movie stars releases can be found in many of the record fairs and magazines, and European icons such as Françoise Hardy and Jane Birkin are relatively easy finds. Much of the more eccentric material stems from the USA and, thanks to the Internet, is daily becoming as easy to research as UK releases.

Beautiful Vinyl – In 1993 Philips released a three-record set of French goddess Brigitte Bardot's recordings, along with a 16-track promo, including artwork objected to by the celebrity. Revised copies are worth around £20 ($30) – the initial versions are now £75+ ($115+). Expect to pay up to £500 ($750) for her rarest release.

The most expensive Marilyn Monroe record currently lists at around $80/£55, a rare Bardot single at £150/$225, and $30/£20 could buy you *Marlene Dietrich at the Café de Paris*. However, don't think it's all cheesecake – there's actually an MGM Jayne Mansfield LP on which she whispers Shakespeare to a backdrop of Tchaikovsky!

Lounge Music *"A WEALTH OF AMERICANA"*

Suggested Strands
Vocal
Orchestral Pop
Elevator Music

Average Record Cost
★★★

Rising Stars
Les Baxter
Nat King Cole
Billy Eckstine
The Three Suns

VOCAL

LPs

Harry Belafonte *Belafonte Sings of the Caribbean*

Tony Bennett
The Beat of your Heart

Nat King Cole
Nat King Cole Trio ★

Perry Como *Como Swings*

Bing Crosby *Bing – a Musical Autobiography* ★ (5 LPs)

Sammy Davis Jr.
Just for Lovers

Billy Eckstine *Mr. B* ★

Ella Fitzgerald
Ella Fitzgerald Sings the George and Ira Gershwin Song Book ★

Peggy Lee *Sea Shells*

Dean Martin *Sleep Warm*

The Mills Brothers
Four Boys and a Guitar

Frank Sinatra
A Swinging Affair

Barbra Streisand *Stoney End*

Dinah Washington
After Hours with Miss D ★

Andy Williams
Under Paris Skies

Whole books have been written trying to categorize precisely the various fractions of Lounge Music – none has been conclusive. However, the American tribute book *Forever Lounge* struggles for a lasting definition of Lounge Music and by chance achieves it in a half sentence... "it concerns itself more with the listener's experience than that of the player(s)". For all those quiet times when you curl up and read or enjoy dinner with friends and your loved rock record won't do, a Lounge album is the perfect musical backdrop.

Vocal

Essentially, "mood" music was born after World War II when big band singers went solo. This created the Hit Paraders (*see* pages 39–43), and left room for the more resourceful bands to cash in on the new long-playing records by making mood albums. Perfect for the early '50s American lifestyle, this Lounge Music became the ideal social backdrop to dinner parties and the inevitable cocktail hour.

Many of the vocal recordings were made by stars synonymous with Vegas-style nightlife, which provoked the later 1950s "playboy bachelor pad" mentality. This was further reinforced by NBC TV's smash hit series *Peter Gunn*, which used such music as written by a young Henry Mancini.

> *Bigger in the UK than USA – Dean Martin, the quintessential Las Vegas Brat Packer of his era, currently generates around 30 collectable releases in the US but in the UK over 160 are listed as worthwhile; the UK just seems to love him.*

Records from household names like Sinatra and Crosby are steady collectors' items but it really does pay to explore. Peggy Lee's *Sea Shells* album, for instance, has a UK value of £15 while it is worth $60 in the US. Nat King Cole sits well above Andy Williams, Billy Eckstine offers long promising US lists, and Ella Fitzgerald easily outsells Barbara Streisand.

Orchestral Pop

This element within Easy Listening is the domain of the big songs. As Pop records grew in status, so too did the demand for celebrations of their melodies without the often jarring production that differentiated them from the original hits.

ORCHESTRAL POP

LPs

Boston Pops Orchestra
Gaîté Parisienne ★

Frank Chacksfield
South Sea Island Magic

Ray Conniff *S' Wonderful*

Bert Kaempfert
Wonderland by Night

Guy Lombardo *Sweetest
Music this Side of Heaven*

Mantovani
All American Showcase

Billy May *Capitol Presents
Billy May and his Orchestra*

101 Strings Orchestra
Down Memory Lane

Nelson Riddle
The Tender Touch

The Three Suns
Hands Across the Table

Billy Vaughn *Melody of Love*

Paul Weston
Music for Dreaming

Orchestral Pop therefore offered what was effectively compilations of material using one beautiful voice: Mantovani, Nelson Riddle, Ray Conniff – the names alone guaranteed quality. The Boston Pops offered their first Promenade Concert of light music in 1885. This orchestra cut its first 40 tracks in 1935, generating the first major orchestral hit with *Jalousie*, which was a US million-seller. Broadcast series, tours, and vast collections of records all followed – even the *Jaws* and *ET* composer John Williams acted as their resident conductor for a time. While almost worthless in the UK, their US repertoire and history would make a fabulous collection. Another American secret well worth exploring is The Three Suns. Combining accordion, guitar, and organ they created a great many classy albums – most of which start at around $50 – including their LP *Hands Across the Table*. They had a million seller in 1950 with *Twilight Time* and some of their LP covers are also collectable in their own right.

A particular brand of Lounge was initiated by Paul Weston in 1945 with themed mood music. His *Music for Dreaming* sold a staggering 175,000 and naturally led to others, such as *Music for Memories*, *Music for Reflection*, and *Music for Romance*. It wasn't just the music that seduced, the sleeve notes worked hard too. The *Daydreaming* sleeve suggests, "A daydream can fly you to the uttermost exotic land, bring you the choicest of the world's luxuries, even transport you to another planet" – isn't that worth $50 of anyone's money? *Music for Dining* recommends the correct food for the music: *Too Young* apparently goes with pâté de foie gras and truffles while *Clopin Clopant* should herald the main course. RCA answered this success with Melachrino Strings, who made 50 LPs during the 1950s including *Music for Dining, Music for Reading*, and *Music for Relaxing*. In 1955 Columbia launched a series called *Music for Gracious Living* with titles such as *After the Dance, Barbecue, Foursome*, and *Buffet*, as well as a wonderful guide to home improvements called *Music for Gracious Living – Do-It-Yourself*. This has a glorious cover photo of a "happy" family – a young mum sewing while the son and dad are at the workbench with all their tools hooked

US Success – The Boston Pops Orchestra was essentially born over a century ago and has a staggering history, recording more albums than any other 20th-century orchestra. However, the UK hardly recognizes they exist – there is only one £6 single in the Record Collector's annual guide. US prices, however, range from $20 to $300.

neatly to a peg board. The sleeve notes give DIY hints and the Peter Barclay Orchestra provide the music; the covers alone are worth collecting.

Elevator Music

Ambient music has been used for decades to induce higher workforce productivity, retail spending, and even to reduce anxieties. It's a tool that was used by many from the military to phone companies, and it also resulted in a body of fascinating recordings from modernists such as Brian Eno and Jackie Gleason. The latter's records have sold over 120 million copies despite the fact that he couldn't read music and claimed that on a good day his sounds were "plain vanilla". But by pitting this ultra-smooth formula along with talented arrangers very imaginative work was created.

> *Mistakes Can Pay Dividends – The pivotal figure of influence, Les Baxter, succeeded with a mistake! His second million-seller was a cover; the song,* La Goulant du Pauvre Jean *(The Ballad of Poor John) was cabled incorrectly from Paris, emerging as* Pauvre Gens, *which means people. Thus it became* The Poor People of Paris*!*

For example, engineer/producer Brad Miller experimented layering atmospheric sound effects behind a Jackie Gleason disc and got an immediate reaction from local radio. Conductor/arranger Don Ralke had spare, unreleased material and got together with Miller to add background effects to the 1966 Mystic Moods Orchestra's *One Stormy Night*. This was a recording landmark.

In general Elevator Music is not as valuable as the other two categories within Lounge, but it is steeped in well-documented history and offers many diverse recordings.

ELEVATOR MUSIC

LPs

Les Baxter *Music for Peace of Mind*

Percy Faith *Malaguena*

Jackie Gleason *Lover's Rhapsody*

Morton Gould *Doubling in Brass*

Earl Grant *Spanish Eyes*

The Hollyridge Strings *The Beatles Song Book*

Michel Legrand *Spaced Out*

Francis Lai *A Man and a Woman*

Johnny Mann Singers *Alma Mater*

Mystic Moods Orchestra *One Stormy Night*

101 Strings *Astro Sounds from Beyond the Year 2000* ★

Norrie Paramor *Plays the Hits of Cliff Richard* ★

Lawrence Welk *Bubbles in the Wine*

Roger Williams *Autumn Leaves*

Exotica *"ADVENTURES IN SOUND"*

Suggested Strands
Worldbeat
Space Age

Average Record Cost
☆☆

Rising Stars
Les Baxter
Martin Denny
Esquivel
Korla Pandit

Exotica was very much a child of its times, and a sibling of Lounge Music. Ironically, this form of Easy Listening wasn't given too much credibility during its core period as it was thought to be quite lightweight. It quietly faded away until a 1990s resurgence gave the form credit for its production qualities, as well as its interest, however superficial this may have been, in foreign cultures.

World Beat

After World War II, returning American soldiers waxed lyrical over the South Pacific. Musicals began to celebrate the theme, as did hotels, restaurants, and amusement parks. The lush sounds of fashionable Lounge music began to feel tame at this time, which tempted pioneers like Les Baxter to introduce the additional colours of World Music. Seemingly daring only to American suburbia, it offered a safe, armchair form of exotic travel on newly introduced long-playing records – complete with glamorous, semi-primitive album covers. Baxter's 1951 pivotal recording *Ritual of the Savage* began the whole movement with its tone poem – a semi-conceptual travelogue through a jungle. Its track *Quiet Village* later became singer Martin Denny's ticket to success.

> *Cult and Pop Status – Les Baxter's influential position in Exotica didn't limit his vision. He was responsible for the orchestral output of mainstream radio shows with Bob Hope and Abbott and Costello, and even joined Mel Tormé's singing group The Meltones. In 1955 he achieved a million-selling hit with* Unchained Melody, *now worth £15.*

Peruvian-born Amy Camus, from New York's Brooklyn, sang folk songs to show off her five-octave vocal range. Capitol hired Les Baxter to produce *Voice of the Xtabay* – a collection of Peruvian folk material featuring a suitably exotic clad Amy under the name Yma Sumac. This went on to sell half-a-million copies. Then followed journeys through the Amazon on *Legend of the Jivaro*, which captured live primitive sounds, and *Voodoo*, which explored Haiti and the unsubstantiated claims that Amy was a descendant of Inca royalty.

New Yorker Martin Denny's 1957 single *Quiet Village* enjoyed a No.1 position while his first LP *Exotica* eventually lent its

WORLD BEAT

LPs

Leo Addeo *Hawaiian Paradise*

Eden Ahbez *Eden's Island* ★

Herb Alpert and Tijuana Brass *Whipped Cream & Other Delights*

Les Baxter *Ritual of the Savage*

Martin Denny *Quiet Village*

Pedro Garcia and Orchestra *Tropical Cruise*

Richard Hayman *Voodoo*

Arthur Lymann *Taboo*

Korla Pandit *Music of the Exotic East*

The Surfmen *Sounds of Exotic Island*

Yma Sumac *Voice of the Xtabay*

name to the entire music genre. This album mixed piano, vibraphones, a rhythm section, and atmospheric jungle and percussion sounds. Four million sales and 37 LPs later he was a legend, while ex-band members also built careers for themselves. His vibraphonist Arthur Lyman had a spectacular 1961 Top 10 hit with *Yellow Bird*, while his first LP, *Taboo*, recorded in an aluminium dome in Honolulu, became a two-million seller. Born on Kauai, he grew up playing along to jazz records and worked with Martin Denny before forming his own trio for an Hawaiian hotel. He introduced ever more haunting sounds, and during the intervals the group would simulate bird calls to amuse the crowds!

Success from the Wilds – Eden Ahbez took the Exotica concept in a more literal direction by living on a tropical island and recording his one Exotic album, Eden's Island ★, *worth $200. In 1948 he left his first composition,* Nature Boy, *at the stage door where Nat King Cole was performing. Cole took it on and his version went to No.1 for seven weeks.*

Latin rhythms had gradually grown in popularity too, largely through Cuban band leader Xavier Cugat. However, it was Perez Prado's first album *Mambo Jambo* (now worth $50) that spread the craze, even influencing Hit Paraders like Perry Como with *Papa Loves to Mambo* (worth £18) and Rosemary Clooney's *Mambo Italiano*, with which she topped the charts in 1954. Perez earned chart status too by creating a US No.1 that stayed at the top for ten weeks (it was No.1 in the UK for two weeks). This was the theme music from the movie *Underwater – Cherry Pink and Apple Blossom White* – which is now valued at £10.

Space Age

America was filled with dreams of outer space in the 1950s – comic strips, classic B-movies, and news magazines were all preoccupied with the romance of the unknown. Broadcasters and film makers requiring space-like music spawned experimental effects material that used primitive synthesized sounds and tape manipulation. Themed LPs followed, creating a kind of lightweight impressionistic version of Exotica. Friends and classical pianists Arthur Ferrante and Louis Teicher toured as duo pianists and were increasingly drawn to experimental sounds, adding sandpaper, metal, and woodblocks to their pianos to evoke new effects. Their

SPACE AGE

LPs

Louis and Bebe Barron
Forbidden Planet

Sid Bass
From Another World

Bobby Christian
Strings for a Space Age

Frank Comstock
Music from Outer Space

Esquivel *Other Worlds Other Sounds*

Ferrante and Teicher
Soundproof

Dick Hyman
The Age of Electronicus

Enoch Light
Persuasive Percussion

Perrey/Kingsley
The In Sound from Way Out

1956 space odyssey *Soundproof* (worth $25) was made using 17 live microphones on swinging booms to exaggerate the sounds. Frank Comstock's offering, *Music from Outer Space*, used an electric violin and a soundwave machine to eerie effect. Juan Garcia Esquivel produced albums exploring the newly available stereophonic techniques – his 1962 *Latinesque* album (worth $60) involved placing sections of his orchestras in different buildings, and was given free to buyers of shiny new stereo record players.

As recording moved into the '60s "Space Age Pop" took a quantum leap with the availability of the Moog synthesizer, which was first shown at a 1964 trade show. Jean-Jacques Perrey and Gershon Kingsley exposed its potential on their 1966 album *The In Sound from Way Out* (now worth $40), suggesting these strange new sounds would soon become familiar on space station jukeboxes. Others also relished stretching sound technology via space themes and undemanding compositions. Enoch Light was a true sound engineer, turning his albums (such as *Persuasive Percussion*) into virtual hi-fi demonstration discs. They also included elaborate cover data – he was responsible for gatefold album covers. He pioneered the use of 35mm film stock instead of tape for higher definition (as used on *Stereo 33/mm Vol 1* and *Vol 2*), yet he also still recorded more traditional tracks like *Baroque Hoedown*, which was used by Disneyland in their Main Street parades.

Widespread Talents – Mexican Esquivel didn't just stretch the boundaries of stereo. By the age of 12 he had a radio show, and by 14 ran a full band. He may have become a stereo space junkie but you will have heard his music as he also wrote for Kojak, Magnum P.I., *and* Charlie's Angels.

Hit Paraders *"LARGELY IGNORED – EASY TO COLLECT"*

Suggested Strands

Italian-American
Instrumentals
First Generation Pop Stars
Copycat Recordings
Teenage Sweethearts

Average Record Cost

☆☆☆

Rising Stars

Fats Domino
Connie Frances
General Instrumentals

ITALIAN-AMERICAN

Singles

Rosemary Clooney
Mambo Italiano

Nat King Cole *Mona Lisa*

Doris Day *Que Sera, Sera*

Four Aces
Three Coins in a Fountain

Ronnie Hilton *Veni, Vide, Vici*

Dean Martin
Volare / That's Amore

The Hit Paraders make up a fascinating musical backwater, charting an almost invisible period between mighty Big Band Jazz and the birth of Rock & Roll. Filled with innocence, charm, and nostalgia, it's frequently lost within catch-all terms such as the "Fabulous Fifties". In fact, it's a very subtle category that has its origins in the decay of Swing Band. It also survived for years after the emergence of Rock & Roll influences such as Elvis Presley, Buddy Holly, and The Everlys.

In order to identify the parameters of Hit Paraders it helps to understand exactly what happened to music following World War II. As is detailed in the Jazz section (*see* pages 123–146), music had become divided between increasingly predictable Big Band Swing and deliberately restless, questioning compositions. Inevitably this left the main stage vacant.

The dance bands era literally collapsed towards the end of 1946, seeing nine large leading orchestras dissolved within a couple of months. Suddenly an entire raft of relatively poorly paid band singers was out of work. They became the immediate future of popular music, thanks to the rapid growth in records and television. A veritable army of ex-crooners fought for best chart songs and best broadcasts; these included Bing Crosby (ex-Paul Whiteman Orchestra), Ella Fitzgerald (ex-Chick Webb), Perry Como (ex-Ted Weems), Frank Sinatra (ex-Harry James & Tommy Dorsey), Peggy Lee (ex-Benny Goodman), and others such as Rosemary Clooney, Al Martino, Frankie Laine, Tony Bennett, and Dean Martin.

A Female Star – Connie Francis enjoyed the status of highest-selling female artist with approximately 10,000 record releases to her name. One early MGM recording session had just minutes left when her father persuaded her to cut one more song – it became the UK No.1 and million-seller Who's Sorry Now.

Italian-American

The popular look of the day was Italian-American, although Nat King Cole was acceptable because he "sounded" like a fashionable white Italian crooner. Hollywood stuck rigidly to the rules, insisting Bernie Schwartz changed his name to a more suitable Tony Curtis while Doris Day was stripped of her name – Kappelhof. The slick, ex-crooner, Mediterranean look

INSTRUMENTALS

Singles

Larry Adler *Genevieve*

Herb Alpert *The Lonely Bull*

Winnie Atwell *Poor People Of Paris / Let's Have A Party*

Kenny Ball *Midnight in Moscow*

Chris Barber *Petite Fleur*

Sidney Bechet *Les Oignons*

Acker Bilk *Strangers on the Shore*

Eddie Calvert *Cherry Pink & Apple Blossom White*

The Champs *Tequila*

Russ Conway *Side Saddle / Roulette*

Duane Eddy *Rebel Rouser / Peter Gunn*

Ted Heath *Swingin' Shepherd Blues*

Bill Justis Orchestra *Raunchy*

Sandy Nelson *Teen Beat*

Les Paul and Mary Ford *Mockin' Bird Hill / How High Is The Moon*

Lord Rockingham's XI *Hoots Mon*

The Tornados *Telstar*

Bert Weedon *Guitar Boogie Shuffle*

forced other artists to shed evidence of their origins too. Robert Cassatto became Bobby Darin, Francis Avallone became Frankie Avalon, Robert Volline turned into Bobby Vee, while ladies such as Concetta Franonera reappeared as Connie Francis – MGM's Soda Pop queen who would score a staggering 20 hits in just four years. It didn't stop with trying to look Italian – the songs often picked up the theme as well.

Instrumentals

So soon after the demise of dance bands instrumental hits were inevitably very popular. These now make a highly affordable theme to start collecting. Caribbean singer Winnie Atwell sat between two pianos, switching between ragtime and popular songs, and generated three Top 5 hits in just two years. Russ Conway's keyboard offered a much more English flavour with a brace of No.1s called *Side Saddle* and *Roulette*, while Eddie Calvert's trumpet gave him the multi-million selling *Oh Mein Papa*. Larry Adler's famous harmonica offered up the movie-inspired gem *Genevieve*, Jazz master clarinettist Sidney Bechet composed and played *Les Oignons*, while Herb Alpert, Bert Weedon, and the Champs all produced American Number 1 hits, the latter being *Tequila* (now worth £12). Then there was the almost forgotten guitar hero Duane Eddy who had 20 UK hits in under five years, including his first million seller *Rebel Rouser* (worth £6 for a round centre, £12 for a tri-centred, £30 as a 78' – $30 in the USA), or the one-off madness of Lord Rockingham's XI playing *Hoots Mon* (worth £6 as a 45', £8 as a 78'). These are all pure Hit Paraders.

> *Rising Prices – The Tornados' fabled* Telstar *single is virtually worthless yet the band's 1963 Decca LP* Away from It All *will set you back around £50 – if you can find one, of course. Their LPs and EPs are generally rising in value, as are their 1965/6 Columbia singles.*

First Generation Pop Stars

At this time there was no interest in teenagers. They were lost souls trapped between childhood and the then magical figure of 21, which spelt adulthood. The war years had been tough, as men had been away for long periods. This had an effect on movies and music, which became heavily laced with jingoisms and propaganda – lyrics squarely addressing the grown-ups' frame of mind. Some songs even related directly to military

FIRST GENERATION POP STARS

Singles

Paul Anka *Diana*

The Coasters *Yakety Yak*

Bobby Darin
Dream Lover / Mack the Knife / Multiplication

Dion *Runaround Sue / The Wanderer*

Fats Domino
Blueberry Hill ★/ I'm Walkin'

The Drifters *Dance With Me / Save the Last Dance*

The Fleetwoods
Come Softly to Me

Connie Francis
Who's Sorry Now / Carolina Moon / Stupid Cupid

Tab Hunter *Young Love*

The Karlin Twins *When*

Jerry Kellor
Here Comes Summer

Frankie Lymon and The Teenagers *Why Do Fools Fall in Love*

Ricky Nelson *Poor Little Fool / It's Late / Hello Mary Lou*

Phil Phillips *Sea of Love*

The Platters
Smoke Gets In Your Eyes / Great Pretender / Twilight Time

Johnnie Ray
Just Walkin' in the Rain

The Rays *Silhouettes ★*

Jim Reeves *Distant Drums*

Debbie Reynolds *Tammy*

The Teddy Bears
To Know Him Is To Love Him

Conway Twitty *It's Only Make Believe / I Need Your Loving*

Bobby Vee *The Night Has a Thousand Eyes*

duties. Some examples include Anne Shelton's 1956 No.1 *Lay Down Your Arms*, Pat Boone's No.1 *I'll be Home* (worth £15), and Alma Cogan's *Bell Bottom Blues* (selling for £40).

As can be seen in other sections, ignoring teenagers led directly to the advent of youth music – Rock & Roll. However, booming record sales and eager adult consumers ensured a continuance of this blissfully escapist form of chart music well into the '60s. Indeed, television sustained figures like Andy Williams and Perry Como for many years, while the movies launched hit after hit for stars such as Doris Day and Frank Sinatra. As youth music stormed its way into the

> *Singles versus 78's – If you can find Alma Cogan HMV singles from the period 1953 to 1957 they are now averaging around £30 each, in mint condition, but the old 78' versions are worth much less.*

limelight the major record companies worked hard to sustain their existing artists and interests. Originality wasn't the order of the day – it was important to conform to a clean all-American image and Pat Boone personified this, delivering hit after hit. He even countered Elvis' powerful 1957 impact by starring in and singing the hit for the movie *April Love*.

Copycat Recordings

Duplicating rivals' recordings was a frequent and quite acceptable activity – even to the public. Andy Williams' 1957 No.1 hit *Butterfly* (worth £20 – $12 in the USA) was actually a copy of Charlie Grace's original version (the gold label lettering version is worth £50, the silver £35, £10 as a 78', and $25 in the USA). Bobby Darin, another renamed semi-crooner, copied Lonnie Donegan's *Rock Island Line* ★ for his first record (Donegan's version is worth £8 as 78', £20 as a tri-centred 45', while Darin's fetches £48 as a 78' and £130 as a 45'). *Splish Splash* and *Dream Lover* would later give Darin one million copies apiece before he turned to update and cover a 1929 song with *Mack the Knife* (worth £30 as a 78', £7 as a 45', $50 in USA). This single sold a staggering three million copies.

In the UK, artists were barred from performing in America by unions so the equivalent British performers retained a rather more domestic feel and include names like Joan Regan, Alma Cogan, Anne Shelton, Dennis Lotus, Ronnie Carroll, Ronnie Hilton, Dickie Valentine, Michael Holliday, and Frankie Vaughan.

FIRST LADY RECORDINGS

Singles

The Beverly Sisters *Sisters*

Eve Boswell
Pickin' a Chicken

Teresa Brewer *Let Me Go Lover /
Till I Waltz With You again*

Petula Clark *Downtown /
Don't Sleep In The Subway /
This Is My Song*

Rosemary Clooney
*This Ole House / Where Will the
Baby's Dimple Be*

Alma Cogan *Dream Boat*

Doris Day *Secret Love / Move
Over Darling / Deadwood Stage*

Carole King *It Might As Well
Rain Until September*

Kathy Kirby *Secret Love*

Peggy Lee
Fever / Mr Wonderful

Jane Morgan
The Day That The Rains Came

Ruby Murray
*Softly, Softly / Heartbeat /
Come-On-A My House*

Anne Shelton
Lay Down Your Arms

Dinah Shore *Buttons & Bows*

Here, too, recording copies of other people's hits was deemed acceptable – particularly if they were American. Tommy Steele "borrowed" both Guy Mitchell's *Singing the Blues* (Steele's

> *Battle of the Bobbies – Bobby Darin's early hit singles are worth hunting out, while rival Bobby Vee's are more varied. Vee's singles appear unwanted but his early 1961 London LPs are worth more than double Darin's. Even the slightly later Liberty releases compare favourably.*

version is worth £18, Mitchell's £50), and Freddy Cannon's *Tallahassee Lassie* (Steele's fetches £22 as a 78', £8 as a 45', while Cannon's is worth £7 as a 45', £75 as a 78', $25 in the USA). Marty Wilde feasted first on Jody Reynolds' *Endless Sleep* (Wilde's is worth £12, Reynolds' £25, $35 in USA), then Richie Valens' *Donna* ★ (Wilde's £12, Valens' £20, £130 as a 78', $30–80 in the USA, depending on label colours), followed by Craig Douglas' *Teenager In Love* (Wilde's £8 as a 45', £50 as a 78', Douglas' £7 as a 45, £16 as a 78'), and Phil Phillips' *Sea of Love* ★ (Wilde's £6 and Phillips' £25, in the USA $30 on Mercury but over $1,600 on Khoury's). These were all released in 1959. The UK expected all-round entertainers who could sing, irrespective of whose songs they sung and what styles they used. Tommy Steele's 1956 *Rock with the Cave Man* (£40 as a 45', £8 as a 78') sits on his CV besides gems like *Little White Bull* (£10 as a 45', £23 as a 78'), while Cliff Richard's *Move It* (£40 as a 45', £60 as a 78') lives alongside the escapist heaven of *Summer Holiday* (worth £5).

Teenage Sweethearts

Original stars did emerge during this time. Johnnie Ray somehow managed to straddle the ever-widening gulf between crooners like Sinatra and Rock & Roll's crusaders. He appeared as a very straight and vulnerable grown-up, appealing to already existing record buyers. He also demonstrably exposed genuine feelings, particularly of loneliness, through his music, thus capturing the youth sector that was so starved of emotions too.

His 50 per cent deafness from a schooldays' accident caused his deflated persona, which literally led him to cry from time to time while performing. This was successfully traded on and helped him to sell millions of records in just three years; it also acquired him the nickname "The Prince of Sobs".

CROONERS

Singles

Harry Belafonte *Banana Boat Song / Mary's Boy Child*

Pat Boone *I'll Be Home / Love Letters In Sand / April Love*

Nat King Cole *When I Fall In Love / Rambling Rose*

Perry Como *Magic Moments / Catch A Falling Star*

Bing Crosby (with Grace Kelly) *True Love*

Emile Ford and The Checkmates *What do You Want to Make Those Eyes at Me For*

Tennessee Ernie Ford *Sixteen Tons / The Ballad of Davy Crockett*

Ronnie Hilton *No Other Love*

Michael Holliday *The Story of My Life*

Frankie Laine *Woman in Love / Mule Train / I Believe*

Mario Lanza *Be My Love*

Dean Martin *Memories are Made of This / That's Amore / Volare*

Johnny Mathis *A Certain Smile / Misty*

Guy Mitchell *Singing the Blues*

Matt Monro *Portrait Of My Love / Walk Away*

Jimmie Rogers *Kisses Sweeter Than Wine*

Frank Sinatra *Love & Marriage / Love is the Tender Trap*

Andy Williams *Butterfly / Can't Get Used to Loosing you*

Richie Valens *Donna* ★

Dickie Valentine *Finger of Suspicion / Mr Sandman*

Bobbie Vinton *Blue Velvet*

Other artists that were moulded to suit these in-between chart years included Conway Twitty, who came out of the Country genre. He wrote *It's Only Make Believe* in seven minutes and then sold one million copies (£7 as a 45', £14 as a 78', $30 in USA). Ricky Nelson was perfect, safe, young white stock from a long-running TV series. He copied a Fats Domino song *I'm Walkin'* ★ (worth £125 as a 45' with gold label lettering, £80 with silver lettering, £60 as a 78', and approximately $70 in USA) and sold a million copies. He was then promptly contracted by Domino to record for his own label.

> *Unknown Valuables – Conway Twitty's 1959/60 MGM LPs are nearing the £100 value but look for the modest 1960 Mercury Record EP* I Need Your Loving ★ *(No: Zep10069) – it currently lists at £175.*

Another Hit Parader star was helped on by his age: Paul Anka was just 15 when he recorded his own composition *Diana* (worth £8, $20 in the USA) for ABC Dunhill. Using youth as his appeal and safe orchestrations to simulate the rock beat, this one record gave him nine million sales, topping charts both sides of the Atlantic and securing over 300 copycat recordings across 22 countries. Well-scrubbed youthfulness without the darker innuendos of the incoming Rock & Roll genre was a solid formula, and so whole armies of all-American teenage sweethearts dived in. New Yorker Marcie Blane personified the spirit with her 1962 hit *Bobby's Girl*, which was copied in the UK by Susan Maughan (worth £6). Andrea Carroll sang *It Hurts to be Sixteen* (worth £8) and *Please Don't Talk to the Lifeguard* (which sells for $15); the latter was also charted by another youngster, Diane Ray. Diane Renay complained she was *Growing Up Too Fast* on her record (worth $10). Little Peggy March got to No.1 with *I Will Follow Him* (£7) and Lesley Gore's *It's My Party* (£6) also shot to No.1 in the USA, while Carole King pledged in her hit to wait all summer for her boy with *It Might As Well Rain Until September* ★ (in USA on Companion Records worth $300+).

The Unexpected *"COMPULSIVE, HARD TO FIND"*

Suggested Strands

On the Edge
Sounds and Visions
Surprising Packages
After Dark
Animal Life
Overkill

Average Record Cost

☆

The arrival of stereo witnessed an avalanche of hardware and consumer interest but a shortage of suitable albums to show it off. The rush to record LPs wasn't restricted to major stars and so for a decade from the mid-'50s almost everybody considered making a record. This section celebrates the extraordinarily diverse output that resulted. Many of the records had very limited pressings or distribution, and so could be seen as worthless. However, if two collectors are after the same song then its price can soar. Naturally this means that there are few listed price guides to assist the collector. This is extreme vinyl collecting, which will test your ingenuity in the hunt and will often yield uncomfortable yet unique recordings.

ON THE EDGE

Singles

Ali Ben Dhown *Mustapha*

LPs

Balsara and his Singing Sitars *Sound of Music*

Han-Sadutta *The Vision*

Rasput and The Sepoy *Mutinys Flower Power Sitar*

Tangela Tricoli *Jet Lady*

SOUNDS AND VISIONS

Singles

Paul Damian *How to Say Llanfairpwyllgwyngyllgog....*

LPs

Max K. Gilstrap *Whistles*

Steve Halpern *Christening for Listening*

Konkrete Canticle *Experiments in Disintegrating Language*

Lady June *Linguistic Leprosy*

Fred Lowery *Whistling for You*

Wind Harp *Songs from the Hill*

On the Edge

As soon as The Beatles used a sitar on a song, many opportunists jumped on the bandwagon – Balsara and his Singing Sitars struggled gloriously with covers of *I Want to Hold Your Hand* and even old classics like *The Sound of Music*. Then there's Ali Ben Dhown's 1967 Piccadilly single *Mustapha*; the B-side *Turkish Delight* features a toy piano, chiming sitars, rushing gongs, and a strange whispering vocal. Dora Hall – heiress to an industry fortune – simply couldn't sing but offered an LP with material like *Hang on Sloopy* and *Satisfaction* – she even organized her own TV show and somehow persuaded Frank Sinatra to appear as a guest!

Indulged – Jeff Gray is an LP of just vocals and drums. This production was assisted by the artist's rich parents. The words on the sleeve include: "Jeff, the man and his music, is where genius begins. Like that wise saying: 'beat the wife, black her eyes, kick her in the shins, break her arm, and you'll end up having to get your own dinner...'"

Sounds and Visions

Private musical voyages are intriguing. British poet Lady June's *Linguistic Leprosy* offers surreal poems spoken in her deep voice over sparse Brian Eno-like exotic tracks on Caroline Records. Wind Harp presented the LP *Songs from the Hill*, which features strange sounds from an 18m (60ft) harp played on top of a hill. More down-to-earth recording comes from Fred Lowery, the blind whistler and preacher – his 10" Decca album *Whistling for You* features *Walking Along*,

Kicking the Leaves, and *Whistle a Happy Tune*. Konkrete Canticle is a group of avant-garde poets and composers who offer strange gurglings, barks, and squeaks to text on the LP *Experiments in Disintegrating Language*. One track, *Seven Numbers*, is a poem, just chanting the digits one to seven.

Surprising Packages

Lynn Carey wrote music for *Beyond the Valley of the Dolls*; under guidance from an admirer she graced the cover of her *Mama Lion* LP behind cut-out bars of a lion's cage. The inside revealed her suckling a lion cub. Scott Bond's series of 45's on Spurt Records are mixtures of avant-garde and piano boogie. His first LP, *Amsterdam Red Light Boogie*, which was limited to 1,000 copies, had a fake cowskin sleeve, marbled pink vinyl, and samples of the infamous *Peter Wyngarde* ★ album (*see* p62).

After Dark

Occult themes are popular in this particular area. Robbie The Singing Werewolf – actually a folk singer from Santa Monica – offered *Live at Waleback* tracks including *Vampire Man* and *Streets of Transylvania*. Frances Cannon, on her *The Singing Psychic* LP, predicted public figures' futures, while real celebrity Vincent Price created a 1970 double LP *Witchcraft and Magic*. As he is a "name", valuation is possible for this LP – expect to pay around £70. Louise Huebner's LP offers hints on *Seduction through Witchcraft* and there's even an LP called *Music to Strip By*, which provides a free G-String!

> *Ulterior Motives – Ann Corio's album* How to Strip for your Husband *offers music to "make marriage merrier". It includes an instruction booklet with gems such as, "Remember the time it takes to roll down a silk stocking can spell the difference between mink and mink-dyed muskrat."*

Animal Life

Plenty of animal sounds have graced LPs. There's even a heavily edited rendition of *A Hard Day's Night* with barking dogs, and Tony Schwartz presents a story in sound of *A Dog's Life*. More enduring is *Going to the Dogs* – a record by Charlie, Bill, and Steve. It's a fundraiser for guide dogs for the blind, and was evidently recorded live in their own backyard as it comes complete with the audible quote, "Oh, are you recording? Should I turn the dryer off?"! Birds are favourites on LPs: Artal Orchestra offers *The Canaries Birds*, mixing bird

ANIMAL LIFE

Singles

San Diego Zoo *I Left My Heart in San Francisco*

LPs

Artal Orchestra
The Canaries Birds

Charlie, Bill and Steve
Going to the Dogs

Jim Fassett
Symphony of the Birds

Tony Schwartz *A Dog's Life*

OVERKILL

LPs

Arthur Godfrey
Strategic Air Command

Dr Hajime Murooka
Lullaby from the Womb

Armand Schaubroeck
A Lot of People Would Like to See Armand Schaubroeck … Dead (3 LPs)

A SINGLE VOICE

LPs

Rev Fred Lane
The One that Cut You

Victor Lundberg
Open Letter to my Teenage Son

Marcel Marceau
Best of Marcel Marceao (sic)

John Ylvasaker *Cool Livin'*

songs with waltzes, while ex-CBS engineer Jim Fassett's 1960 *Symphony of the Birds* uses nothing but field bird recordings that have been processed into an electronic symphony. Brazilian canaries sing *Swanee River* while parakeets invite you to *Come on in the Door is Open* and sing *Come Up and See Me Sometime*. And Pancho the Parrot from San Diego Zoo sings *I Left My Heart in San Francisco*.

Overkill

The seduction of vinyl was never limited to oddballs and hippies – the "Establishment" saw its potential too. Truly strange is the 1962 LP *Norad Tracks Santa*, which promotes the North American Air Defence Command's Dew Line (Distant Early Warning). It offers standard Christmas music along with regular reports on Santa's progress indicating whether he'll be shot down en route. This apparently illustrates the threat of accidental nuclear war. The Norad/Santa association stems from a 1950s incident during which a boy tried to call a department-store Santa and accidentally got through to Norad instead!

A Single Voice

Individuals on vinyl are the stuff of curiosity. Wide-ranging in talent and topic, you might discover *Born to Trouble* – the 1966 recorded testimony of a psychopath, or Buck Warner's entirely spoken album about his love affair with Chicago's O'Hare airport.

Victor Lundberg's *Open Letter to my Teenage Son* features patriotic music, sermons on freedom, and threats to disown his son if he burns his draft card. Somewhat closer to the edge is Rev Fred Lane's *The One that Cut You*, which features a cover portrait with graffiti, sticky plasters, and weird lens glasses. The album has tracks such as *I Talk to my Haircut*.

More whimsical are a pair of LPs that are associated with the famed French mime artist Marcel Marceau. *Marcel Marceau Speaks in English* is on Caedmont and, my favourite, *Best of Marcel Marceao* (sic), features 19 minutes of silence plus applause, on Gone-If Records/MGM Records.

> *Flights of Fancy – Evangelist Forrest McCullough's mock documentary* Flight F.I.N.A.L.: A Dramatic Comparison to Death *on Word Records reveals a radio reporter who has been let into the "Terminal of Death" and joins a newly departed soul on a supersonic flight to heaven.*

Celebrities *"THE CURIOSITY SHOP"*

Suggested Strands
Wordsmiths
Headliners
Second Careers
Sporting Voices

Average Record Cost
☆☆

Rising Stars
Maureen Reagan
Sugar Ray Robinson

WORDSMITHS

Singles

Russell Grant *No Matter What Sign You Are*

Derek Jameson
Do They Mean Us

William Saroyan
Come on-a my House

LPs

Rona Barrett
Sings Hollywood Greatest Hits

Bredan Behan
Irish Folksongs & Ballads

Barbara Cartland
Album of Love Songs

Alistair Cooke
An Evening with Alistair Cooke

Allen Ginsberg
First of Blues

Naura Hayden
And Then She Wrote

Ron Hubbard *Space Jazz*

Tom Lehrer
Songs by Tom Lehrer

Carol Sandberg
America Songbag

J.R. Tolkien *Reads & Sings Lord of the Rings*

The whole area of collecting Celebrity recordings is as confused as many of the misguided individuals that put themselves in front of microphones and so for our guide we've separated the worlds of TV, Movies, and Stage Musicals (*see* later sections), and created a further "Glamorous" category (which follows on page 51). Andy Warhol's quotation about 15 minutes of fame is curiously pertinent here, as celebrity status is often brief. This has meant that many have extensively capitalized on the moment by making records. Some of these are unexpectedly interesting while others are so painful they are compelling!

Ironically, it's quite a challenging field within which to build a collection as the records themselves were often released only for very short periods of time – and for some sports stars distribution might have been restricted to their team's location. So hunting out almost any record within this field will test your ingenuity and the likelihood of profiteering is very slight. That said, you will definitely create a fascinating archive and a unique insight into an era.

Back in the 1920s star recordings were promotional tools for stage shows and movies, and many delivered respectable results as that era's stage training included song and dance. The surging worlds of cinema and radio helped raise morale during World War II and many future broadcast stars emerged.

As the '60s youth revolution took hold achieving fame was an imperative, and so began decades of the unlikely queuing up to commit their vision to vinyl. It could be speeches, poetry, literary readings, press conferences, how to keep fit and healthy, or desperate attempts to sing meaningful songs. In more recent times semi-spoken styles of music such as Rap have given celebrities an easier route towards the music charts, while studio technology can now virtually guarantee apparently acceptable vocal performances. All this adds value to the earlier, more naked efforts of the famous.

Wordsmiths

The urge to stray beyond the written word and onto disc has seduced an extraordinary collection of writers, from the high-priestess of romance Barbara Cartland, with her 1978 *Love Songs* LP, to J.R. Tolkien's 1975 reading and singing of *The Lord of the Rings*. Interestingly, Cartland's effort, which wanders through songs like *Dream Lover* and *Goodnight Sweetheart* backed by the Royal Philharmonic Orchestra, is

HEADLINERS

Singles

Senator Sam Ervin *Bridge Over Troubled Water*

Fed Judge William Hungate *Down at the Old Watergate*

President Kwame Nkrumah *Ninth Son*

LPs

Senator Robert Byrd *Mountain Fiddler*

Winston Churchill *The Voice of Winston Churchill*

Lord Adrian Foley *At the Piano*

Howard Hughes *Press Conference*

Governor Lester Maddox *God, Family and Country*

Charles Manson *Live at St Quentin*

King Samdech Norodom Sihanouk *Cambodian Suite*

Lee Harvey Oswald *Lee Harvey Oswald Speaks*

Pope John Paul II *Lieder des Papster*

Maureen Reagan *Guess Who's Happy at Home*

Margaret Truman *American Songs*

currently worth twice Tolkien's interpretation of his masterpiece. Then there are the questionable "bargains", such as astrologist Russell Grant's rendition of the old Supremes song *No Matter What Sign You Are* or journalist Derek Jameson's Polydor single *Do They Mean Us* – neither of these is worth more than a few pence. More weighty efforts include distinguished writer/broadcaster Alistair Cooke's 1955 *An Evening with ...* album, valued at around $40. (The reissue that appeared 20 years later currently sells for around $20).

Headliners

The prospect of leaving a permanent mark on vinyl is far too seductive to be left merely to hopeful pop groups. The world's great and mighty have taken little persuading... Lord Adrian Foley slipped from the House of Lords in 1955 to record his piano skills on MGM – yours for around $40. Or perhaps you prefer American Senator Robert Byrd's *Mountain Fiddler* LP or his 1978 single *Strawberry Stomp*, worth around $25. Georgia Governor Lester Maddox sings, whistles, and plays harmonica on his *God, Family and Country* disc, while President Harry

> *Prison Voice – Prison has long been a popular record theme for country artists, yet it's the real-life killer of Sharon Tate, Charles Manson, who created the reality. He wrote and performed his own LPs,* Love and Terror Cult *and* Live at St Quentin. *Expect to pay £10–£150 per copy.*

Truman's daughter Margaret studied as a coloratura and toured with orchestras before her 10" record *American Songs* prompted a Washington Post critic to print that she sang flat. Copies of the record are now worth around $80. For less than that you might find collections of Winston Churchill's oratory, choose from a huge range of John F. Kennedy speeches and commemoratives, or maybe enjoy Pope John Paul II singing in foreign tongues. In a rather more desperate attempt to capture the spotlight there are records such as that by Ghana's 1960s President entitled *Ninth Son* (worth $25), infamous ex-Philippine First Lady Imelda Marcos with her bilingual offering *Imelda Marcos* (English and Tagalog – both $18), or you can travel further afield to enjoy *Cambodian Suite*, the 1955 composition by the then king of that country (available for $35).

This is a zany corner of the record world, yet such curiosities present great challenges and provide a true archive of the time.

Nonconformist

- Wealthy US socialite Florence Foster Jenkins dreamt of being an opera star so she self-funded her own concerts. She sang off key so badly that she ended up becoming a cult figure! Her 1961 RCA LPs *The Glory of the Human Voice* and 1956 *In Recital* now fetch $30–40 each.

- Ex-embroiderer and late developer Grandma Moses had her first art exhibition at the age of 80. She created 1,600 works and a US national holiday was declared when she turned 100. She also found time to record a 1958 LP *Christmas with Grandma Moses* – examples now cost $50.

- Fabled New York party animal Elsa Maxwell satisfied her ego with an album entitled *Her Music and Her Voice*, which was released in 1958 and is now worth $35.

- Fast-food icon Colonel Sanders lost control to big business in the early '60s but they continued to use his image, even creating Colonel Sanders recordings. These were simple Tijuana Brass-type efforts, with his face on the cover.

- More abstract still, the computer-born star of TV and adverts Max Headroom was "responsible" for four 1980s singles, which are sadly worth very little today.

Falling from Grace – 1960s vice queen Janie Jones rubbed more than shoulders with the jet set until her fall from grace and resulting imprisonment. At her height she cut a series of truly kitsch singles that are so bad they are fascinating. The singles generally fetch up to £15.

SECOND CAREERS

Singles

Eamonn Andrews *Shifting Whispering Sands / The Ship that Never Sailed / High Wind*

Simon Dee *Julie*

Mike Douglas *Pass Me By / Mother's Day*

David Frost *Zookeeper*

Merv Griffin *Bobby Sox Bounce*

Wink Martindale *Deck of Cards / Lincoln's Gettysburg Address*

LPs

Johnny Carson *Here's Johnny*

Mike Douglas *It's Time for Mike Douglas*

Arthur Godfrey *And his Talent Scouts / 7 Years before the Mike / I'm a Lonely Little Petunia*

Merv Griffin *Midnight Music / Remembering the '40s*

Wink Martindale *Big Bad John*

Second Careers

Having hosted artist after artist on their shows, television hosts often fancy their chances on record. At his height, swinging '60s celebrity Simon Dee recorded a single for Chapter One Records called *Julie* – this is now worth just £6. David Frost released a now forgotten 1966 single entitled *Zookeeper*, as well as a couple of albums, while across the Atlantic Merv Griffin, who created shows like *Jeopardy* and *Wheel of Fortune*, had a secret asset – he'd previously been the singer in the Freddy Martin band. The result was a dozen albums and over 80 single releases, but there are no huge valuables among them as yet. Rival Johnny Carson had to be content with a 1978 commemorative show release *Here's Johnny*. Veteran 1950s TV personality Arthur Godfrey racked up a couple of dozen albums and around 50 singles, which are

SPORTING VOICES

Singles

Bobby Allison
Baby It's Because of You

Terry Bradshaw
I'm So Lonesome I Could Cry

Jackie Charlton
Simple Little Things

Joe Frazier
Try It Again

Graham Hill
Takes You Round Snetterton

Hulk Hogan *Hulk Hogan II*

Junk Yard Dog
Grab Them Cakes

John McEnroe, Pat Cash,
and Roger Daltrey
Rock and Roll

Stirling Moss
Motor Racing with Stirling Moss

Akeem Olajum
The Unbeatable Dream

Refrigerator Perry
Rappin' Together

Terry Venables
*What Do You Want To Make
Those Eyes At Me For*

LPs

Lou Albano
NBRQ & Captain Lou Albano

Chicago Bears
Sing Holiday Halftimes

Henry Cooper *Knockout Party*

Denny McLain *In Las Vegas*

NASCAR *Goes Country*

EPs

Sugar Ray Robinson
Hot Soup

all now beginning to mature on the market. Eamonn Andrews, the original host for the TV show *This Is Your Life*, wrote some songs that have failed to surge in value but his 1956 version of the Billy Vaughn record *Shifting Whispering Sands* actually spent three weeks in the UK charts, peaking at No.18.

Naff but Fun – While long lists of female celebrities struggled with personalized "keep-fit" LPs, UK's choreographer Lionel Blair released Aerobic Dancing in 1983. Even worse, but with great cringe appeal, are George Best and a Miss World on Shape Up and Dance.

Sporting Voices

Sport and show business are natural bedfellows, which is more than can be said for many sporting celebrities and microphones. The mass attack of whole squads of players such as the New York Jets or LA's Rams goes some way towards concealing the pain. And in the UK dozens of football teams' albums are avidly collected by their followers. Individual sports stars also tried their hand at record making: the famed Chicago Bears hulk "Refrigerator" Perry offered a 12" single *Rappin' Together* (now worth $8), while Detroit Tigers' pitcher Denny McLain gained TV and Vegas work following his *At the Organ* LP. In the UK, filled with World Cup squad *Back Home* chart success, Jackie Charlton tried a sole venture on Bell Records that hurled musicians, singers, and even church bells at the record with tragic results. Equally uneasy were clutches of racing drivers such as Stirling Moss, Graham Hill, Richard Petty, Bobby Allison, and the NASCAR Champs collectively contributing to *NASCAR Goes Country*. One of Stirling Moss' records promised the unique experience of lapping with him in a single seater but in reality contained a pedestrian Lord Aberdare asking wooden questions to a backdrop of overworked sound effects. Such records really hold curiosity value only.

Wrestling stars also got involved in making records – Henry Cooper has an LP of *Knockout Party* music while middleweight champ Sugar Ray Robinson's 1964 offering was called *I'm Still Swinging*. It is the latter's 1959 single *Hot Soup* ★ that is worth hunting out, as it is currently listing at $100. There are bargains to be had – world wrestling hero Junk Yard Dog's single *Grab Them Cakes* is yours for just $4. And, though valued at much the same, heavyweight Joe Frazier's 1974 Jobo record *Try It Again* really is a pretty decent track.

Glamorous *"DREAMS AND NIGHTMARES"*

Suggested Strands

Ambitious
Action Women
Continental Spice
Waifs and Strays
Old-Fashioned Charms

Average Record Cost

✩✩✩

Rising Stars

Brigitte Bardot
Honor Blackman
Diana Dors
Marilyn Monroe
Ann-Margret
Jane Russell

AMBITIOUS

Singles

Marilyn Chambers
Benihans

Joan Collins *Imagine*

Sue Lyon *Lolita Ya-Ya*

Elizabeth Taylor
Wings in the Sky

Raquel Welch *This Girl's
Back in Town*

LPs

Ann-Margret
And Here She Is / Dames At Sea ★

Samantha Fox *Touch Me*

Mae West *Mae West Songs
Vols. I & II*

ACTION WOMEN

Singles

Farrah Fawcett *You*

Diana Rigg
Sentimental Journey

If you listen to conversations at record fairs or spot music journalists' frequent remarks it will soon become clear that there's a complete layer of collecting that, until now, hasn't been granted full status. Officially it transcends the boundaries of Celebrity, TV, Movie, and Stage yet is still precisely driven by a single criteria – how it looks. Collecting period records for their glamour only, without any emphasis on the music itself is really no stranger than collecting tea caddies without filling them with tea. Record covers are wonderful souvenirs of an era, or a particular style, and are full of memories. In this section we explore the decades of glamorous women who've looked to records to give them a second slice of the celebrity cake.

Ambitious

Combining two high-profile names does not automatically guarantee that a record will achieve any great value. For example, pairing Joan Collins and Bing Crosby on *Let's Not Be Sensible* resulted in a single worth only a few pence. Raquel Welch's *This Girl's Back in Town* is also virtually worthless, yet the ex-Ivory Soap advert girl-turned porn star Marilyn Chambers' 1977 single creeps ahead in value at $12. However, screen vamp Mae West can command up to $80 a disc (*Mae West Songs* Vol I or II), while Ann-Margret, who has droves of credible recordings, also has a little-known collectors' gem – a pink LP called *Dames At Sea* ★, released by Bell System Family Theater and worth around $200.

> *Ever Optimistic – Barbi Benton, the one-time hopeful partner of* Playboy *magnet Hugh Hefner, made five LPs, including a country and western LP for* Playboy's *own label called* Best Live In Japan *($40). She later turned to New Age style and recorded* Kinetic Voyage, *worth just $10.*

Action Women

The Television section positively bulges with actors spreading their wings (*see* pages 58–61) but here we look briefly at the glam action women that were blessed with good looks, if not always with a matching voice. TV's *Charlie's Angel* Cheryl Ladd chalked up three LPs and numerous singles including *Think It Over*, which edged into the lower end of the music charts in 1978. Her *Best Of...* album now commands around $25.

LPs

Honor Blackman
Everything I've Got

Lynda Carter *Portrait*

Cheryl Ladd
Best of Cheryl Ladd

CONTINENTAL SPICE

Singles

Brigitte Bardot *Mr Sun* ★

Claudia Cardinale *Love Affair*

Leslie Caron *Hi Lili, Hi Lo*

Marlene Dietrich (with
Rosemary Clooney)
Too Old to Cut the Mustard

Britt Ekland
Do it to Me

Vanessa Paradis *Joe le Taxi*

LPs

Sophia Loren *Peter Sellers
& Sophia Loren*

EPs

Françoise Hardy *En Anglais*

Predecessor Farrah Fawcett managed just one single, *You*, in 1978, but selling eight million posters of herself in a single year must have been some comfort. A modest contribution by TV's *Wonder Woman*, Lynda Carter, was well eclipsed by *Avengers* star Honor Blackman. Her first record outing resulted in the UK Top 5 *Kinky Boots* duet with Patrick MacNee (worth £30) and she then went on to make a half-sung album *Everything I've Got*. It was valued in 1999 at £35 and is now worth over £50.

Continental Spice

The allure of continental glamour created recording opportunities for the likes of Britt Ekland, who produced three versions of *Do It To Me*. Not surprisingly, the picture disc version has the most value at $25. Vanessa Paradis' single *Joe Le Taxi* – complete with its all-important poster – is worth £25. Françoise Hardy produced quite a body of work – 18 UK singles and more than 20 LPs/EPs. The most valuable is the 1968 *En Anglais* (£25). Marlene Dietrich perfected the art of semi-singing and created dozens of delicious and collectable recordings that average around $50 a disc. High-priestess Brigitte Bardot delivered over 70 recordings with borderline skills and great style. Interestingly a lack of US interest reveals her *Mr Sun* ★ single to command just $12, while in the UK it could fetch £150 if accompanied by its picture sleeve.

Starry Eyed

If Miss World could become *Wonder Woman* (Lynda Carter) and Miss Italy (Sophia Loren) could get on the show business "A List", it naturally followed that numbers of opportunist Miss Americas headed for the recording studio:

- 1945 winner Bess Myerson then went on to be a commissioner of cultural affairs; her 1959 LP *Fashions in Music* values at $35.

- Miss America 1958 was Marilyn Van Derbur. She offered *Miss America Plays Hammond*, which now lists at $40.

- In 1959 Mary Ann Mobley won, picking up a part in the movie *Diff'rent Strokes* as well as a chat show-host husband. Her 1961 single *Down the Aisle* is now worth $15.

- Maria Beale Fletcher took the crown in 1962 on behalf of North Carolina and celebrated with a single *The Grass Looks Greener*, worth $6.

- Miss America 1965, Vonda Kay Van Dyke from Arizona, went on to create four LPs. Her first, *Teenage Diary*, has the highest value at $15.

WAIFS AND STRAYS

Singles

Barbie and Ken *Nobody Taught Me (how to fall in love)*

Rula Lenska *I Wanna be in a Movie with You*

Michelle Pfeiffer *Cool Rider*

Adrienne Posta *Only 15*

LPs

Gypsy Rose Lee *That's Me All Over*

Hayley Mills *Annette and Hayley Mills* ★

Cybill Shepherd *Does it with Cole Porter*

Twiggy *Twiggy and the Girl Friends*

OLD-FASHIONED CHARMS

Singles

Sandra Dee *When I Fall in Love*

Audrey Hepburn *Oh How to be Lovely*

Gina Lollobrigida *Vissi d'arte*

Julie London *Cry Me a River*

Marilyn Monroe *I Wanna Be Loved by You*

Tuesday Weld *Are You the Boy*

LPs

Diana Dors *Swinging Dors*

Jayne Mansfield *Busts up in Las Vegas* ★

Debbie Reynolds *Am I That Easy to Forget*

Jane Russell *Jane Russell*

EPs

Susan Heywood *I'll Cry Tomorrow*

• In 1973 it was Terry Ann Meeuwsen's turn. She became co-host of CBN's *700 Club* and even briefly sang with the New Christy Minstrels. Her one album, *Meet Terry*, is worth $30.

• Susan Powell was the 1981 victor. She joined the cast of *Nashville on the Road* and released two singles – *Midnight Flyer* and *There's No Me Without You*, worth $5 each.

• Controversial 1984 winner Vanessa Williams was later disqualified for posing nude in a magazine, but she went on to build a modest recording career with 15 US singles.

Waifs and Strays

Those with more restrained images sadly suffer in the value stakes. Ex-model and *Moonlighting* star Cybill Shepherd's LP *Does it with Cole Porter* requires just $20 (including poster), while a Michelle Pfeiffer single is worth only $5. Twiggy produced a number of records that are now worth £15–20, but the surprise package is British actress Hayley Mills – her 1962 soft-covered record *Annette and Hayley Mills* ★, from Buena Vista, will set you back $600! Talking of strays, Barbie once teamed up with her friend Ken and came out with *Nobody Taught Me* – no one has tendered a price for this as yet!

Old-Fashioned Charms

Inevitably nostalgia drives much of record collecting. Building up a library of vinyl seductresses offers a chance to listen to the music as well as feast upon the period artwork. Select from the heart – if it looks good it's likely to appreciate in value. Diana Dors' single *Where Did it Go* is worth just £6 yet her *Swinging Dors* LP, complete with red vinyl, is worth £60 in the UK ($40 in the USA). Jane Russell's 1959 self-titled LP is now topping $100 in stereo form. In their early days Jane Mansfield and Mary Tyler Moore posed for other people's LP covers. Mansfield's own LP *Busts up in Las Vegas* ★ is now almost $200 and her recitations on *Shakespeare, Tchaikovsky and Me* is worth up to $50. Easy Listening queen Julie London strikes the best balance between period sex appeal and excellent recordings – making dozens of singles and LPs. *Cry Me a River*, her 1956 million-seller single, is now worth £40.

Second Career – Actress Debbie Reynolds had a million-seller in 1950 with Ada Daba Honeymoon, *which was written 36 years earlier. In 1957 she scored a No.1 US hit (and UK No.2) with* Tammy *from her movie* Tammy and the Bachelor. *US copies of her LPs are $30, but UK ones make £30.*

COMEDY

This section releases all of the usual inhibitions about collecting – for example, the fear of not knowing the correct year or value of an item spoils so much in the collectable arena. Not so with comedy records – you should simply hunt out records or artists that appeal to you. There are no sleeping giants to discover, no huge profits to be made, and, most appealing, no huge prices to pay. You are free to collect favourite performers, or maybe troupes such as *Carry On* stars or clusters of related humour like the worlds of Monty Python or The Goons.

Recorded comedy is nothing new – it was committed to cylinders at the beginning of the last century and cuts like *I Like Bananas Because They Don't Have No Bones* existed before World War II. Broadcasting then overpowered recorded comedy until the boom of the 1950s, when recording technology suddenly provided fresh creative freedoms. It is interesting to note that Sir George Martin was producing '50s comedy records with Peter Sellers, Bernard Cribbins, and the *Beyond the Fringe* team long before his Beatles sojourn. New breeds of comedians discovered less censorship on long-playing records and so monologue stars such as Shelley Berman, Bob Newhart, and Allan Sherman were launched. In the UK Tony Hancock's observations and the madness of The Goons unleashed a decade of often lightweight, sometimes very successful, comedy recordings. During the psychedelic '60s American comedy was seen as particularly cool and included the likes of Cheech & Chong, the National Lampoon, Flip Wilson, Richard Prior, and Bill Cosby. They covered fresh topics like drugs, race, and politics, and often quite sophisticated productions such as Firesign Theatre's sound collages were made. Alternative comedy outlets gradually began to reduce enthusiasm for recording, although occasionally a TV show helped to launch a band or record. This is certainly true of The Beatles parody by The Rutles (*see* page 70 for the album covers).

Madness Itself – The 1950s US magazine, Mad,*was a genuine cult and it even issued four LPs plus a number of cardboard singles within the magazine. Expect to pay between $50 and $80 for these gems, which include* She's Got a Nose Job, Somebody Else's Dandruff, *and a parody of a suitably '50s crisis single* All I Have Left is My Johnny's Hubcap *– he had been "nicked" for stealing cars. All these tracks are from* Mad Twists Rock 'n' Roll, *which is worth $40.*

Offering price guides is very difficult within comedy as the UK and US markets frequently don't acknowledge the other's comic stars and the published price lists have only token entries. However, the prices shown here will soon give you a sense of the ranges involved, and indeed will occasionally reveal that a cherished US artist/recording is actually considerably cheaper in the UK – which may appeal to buyers across the world with access to the Internet. Comedy discs are generally very cheap so it's fine to gamble on odd records that you discover but don't know much about. Let your hair down and simply enjoy the adventure.

Comedy *"A PATCHWORK OF STYLES"*

Suggested Strands

Airways Landmarks
Series Animals
Fun & Games
Class Acts
American Gems

Average Record Cost

☆

Rising Stars

Stan Freberg
Bonzo Dog Doo Dah Band
Joyce Grenfell

CLASSIC SINGLES

Milton Berle
Bibbidy-Bibbidy-Boo

Bernard Bresslaw
*Mad Passionate Love /
I Only Asked*

Jasper Carrott *Funky Moped*

Kenneth Connor
Rail Road Rock

Billy Connolly *D.I.V.O.R.C.E*

Harry H. Corbett
Flower Power Fred

Bernard Cribbens
*Right Said Fred / Hole in
the Ground*

Windsor Davies/Don Estelle
Whispering Grass

Charlie Drake
*Splish Splash / Hello, My
Darlings / My Boomerang
Won't Come Back*

Clive Dunn *Grandad*

Jimmy Edwards *I've Never
Seen a Straight Banana*

Flanders & Swann *I'm a Gnu*

Bruce Forsyth
I'm Backing Britain

Being a matter of personal perception, divisions in comedy are virtually impossible, so the categories below are quite arbitrary, although certain criteria do prevail. Vinyl continued to be used in the 1980s but CDs were emerging, so that decade's gems – such as the infamous Spitting Image *Chicken Song* or Alexei Sayle's *'Ullo John! Got a New Motor?* (both just £3) – have been left out. Neither does the book extend back to the rich heritage of early humour from the 1930s, such as W.C. Fields' *Temperance Lecture* (now worth $25).

Airways Landmarks

So much of recorded comedy owes its success to broadcasting, which brought everything from political revue to slapstick directly into our homes. Tony Hancock captured 1950s suburban Britain with painful accuracy through masterpieces like *The Blood Donor* and *Radio Ham* (on LPs worth around £18 each) but the collectors' gem is the emotional interview LP with revered journalist John Freeman, *Face to Face*, which now fetches £80. Radio ensemble The Goons also had enormous impact. Born of wartime camaraderie, Peter Sellers, Harry Secombe, Spike Milligan, and Michael Bentine created airways mayhem and two Top 5 hit singles – *I'm Walking Backwards to Christmas* reached No.4 (now worth £12) while the *Ying Tong Song* peaked at No.3 (this version worth £9) and reappeared again at No. 9 in 1973 (fetches £3 today). Eventually Michael Bentine enjoyed his own comic visions in the series *It's a Square World* – the 1962 LP of this is now rising towards £20. The US run of the revue *Beyond the Fringe* led to the TV series *Not Only ... But Also*, and a range

> *Circus Troop – Monty Python's Flying Circus included John Cleese, Graham Chapman, Eric Idle, Terry Jones, and Michael Palin. Their first LP was a BBC affair (£6–10). Their Charisma Records' Another Monty Python Record and Monty Python's Previous Record are worth £10 each.*

of Peter Cook and Dudley Moore LPs, and the TV theme *Goodbyee* entered the UK charts. Dudley Moore's 1970 *From Beyond the Fringe* is worth around £12, Peter Cook's 1965 *Misty Mr Wisty* LP £15, and their joint albums fetch around the same figures.

The Goodies *The Funky Gibbon*

The Goons *I'm Walking Backwards to Christmas / Ying Tong Song*

Rolf Harris *Jake the Peg / Tie Me Kangaroo Down Sport*

Henhouse Five Plus Too *In the Mood*

Benny Hill *Ernie*

Frankie Howerd *Nymphs and Shepherds*

Sidney James/Liz Fraser *The Ooter Song*

Rambling Syd Rumpo *Green Grow my Nadgers Oh*

The Rutles *I Must be In Love*

Monty Python *Always Look on the Bright Side of Life*

Terry Scott *My Brother*

Peter Sellers *Goodness Gracious Me, Sophia Loren / A Hard Day's Night / Any Old Iron*

Tiny Tim *Tip Toe Through the Tulips with Me*

The Goodies ran for eight series in the 1970s. They frequently used parodies of pop music within the shows, which inevitably spawned relatively worthless LPs. However, they did enjoy UK chart hits with *The Funky Gibbon*, which reached No.4, and *The In Betweenies* that made it to No.7 (both worth just £3 today).

Series Animals

One time hits by TV's funny men are generally easy and cheap to collect. Benny Hill's No.1 *Ernie*, for example, can be picked up for just a couple of pounds (LPs from £7–10). Frankie Howerd joined forces with the wonderful Margaret Rutherford to offer the single *Nymphs and Shepherds*, while his best LP *At The Establishment* is worth £15. Terry Scott issued the forgotten *My Brother* in 1962 (now worth £12), Ronnie Corbett's *Big Man* fetches £6, Bill Oddie's *Knitting Song* is worth £5, and Mike & Bernie Winters *That Man Batman* fetches £8–15, depending on whether it has a picture sleeve. Tommy Cooper appealed to a different audience, and his single *Don't Jump off the Roof Dad* is worth £15. Spike Milligan singles remain cheap unless you find a 78' version of his 1958 *Will I Find My Love*, for which you should expect to pay £20. His more desirable LPs, such as *Milligan Preserved* and *Muses with Milligan*, are also more expensive at £15–20.

Fun and Games

Simple, honest, funny singles are cheap and full of memories, if not always good taste! Bernard Bresslaw offered *Mad Passionate Love* in 1958 and *I Only Asked* in '59, both of which fetch approximately £10, and Clive Dunn's infamous 1970 *Grandad* reached No.1 but is now worth just £3. Cult figure Kenneth Williams' 1967 LP *Pleasure Bent* is now worth £20 and his single under the pseudonym Rambling Syd Rumpo, called *Green Grow my Nadgers Oh,* is £5. Barbara Windsor's forgotten LPs *Don't Dig Twiggy* and *Grin and Bare It* fetch around £8 each.

American oddball Tiny Tim burst into the charts in 1968 with a 40-year-old song *Tip Toe Through the Tulips with Me*. This is only worth £5, although his Australian EP *The Wonderful World of Romance* ★ is now worth around £200. Jackie Gleason's non-music album *And Awaaay We Go* is now edging towards the $100 mark while Phyllis Diller's mad domestic humour on *Wet Toe in the Socket* is yours for $20. Animals feature on comic records too – there really is an LP called *Songs for Gay Dogs* by Paddy Roberts, while record veteran Ray Stevens produced a wonderful version of Glenn Miller's *In the Mood* in 1976 by Henhouse Five Plus Too, which is "sung" by chickens – definitely well worth $10!

CLASSIC LPS

Milton Berle
Uncle Miltie on Radio

Firesign Theatre *Dear Friends* ★

Stan Freberg
The Best of Stan Freberg Shows

Joyce Grenfell
Requests the Pleasure

Tony Hancock *Face to Face*

Arthur Lowe *Bless 'em All*

Arthur Mullard
Arthur Mullard of London

Arthur Mullard/Hylda Baker
Band on the Trott

William Rushton
The Collected Works

Peter Sellers
The Best of Sellers

Eric Sykes/Hattie Jaques
Eric, Hattie and Things

Kenneth Williams/Hugh Paddick *The Bona Album of Julian and Sandy*

Unlikely Hero – Forty years a general-purpose celebrity, Rolf Harris has somehow generated a true cult music status. His records range from a cover of Led Zeppelin's Stairway to Heaven *to his No.1* Two Little Boys. *Anything of his can be picked up for under £15.*

Class Acts

Those listed within this section produced productions well beyond just "funny". Bonzo Dog Doo Dah Band fused jazz, pop, and the surreal to make clever but fun music. Singles include *My Brother Makes the Noises for the Talkies* (worth £35) and *Alley Oops* (£30), while the LPs *Gorilla*, *Tadpoles*, and *The Doughnut in Granny's Greenhouse* are all £30. The classic Joyce Grenfell *Nursery School* single is worth £5, while her 1954 LP *Requests the Pleasure* is £20. Both of satirist David Frost's *Frost Report* LPs are around £12. Victor Borge albums are all about $25 but a rare one-sided LP, *To Denmark – The Legend* ★, fetches $100. Wheelchaired Flanders and pianist Swann held Broadway records for their brilliantly witty shows that sold uniquely British humour to the USA. The three LPs using the *Drop of a Hat* title theme are worth $30 each. From the shadows of Monty Python emerged the TV and LP parody of the whole Beatles madness by The Rutles. The brilliantly conceived *All You Need is Cash* LP can be bought for £10.

American Gems

Bob Newhart was an accountant doing amateur radio comedy (he had never performed a live show), when he made the first of his memorable Warner LPs. Somewhere between Hancock and Berman, his accounts of driving lessons, use of tobacco, and other ordinary life issues quickly gained cult status. His 1960 LP *Button Down Mind* was followed with other *Button Down* derivatives – $25/£12 should buy you one.

Stan Freberg produced successful early topical US satire, and although his LPs are dated they are perfect mirrors of their times. Hunt out his 1951 love-smitten duet *John & Marsha*, which provides endless whisperings for $40. *The Best of Stan Freberg Shows* LP is $60 in the US and just £20 in the UK.

The recordings of established music figures Jo Stafford and Paul Weston under the pseudonyms of Jonathan and Darlene Edwards are extremely clever – deliberately slightly offkey or out of time. UK prices are around £10 but in the USA *Piano Artistry of Jonathan Edwards* commands $50–60 and *Jonathan and Darlene Edwards in Paris* is worth around $40.

DISCO

War *Lowrider* This was a fashion so strong that Disco Banners became quite commonplace.

Not only is "Discothèque" a French word but the roots of this genre stem from France during World War II, during Nazi occupation. At this time fashionable live Jazz was banned and so dances were held to records. The US growth of the genre stemmed from inner city gatherings of black communities to listen to Funk music in the late 1960s, but Disco quickly became the popularized and sanitized form for white clubbers, although it was often restricted to gay clientele. For white folk it was really a product of the '70s. Its East Coast explosion was aided by radio stations like Disco 92. However, clubs were the real driving force as Disco was about having a great time. At the time of its explosion onto the music scene it was an antidote to Vietnam and the Nixon scandals.

Disco was very overworked and in 1979 the backlash against it reached a point where a Disco Demolition rally took place in a Chicago Stadium to destroy thousands of records. As it has not yet returned to favour, any Disco record can be bought cheaply. This makes it the perfect time to build up what will definitely be a future asset.

As stars themselves weren't always central figures in Disco, collecting themes are very different. Producers and re-mix engineer portfolios make an interesting route. Alternatively, you could choose to collect the outputs of one of the era's key labels such as TK, Prelude, Salsoul, and Philadelphia International. A collection of the genuine black Funk dance music would be a fascinating journey through artists and records that never crossed over into mainstream charts, yet whose fingerprints are all over pop stars' Disco efforts.

The 1970s Rock era had been very masculine-dominated, full of denim and beer cans. Disco inverted this with glamour and armies of new assertive female stars from Blondie and Grace Jones to Gloria Gaynor, who declared *I Will Survive*. The female invasion itself would make a fascinating subject for a collection. Because the majority of the core material is made of singles, albums obviously don't dominate this scene – except perhaps the more original Funk bands like BT Express or Brass Connection. However, 12" pressings and re-mix issues of singles are the more elusive releases that will get collected first.

Disco Heaven – New York's Studio 54 grossed a cool seven million dollars in its first year. The building was originally built as an opera house, but it never staged an opera and instead became the Casino de Paree, then the Palladium, the Federal Theatre, and even a CBS studio, before evolving into New York's hottest discotheque.

Disco *"WAITING ITS TURN"*

Unlike other sections Disco is driven by music and dancing rather than by huge stars. Therefore collecting this genre remains uniquely free form – discover the vintage you enjoy the most and hunt it out. Right now everything is relatively cheap.

Grass Roots

Early years were influenced by Soul artists like Aretha Franklin and James Brown who pioneered the '60s dance singles *Out of Sight* (£12) and *Papa's Got a Brand New Bag* (£10). It was from Dyke and The Blazers' 1967 single *Funky Broadway* ($8) that the name Funk derived. This influenced a stronger "groove" feel from artists such as Isaac Hayes who made *Theme from Shaft* ($5/£5) and also Kool and The Gang's *Celebration* ($4).

Popularists

The Disco boom stormed radio thanks to artists like Donna Summer who sang *I Feel Love* (12" worth £12) and *Love to Love You Baby*. The latter's first pressing No.401A/B is worth $12, while the others (AA/BB) are just $6. Michael Jackson, The Rolling Stones, and Rod Stewart all cashed in on the boom, along with Chic's *Dance, Dance, Dance*, which sold a million in a month on Atlantic and is worth $4 today, although the very first ones that came out on Buddah are valued at $20. Fabricated group The Village People sang their hearts out on *YMCA* (worth $5). Their promo-only picture sleeve, *In the Navy*, is worth $20.

The real Disco-mania came with the 1977 movie *Saturday Night Fever* – the soundtrack is $12 while the Bee Gee's singles *You Should be Dancing*, *Stayin' Alive*, and *Jive Talkin'* are all $4.

European Voice

Disco started in Europe so naturally European acts contributed to its success. These included Giorgio Moroder, who created hits for Donna Summer and the movie scores for *Flashdance* (1983) and *American Gigolo* (1988), and Sweden's ABBA, whose *Dancing Queen* is worth $4. Scotland's Average White Band sang *Pick up the Pieces* (£5 or $5), French Cerrone created *Supernature* (12in worth £10), and the UK's Hot Chocolate wrote *You Sexy Thing* (£5 or $5). New Electronica movements emerged from the German group Kraftwerk, whose albums include *Trans Europe Express* (worth £6 or $5), and *Showroom Dummies* (£6–15).

TELEVISION

The George Mitchell Minstrels *Black and White Minstrel Show* A great many series enjoyed record-releases, and with huge audience figures most have collectors – even the old interlude music has appeared.

Prime-time programmes command enormous audiences and it's no surprise that their title music often gets more attention than many pop records. Broadcasters do now sell background music CDs, but most vinyl adventures fell to actors who were trying to capitalize on their screen status. However, this wasn't always a success. In the case of the *Dr Who* character Jamie, his manager actually discouraged a second record in case it damaged his acting status!

Initial TV growth in the USA coincided with fierce Musicians' Union battles over radio eroding income. This led to unfettered independent programme-makers using faceless library music. The 1950s saw compromises, and flagship TV programmes such as *Victory At Sea* commissioned leading composers. For example, Bernard Herrman and Jerry Goldsmith worked for *Twilight Zone*, *Dr Kildare*, and *Voyage to the Bottom of the Sea*. However, it was the fashionable westerns that fought one another for the most popular title music. *Bonanza's Maverick* perfectly caught the show's mood while *Cheyenne* commissioned Stan Jones who created the evocative *Rider in the Sky*. Henry Mancini soon unveiled his landmark jazz-tinged *Peter Gunn* theme. This had a huge impact on Lounge Music growth (*see* pp 33–5) and turned many TV executives into Jazz fans.

There are few general collectors of television music – most prefer to specialize in a brand of show, a composer, or even a specific series. It's perfectly possible to build up a fascinating collection of records associated with *Dr Who*, *The Avengers*, or Patrick McGoohan's twin gems *Danger Man* and *The Prisoner*. With such a wealth of programming choice it's hard to provide central price guidance. Some examples are only worth a few notes while others are worth many hundreds. This is really a world of two halves – the cheap, loved, but forgotten and the cultish, desirable, and appreciating. Utopia is second guessing the next record to cross over from one to the other.

Kids' Delight – The 1960s American favourites The Banana Splits *were always hunting out the action and somehow found their way onto vinyl. Two US EPs from the first series were issued in association with the network sponsors Kelloggs. The 1969 LP* We're The Banana Splits *was conducted by Jack Eskew. On it Snorky, Bingo, and the gang attack Barry White and Gene Pitney songs as well as singing their Tra La La Song. Around £80 will let you join in the fun.*

TELEVISION *"FEASTS AND FAMINES"*

Suggested Strands
Soaps & Series
Crime
Family Shows
Other Worlds

Average Record Cost
✩✩

Rising Stars
Honor Blackman
Patrick McGoohan series
Mickey Mouse TV Club
Star Trek series
Soaps & Series

SOAPS AND SERIES

Singles

Roy Castle *Doctor Terror's House of Horrors*

Harry H. Corbett *Junk Shop*

Danny La Rue *On Mother Kelly's Doorstep*

Bob Monkhouse *I Remember Natalie* ★

Des O'Connor *Thin Chow Min*

LPs

Bonanza Cast *Christmas on the Ponderosa*

Patrick Cargill *Father Dear Father*

The Cast of Dallas *Dallas: the Music Story*

Dick Emery *Dick Emery Sings*

Bruce Forsyth *Mr. Entertainment*

Larry Grayson *What a Gay Day*

Jack Howarth (Albert Tatlock) *'Ow Do*

Soaps and Series

Big TV series command great fan loyalty and Britain's long running *Coronation Street* provided a hit in 1963 for Chris Sanford (Brett Falcon) with *Not too Little, Not too Much* (worth £8), which reached No.17. Grumpy old Albert Tatlock, played by Jack Howarth, offered an LP *'Ow Do* (£12), while Violet Carson and David Hill's LP *The Lad from Coronation Street* values at £10, as does the album *On the Street Where you Live* by the Street's famous character Rita (Barbara Mullaney).

Crossroads' Meg had sung in musicals – her *Noele Gordon Sings* fetches around £10, while Sue Nicholls' (Marylin) 1968 *Where Will You Be* is worth £5. There was even an album to celebrate Meg's marriage in 1975 – *Crossroads Wedding Party* (£10).

> *Over the Top* – Dallas *produced little vinyl success. Larry Hagman (J.R. Ewing) was best with his 1950 duet single with Mary Martin,* You're Just in Love *($30). Audrey Landers' (Afton) LP* Little River *is worth $20 but Victoria Principle's (Pamela)* All I Have to Do is Dream *fetches just $8.*

The evergreen *Dad's Army* spawned a number of actors' efforts including Clive Dunn's LP *Permission to Sing* (worth £8), Arthur Lowe's *Bless 'em All* LP (£11), and John Le Mesurier's LP *What's Going to Become of Us All* (£14). The star of *Ben Casey* released the 1962 LP *Vince Edwards Sings* ($22), Patrick Cargill attempted a strangely wry LP *Father Dear Father* (£16), and comedian Dick Emery failed to reveal his classical training on *Dick Emery Sings* (£16). Ironically, Emery is considered more valuable than Richard Chamberlain, who cashed in on his fame with a *Dr Kildare* LP (worth just £12).

Crime

Whether it's *Inspector Morse* or *Highway Patrol*, *Dixon of Dock Green* or *Z Cars* we all love crime detection. *Hawaii Five-O's* 1959 soundtrack album is currently worth $30 and James MacArthur (Danno) released three singles – his best, *In-Between Years Pt 1*, is worth $12. Edward Woodward (*The Equalizer*) amassed a staggering 11 albums of work, his *This Man Alone* LP can be bought for £12. David McCallum (*The Man From UNCLE*) arranged/conducted some interesting instrumental LPs like *McCallum* $20, but his single,

Arthur Lowe (Captain Mannering) *Bless 'em All*

Barbara Mullaney (Rita Littlewood) *On the Street Where you Live*

Meg Richardson *Noele Gordon Sings*

EPs

Max Bygraves *A Good Idea Son ★*

CRIME

Singles

Ron Grainer *The Maigret Theme / The Prisoner Theme*

Tony Hatch *Ben Casey Theme*

David Soul *Don't Give Up on Us*

Jack Webb (Dragnet) *You're My Girl*

LPs

Edwin Astley *Secret Agent ★ (Danger Man Soundtrack)*

Honor Blackman *Everything I've Got*

Tony Crombie *Man From Interpol*

Laurie Johnson & Orchestra *The Avengers Theme*

George Maharis (Route 66) *Portrait in Music*

David McCallum *McCallum*

Hugo Montenegro *Man from UNCLE Soundtrack*

Lalo Schifrin *Mission Impossible*

Morton Stevens *Hawaii Five-O Soundtrack*

Peter Wyngarde *Peter Wyngarde ★*

Communications, was less successful (£5). The actual *Man from UNCLE Soundtrack*, conducted by Hugo Montenegro, is desirable (worth $70/£40).

Some stars did quite well crossing over into singing territory while others fared badly. Roger Moore's UK single *Where Does Love Go* is worth less than £10 today. Dennis Weaver's album *McCloud Country* is worth $20. Telly Savalas (*Kojak*) got to No.1 in the UK with *If*, but it is only worth £3 today, while *Route 66* star George Maharis' best LP, *Portrait in Music*, is prized for its 3D cover ($45). Peter Wyngarde starred in *Department S* and then the '60s classic *Jason King* as the definitive male egotist. His flamboyant ways were personified in the unique, and

> *Rising Saint* – Edwin Astley made the 1965 TV theme single for The Saint (£50) as well as Danger Man and the original Randell & Hopkirk. RCA in America created an LP of series music that is worth $200, and a combined LP of Secret Agent (Danger Man in UK) and The Saint is worth $230.

extremely collectable, 1970 *Peter Wyngarde* LP ★. Nothing prepares you for the stereo mixing, the vocals, and the literal seduction – its part "theatre" opening includes a whispering courtship about where to sit; he appears to guess what perfume the listener has used, and then muses on how things begin, before launching into a controversial, multi-national review of the act of rape. Expect to pay £200–400 for a copy.

The Avengers

Frivolous, escapist, and very 1960s, *The Avengers* quickly became one of the UK's biggest successes. The initial title music came from Johnny Dankworth (his 1961 single *The Avengers* is worth £16) while Laurie Johnson later replaced it with his '65 *The Avengers* (£35). This was itself replaced by *The New Avengers Theme* (£10). The series stars made records too. Linda Thorson's single *Here I Am* was worth just £5 in 1993 but fetches £45 now, while Diana Rigg's single *Sentimental Journey* was £8 then – £10 today. The fact that her records remain virtually static could be a good reason to hunt out ignored singles now. The collector's choice, however, is Honor Blackman. Her single *Before Today* was, in '93, £15 and now commands £50+ and her LP *Everything I've Got* fetches £50–60. Her 1964 duet with co-star Patrick MacNee was *Kinky Boots* (£25); a 1990 reissue got into the UK Top 5.

SPACE TRADERS

Singles

The Go Gos *I'm Gonna Spend My Christmas with a Dalek*

Tony Hatch *Out of this World*

Malcolm Lockyer *Eccentric Dr Who*

Jon Pertwee *Who is the Doctor?*

LPs

Barry Gray *Space 1999*

Leonard Nimoy *Mr Spock's Music from Outer Space*

Nelson Riddle *Batman*

William Shatner *The Transformed Man*

Various *Inside Star Trek*

EPs

Barry Gray *Thunderbirds Are Go*

Cliff Richard and The Shadows *Thunderbirds Are Go* ★

The McGoohan Phenomenon

In 1960 respected actor Patrick McGoohan became TV's *Danger Man* and Edwin Astley created the theme music for the show. A year later came Parlophone's *Danger Man Theme* single by Red Price Combo (worth £18), followed by Ska artist Tommy McCook's version (£15). In 1964 the series was revamped and renamed for the USA as *Secret Agent*, using its own US title music, *Secret Service Man*, sung by Johnny Rivers ($12). Astley's tune was also re-recorded under the title *High Wire* by the Ivor Slaney Orchestra (now worth £10). Astley's own selection of series music became the ultra collectable US LP – *Secret Agent* ★ – for which you can expect to pay up to $300.

Restless McGoohan dreamed up *The Prisoner*, fascinating audiences for decades with a surreal drama about enforced retirement in an Italianate coastal village. For music, Ron Grainer reworked an old tune of his, *The Age of Elegance*, as a single and *The Prisoner* is now worth £60. It's difficult to overestimate the strength of the McGoohan cult as there are tributes aplenty. These include Teenage Filmstars' 1980 single *I Helped Patrick McGoohan Escape* (£10) and Roy Harper's *McGoohan Blues* on his *Folkjokeopus* LP (worth £30). Dr. Feelgood used *The Prisoner* catchphrase for their *Be Seeing You* LP, and Iron Maiden's *Number of the Beast* LP track *The Prisoner* (£30) even opens with dialogue from the show. Taboo's single *Number Six* simply chants McGoohan's identity number from the series. The appreciation society Six of One created its own LP, *The Prisoner – Original Soundtrack*, a double gatefold with a 24-page booklet on *The Making of...*, a village map, and a poster. This was revamped for the public, bootlegged, and later repackaged – an original is a shrewd investment at £35.

Family shows

Fess Parker created many children's LPs but struck gold with his Davy Crockett single, which reached the US Top 5 (worth $10). The actual *Davy Crockett Soundtrack* album is now worth $50, as are many show episode LPs. Staying with youth, LPs by the casts of *The Muppet Show* and the *Beverly Hillbillies* are both worth $12. *The Partridge Family* had many releases – a typical LP *The Partridge Family Album* is worth $15. Cast member David Cassidy also sold over four million of his single *I Think I love You*. *The Dukes of Hazzard* cast LP is worth just $15, while star Tom Wopat's *Don't Look Back* LP fetches $12 and John Schneider's *Quiet Man* LP is $10. Both of these men eventually moved into country music, leaving their TV careers behind. The light-hearted *Munsters Soundtrack* ★ is much more valuable, commanding $100. *Mickey Mouse TV Club*

"Mouseketeer" Annette Funicello made a vast 48 LPs. Her best, *Annette and Hayley Mills* ★, fetches $600, while the more average-priced *Annette Sings Anka* is worth $60. Her 70 singles include *Walkin' and Talkin'*, which is worth $50. Eleven other Club members also list recordings.

Other Worlds

Pre-Christmas 1963 saw the birth of a British TV institution – *Dr Who*. The programme captivated all ages, despite amateur sets and frequent cast changes. Australian Ron Grainer (of *Maigret* and *Steptoe and Son* fame), Delia Derbyshire, and Dick Mills of Radiophonic Workshop created the infamous main theme. The original 1964 Decca single is worth £15, various reissues much less. Jon Pertwee joined Deep Purple's label for the 1972 single *Who is the Doctor?*, which fetches £15 (1985 reissue £5), while the Peter Howell single with Radiophonic Workshop, *Doctor Who*, is worth just £6. The Doctor's assistant Roberta Tovet's single *Who's Who?* fetches £40 for the picture sleeved version, while the single by Frazer Hines' (Jamie), *Who's Doctor Who?*, is worth £30. The Peter Cushing movie version gave us Malcolm Lockyers' single *The Eccentric Dr. Who* (£35), the Gerry Anderson label *Century 21* issued a 1966 EP *The Daleks* (£50), and the Jack Dorsey Orchestra's single was *Dance of the Daleks* (£10). Tributes came from The Go Gos single *I'm Gonna Spend my Christmas with a Dalek* (worth £40 with picture sleeve), punk band Art Attacks' single *I am a Dalek* (£15), and house band The Timelords' *Doctorin' the Tardis* – the latter even got to No.1 in the UK! However, a 1985 all-star charity single, *Doctor in Distress*, is only worth £5.

Rising Well – Thunderbird *theme singles were done by the Barry Gray Orchestra (£25), Joe Loss Orchestra (£18), and Billy Cotton (£10). Gray's* Thunderbirds are Go ★ *EP fetches £100. Another with the same title features Cliff Richard and The Shadows. This recently rose from £40 to £100+.*

Although *Star Trek* has had various soundtracks the best is the 1976 Columbia LP *Inside Star Trek* – an interview LP worth $80. The stars' efforts include William Shatner reciting Shakespeare to music on the LP *The Transformed Man* ($60), and Leonard Nimoy's *Mr Spock's Music from Outer Spac*e, which includes Spock narrating *Twinkle, Twinkle Little Star* ($80). Lieutenant Uhura (Michelle Nichols) offers the LP *Down to Earth* ($40), which features the 1968 single *Know What I Mean* ($25).

Reflecting an era's graphics, single sleeves are themselves
collectable. The correct generation of company sleeve-styling is
critical to complement a mint record and will reinforce its value.

Coloured records existed before World War II and became high-fashion limited editions during the 1970s, which in turn led to the '80s cutouts. Value is related to the artist or edition size, not design.

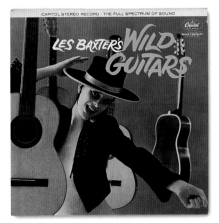

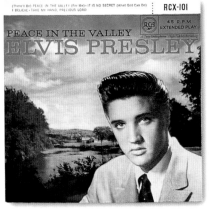

Easy Listening caters for everything, from dinner parties to meditation, with unfamiliar orchestral musicians often fetching higher prices than the major pop stars.

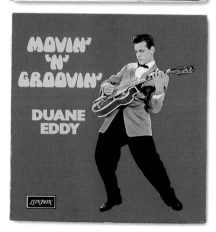

Between the eras of Jazz and Rock rests the innocent genre of
Hit Paraders – many are valuable and less and less are found as
first pressings. This cross-section would cost around £100 ($150).

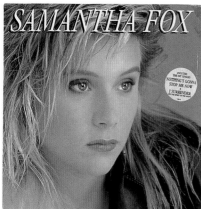

Collecting goddesses includes music and images from every era. Of the songstresses pictured above, Julie London offers the widest choice of records, with values between £25 and £40.

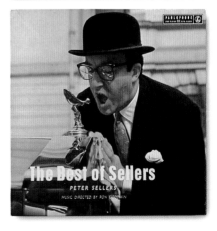

There are enormous choices available within Comedy, but a huge
cultural divide exists between the records produced in the UK and
those in the USA. Prices are compatible – Sellers costs £15/$20.

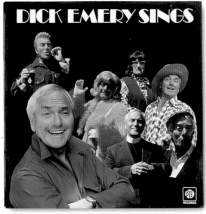

Comedy, drama, music, and background themes –
collecting TV records offers everything. The *Thunderbirds
Are Go* LP shown above right could set you back £100.

The Disco craze provided both great and grim releases; in the current market Disco collections are cheap to establish. It was essentially an American East Coast trend and centred on the rhythms of music rather than artistry. Collecting is therefore focused on the music rather than the stars. The pivotal record was The Bee Gees' *Saturday Night Fever* soundtrack, but so many of these still exist that it is worth only a few pounds. Potentially more interesting, and valuable, are the piles of Disco oddities, such as this *Star Wars* example.

ROCK

Here we enter one of the hallowed halls of contemporary music. Treated by many as a virtual religion it carries many of the same pressure points, as each faction believes theirs is the only path to follow. Even our general heading, "Rock", is contentious from an aficionado's point of view, as Rock is quite distinct from Rock & Roll. Essentially, the true common denominator is a musical freedom of spirit, an expression from the streets. On occasion the music itself has been the very catalyst for social change, as with Elvis Presley's Rock & Roll or the wider declarations of Punk.

Generally, the collecting of Rock music is divided into two loose schools. The first is collecting by type, in which cross-sections of artists and releases are built up into an archive of, for example, Punk, Glam Rock, or Doo Wop. Then there are avid single-subject collectors who will focus on specific acts, or sometimes labels, within the worlds of Rock Bands, A.O.R., New Order, and Prog Rock. Collecting offers a unique chance to look back at your most-loved music, and there is real fascination in viewing the wider music landscape. Rock didn't just appear from nowhere – it grew from differing strands, and often old songs, giving them a new voice and face in order to speak for a fresh, restless generation. One late-'80s movement specialized in playing vast walls of discordant rock music while standing still, staring at the ground. A perfect example of this "shoegazing" is music by the group My Bloody Valentine, whose 12" EP *The New Record By My Bloody Valentine* is worth £40. There were also those within the "Oi" movement (fast, violent music), such as Business, with their *Suburban Rebels* LP (£20). As you can see, Rock provides something for everyone: skilled and knowledgeable collectors will enjoy getting their teeth into Doo Wop and early Rock & Roll, while adventurers will have fun with Punk; for the amateurs or speculators A.O.R. and Prog Rock provide great places to start. As with any other genre of music you will benefit from doing your homework, but hopefully one part within Rock will fire your imagination to start collecting what is the music of our generations.

Rock Roots
For anyone with a love of Rock music, exploring its birthplace is absolutely fascinating. In this section you meet not only the obvious pioneers but also an entire raft of lesser-known but hugely influential figures and records – sometimes with price tags to make your jaw drop. Some key figures like

Label Conscious – Many labels go through image changes and each of these is extremely important to collectors. Free's Tons of Sobs album was on Island Records. Its first pressing was a pink Island label with a black/orange circle logo, worth £50. The second pressing of the same record had a block logo, worth £30, while the third pressing had an 'i' logo, worth £20. The fourth pressing had the now recognizable Palm Tree logo (£15).

Billy Fury *Halfway to Paradise* Although coloured by artists from the USA, UK Rock & Rollers also generated excitement. A 1961 Billy Fury LP like the one above fetches £30–40, and once-fashionable EPs now command three times that figure.

The Everly Brothers and Buddy Holly feature under other sections (*see* Pop) while figures like Britain's Billy Fury could just as easily qualify within Pop Stars (it's his style of presentation that edges him into Rock). You don't have to be an historian to get started and before long you'll be discovering "new trends and songs" aren't quite what they appear to be, while meaningless lyrics like "Boom Bada Boom", "Boom Chic-a-Boom", and "Boom Diddly Boom" helped create second-hand records now worth thousands. This certainly worked for The Penguins: their 1955 London Records single *Earth Angel* ★ did really well in the USA but utterly failed in the UK charts. Today it is one of Britain's five rarest records and has a price tag of £2,000 for gold label-lettering and tri-centre versions.

Rock Bands

Such a generalization throws together some real extremes of talent and makes price categories impossible. The Rolling Stones, The Who, and Led Zeppelin are Top 10 collectors' targets but what you'll see within this section is the importance of detail. Thanks to websites, books, and magazines it's possible to research your chosen subject from home. The colour of a label or changes in artwork-printing can make a huge difference to values. Don't just pick a single band to collect, spread out across the various groups that members have been part of, or maybe lay down a future investment by gathering in something like U2's original Irish recordings. You could also try to muster all the worldwide versions of a hit such as Hendrix's *Hey Joe*. Lacking full recognition is Southern Rock, a cocktail of Blues and Riff Rock personified by the Allman Brothers' LP *Allman Brothers Band* (£12), and later Lynyrd Skynyrd's *Street Survivors* LP (£12); when two of the band were killed in separate accidents the movement lost its spearhead.

Glam

Glam Rock was really a kind of musical schizophrenia. Think of the worst office party you can possibly imagine, with silly clothes, silly songs, and silly people and there you have it – but everyone involved thought themselves very hip at

Won't Take No for an Answer – US Records chief refused to release Bay City Rollers records. A campaign raged as a result, which ended in the strange marriage of Bay City Rollers and TV network Sports Superstar commentator, Howard Cosell, who was hosting a Saturday night entertainment show. A Rollers track was featured on the first three programmes and the group became No.1 within weeks. Bagged picture-single versions of Saturday Night are worth $6.

Marc Bolan *The Beginning of Doves* Glam Rock wasn't always about trivial excesses – artists like Marc Bolan helped shift musical taste and created collectables that range from just £4 to almost £3,000.

the time. Glam Rock was also about a fascinating cultural groundswell of implied sexual debauchery and cross-dressing, although for the most part the performers' real masculinity was never in question. However, it was extremely cool to look as they did and such rule-breaking became the very seeds of later Punk movements. The perennial Good Time Glam Rockers may never appreciate in value as others will (though check out early Slade) but the more artistic, cult pioneers could one day prove a significant collecting zone.

A.O.R.

A.O.R. is primarily for grown-ups – it is generally taken to mean "Adult-Orientated Rock", although other similar definitions are sometimes used. A.O.R. was born in the late 1970s and is currently unfashionable, which makes this a great time to collect as prices are still low. American radio's favourite brand of Rock, the core of A.O.R. is soundly based on memorable songs. Once all-powerful, it's become Easy Listening for Rock generations and such music has a habit of suddenly appreciating. A Toto LP like *Toto IV* ($40), with its songs *Rosanna* and *Africa*, Boston's second album *Don't Look Back* (£12), or Peter Frampton's LP *Frampton Comes Alive* ★ ($100 for an audiophile copy), all provide the classic sounds for the next generation to glory over.

Punk

The Beatles were the right band at the right time to create an explosion, while both Elvis Presley and the Punk era actually brought about much-needed change. The mid-'70s were full of "Supergroups" who were cocooned in limos and private jets, but American East Coast Glam bands like The New York Dolls were living wild lives, putting on chaotic stage shows, and playing a harder form of Glam Rock. However, the UK's youth had lost that '60s "feel good" factor and in disillusionment returned to basics – homemade music, rudimentary skills, and street messages. This quickly escalated into an anti-culture and rode a typical wave of British media to deify Punk. There are dozens of sub-groups within Punk – all slotting into each other like a musical jigsaw. This is fascinating collectors' territory, but with ever-shifting names but it does require some careful study to separate the masters from the students and wannabes.

New Wave

A genuine muddle, that category of music known as "New Order" can do no more than attempt to represent its extreme diversity. During Punk the mass population waited dazed and confused for something attractive to latch onto again. Suddenly

Curved Air *Air Conditioning* The first 10,000 copies of the band's debut LP were released as picture discs, the rest as regular covers. Heavy promotion ensured they charted with it but this damaged the band's overall credibility. Expect to pay today around £12 for the regular release and £40 for the picture disc.

MTV gave that generation a perfect mirror to admire themselves in all their finery. Some quality mainstream artists grew out of this period, such as The Eurythmics and The Police – they, like many others, still survive thanks to gifted songwriting. Popularized Punk imagery offered Adam and The Ants, Billy Idol, and more eclectic bands like Missing Persons and The Motels a brief chance to shine. In truth New Order is a fairly meaningless category that in the course of time will separate out latter-day Punk, arty experimental groups, and a neo-Glam keyboard-led fraternity. Values are rock bottom so the collecting fields await.

Prog Rock

Progressive Rock has an interesting background as it was partly inspired by US West Coast Psychedelic groups but remained an almost exclusive European genre (although it was often best appreciated by US audiences). Many came from art schools and were educated in European cultural history and its various musical concepts. For example, Supertramp was named after W.H. Davies' *Autobiography of a Supertramp*. The group gained support from private Dutch backers until their award-winning concept LP *Crime of the Century* launched them into the Top 20 and provided the hit single *Dreamer*. Later *Breakfast in America* gave them a Top 10 in the USA. There is little UK collectors' interest, but Stateside a super audio version of *Crime of the Century* ★ is worth $120, and a limited *Breakfast in America* ★ picture disc of the record company's employees is $500.

On its Head – Unsure how to sell David Bowie, Decca moved him to their Deram label and released the novelty song The Laughing Gnome ★, *which promptly shot to No.6 in the charts. Its first release is now worth £140 but watch out, there are many re-releases that are worth £50 or less. The valuable ones have their matrix numbers printed upside down on the labels.*

Pete Sinfield *Still* and *Under the Sky* Lyricist to King Crimson and ELP, Sinfield released this 1973 solo project through ELP's own label, Manticore Records. Only 5,000 copies of the rare companion paperback, containing his lyrics and poems, were published by Boydell Press.

Alan Parsons *The Complete Audio Guide to the Alan Parsons Project* This complete box set of Parsons' work, made in 1980, includes three interview LPs containing his story, and examples of his other work with bands such as The Beatles and Pink Floyd. It was never released for sale to the general public but was given away as a promotional device to people in the music industry.

Rock Roots *"CONNOISSEUR'S CHOICE"*

Suggested Strands

Doo Wop
Ring Leaders

Average Record Cost

★★★★☆

Rising Stars

Clyde McPhatter
The Orioles
Elvis Presley

DOO WOP

Singles

The Channels *The Closer You Are* ★

The Cleftones *Little Girl of Mine*

The Clovers *Don't You Know* ★ / *Love, Love, Love* ★

The Cuff Links *Guided Missiles*

The Dell *Pain in My Heart / Tell the World* ★

Dion *The Wanderer / Runaround Sue*

Dion & The Belmonts *Teenage Clementine / A Teenager in Love*

The Drifters *Soldier of Fortune* ★

The Flamingos *The Ladder of Love* ★ / *Would I Be Crying* ★

The Four Buddies *I Will Wait* ★

The Harptones *Three Wishes*

The Heartbeats *Wedding Bells* ★

The Larks *Hopefully Yours* ★ / *Darlin'* ★

Frankie Lymon & The Teenagers *Why Do Fools Fall in Love*

Clyde McPhatter *Seven Days* ★

Many have attempted to pinpoint the first ever Rock & Roll record, but most people agree upon its roots – Blues and Country are certainly the likely parents. The name "Rock "n" Roll" was steeped in black sexual connotations and the early white champions included American DJ Alan Freed from Cleveland radio, who'd witnessed whites buying black "Race" records, and noticed a new Country band leader called Bill Haley.

This area necessitates serious collecting but with high rewards; the secret is study. Success comes from knowing what counts, not just what's a familiar name.

Doo Wop

This section mainly covers vocal groups, with members weaving differing vocal parts together, often using nonsense words. Although groups frequently performed a cappella live, most Doo Wop records were cut using instruments in support.

The late 1940s to mid-'60s saw a huge number of influential Doo Wop recordings. Only a few were big hits yet many would influence talent like The Beach Boys, The Four Seasons, and The Beatles. Doo Wop's immediate heritage was Jazz Big Bands and groups like The Ink Spots and The Mills Brothers. However, Rock roots go much further back. In 1938 two radio entertainers, Slim and Slam, invented a nonsensical language called Vout and made a Vocalion 78' upon the theme of Italian fruit, *Tutti Frutti,* which, 17 years on, inspired Little Richard.

In 1939 Louis Jordan experimented by fusing his fashionable Jump music style with a 1928 Bert Mays piano Blues song called *(No Use a-Knockin' 'cause) You Can't Come In*; his Decca version was *Keep a-Knockin'*. Other examples are Arthur 'Big Boy' Crudup's 1946 *That's All Right,* which was revamped by him in '49 as *That's All Right (Mama)*, and Lloyd Price's *Lawdy Miss Clawdy* from 1952. Both these records fed Elvis Presley hits much later. Another gift to Rock – and to Presley – was Big Mama Thornton's 1953 gem *Hound Dog*, written by duo Leiber and Stoller especially for this forceful lady. Three years on Elvis would make it a huge hit for himself.

The Orioles got their break on a talent show and their 1953 million-seller *Crying in the Chapel* (£80 or $80) is just one example of their contribution. Early and important in Doo Wop terms, they represent collectors' heaven. Fourteen of their records currently hold a value of $1,200–4,000, including

The Mello-Harps
Love is a Vow ★

Mello-Moods *Where Are You?
(When I Need You)* ★

The Orioles *Its Too Soon
to Know* ★

Johnny Otis *Ma He's Making
Eyes at Me*

The Platters *Only You* ★

The Ravens *Count Every Star* ★

The Swallows *Will You Be
Mine* ★

The Swans *My True Love* ★

The Tru-Tones *Tears in
My Eyes* ★

The Valentines *Why* ★

The Vocaleers *I Walk Alone* ★ *I
Be True* ★

LPs

Frankie Lymon *Rockin' with
Frankie Lymon* ★

The Platters *The Platters* ★

EPs

The Coasters *Rock / Roll*

Little Anthony & The
Imperials *Little Anthony
& The Imperials*

Clyde McPhatter
Clyde McPhatter

---

*Unexpected Hero – Sporting a kiss curl in his hair to distract
from a dysfunctional left eye, Bill Haley made* Crazy Man
Crazy *in 1953 (£30 or $60). In '54 came* Rock Around the
Clock *($60), which became a smash in 1955 (now worth $20).
His 1955 10" LP* Shake, Rattle and Roll * *fetches $800.*

---

their best single, 1951's *It's Too Soon to Know* ★, which
is valued at the top end of that spectrum. A further 18
range from $400–800 each. Still in the big league, The
Clovers' *Love, Love, Love* ★ will set you back as much as
£550, while their most costly is *Don't You Know* ★ at
$1,000. The more Bluesy band The Flamingos boast the
singles *The Ladder of Love* at £500 and *Would I Be
Crying* ★ for £550, although both are worth just £80 as a 78'.

As the '50s developed so Doo Wop moved to capture the
new youth market. Youngster Frankie Lymon, with his group
The Teenagers, scored a hit with *Why Do Fools Fall in Love*
(worth £45); their 1956 album *The Teenagers Featuring
Frankie Lymon* ★ is now worth $500. Frankie also ventured
into solo territory – his *Rockin' with Frankie Lymon* ★ is
worth £400. Ironically, his brother Lewis was with rival
group The Teenchords, whose lesser known *Too Young* ★
also commands £400 today.

Other acts worthy of looking out are The Drifters with *Soldier
of Fortune* ★ (£1,200 as a 45', £100 as a 78'), Johnny Otis'
Ma He's Making Eyes at Me ($50), and The Dells' *Pain in
my Heart* ($40 as a 45') or the rare red vinyl *Tell The World* ★
at $5,000. More modest, at least by Doo Wop standards,
are Dion & The Belmonts' *Teenage Clementine* ($60) and *A
Teenager in Love* ($50). Dion's solo hits include *The Wanderer*
(worth $50) and *Runaround Sue* ($40). The LP *Presenting
Dion and The Belmonts* ★ is listed at £175 in the UK but
in the USA the price ranges from $150 up to $900 for a
reworked stereo version. The Platters' *Only You* ★ is now worth
£200, while their 10" self-titled LP is £350. The more gospel-
tinged material by Clyde McPhatter is well worth finding –
his single *Seven Days* ★ is worth £350 in the UK, but far less
Stateside. Still more confusing are the values for New York
group The Channels – *The Closer You Are* ★ single is worth
£100 in the UK and $250 with block lettering on Bob-Dan
Music in the USA. However, the same block-lettered record is
worth $200 on Spinning Wheel Music, and $100 if the label
name is in caps rather than block letters on the Whirlin' Disc
label. The Port label reissues are worth just $25! Confused!

RING LEADERS

Singles

Chuck Berry
Johnny B Goode / Maybellene / No Particular Place to Go / You Can't Catch Me ★

Eddie Cochran
Hallelujah, I Love Her So ★ */ Summertime Blues / Three Steps to Heaven* ★ */ Twenty Flight Rock* ★

Bo Diddley
Hey, Bo Diddley / Say Man / You Can't Judge a Book by the Cover

Bill Haley
Green Tree Boogie ★ */ Rock the Joint* ★ */ Ten Little Indians* ★

Little Richard
Long Tall Sally / Lucille / Rip it Up / The Girl Can't Help It

Carl Perkins
Blue Suede Shoes / Gone, Gone, Gone ★ */ Matchbox* ★

Elvis Presley
Good Luck Charm ★ */ I'll be Back* ★ */ Jailhouse Rock* ★ */ That's All Right* ★

Gene Vincent
Be-Bop-a-Lula / Right Now ★

LPs

Chuck Berry
After School Sessions ★ */ Fresh Berry's / One Dozen Berrys* ★ */ Rockin' at the Hops* ★

Eddie Cochran
Never To Be Forgotten ★ */ Singing to my Baby* ★ */ Summertime Blues*

Bo Diddley
Bo Diddley ★ */ Go Bo Diddley* ★ */ Spotlight on Bo Diddley* ★

Billy Fury
Angel Face / Maybe Tomorrow / My Christmas Prayer ★ */ The Sound of Fury* ★

Ring Leaders

This section highlights the key architects of Rock & Roll. The music was alive long before Bill Haley appeared but his moment of fame underlines the importance of timing. In 1951 Haley sensed a mood change and made a record with his backers, The Saddlemen, which failed. Two years later he tried again under a new group name, The Comets, but that also failed. The next year he recorded *Rock Around the Clock* again and this time it became an anthem within months, making No.1 in both the UK and USA. Teenagers had finally reached the critical age.

Carl Perkins' Rock passport was Rockabilly (*see* p217), which was his undisputed triumph as he simultaneously topped the US Pop, R&B, and Country charts with his song *Blue Suede Shoes* ★ (£50 as a 78', £200 as a 45'). His follow-up single was *Matchbox* (£130 or $30), but Perkins had a serious car accident allowing new boy Elvis Presley time to steal the limelight; Presley's own *Blue Suede Shoes* ★ is worth £250.

Chuck Berry arrived under the banner of Blues and created a series of Rock masterpieces, openly influencing The Beatles, The Beach Boys, The Rolling Stones, and Bob Dylan. His first record was *Maybellene* (£40, $50), apparently named after a cow; his seminal singles include *Johnny B Goode* (£40 as a 78', £20 as a 45') and *No Particular Place to Go* ($50 or £6). A gold-printed-label version of *You Can't Catch Me* ★ is worth £250 and his *One Dozen Berrys* ★ LP fetches £110 ($200).

Bo Diddley ventured into Rock from an authentic R&B world, bringing with him a distinctive pulsing beat – as is found on *Hey, Bo Diddley* ($50), which would in time become a signature rhythm for bands like The Yardbirds and The Rolling Stones. Somewhat rarer is his 1959 picture-sleeved *Say Man* ★ ($400 or £60) and his EP with gold label-lettering, *Rhythm & Blues with Bo Diddley* ★, worth £175.

Little Richard hounded Speciality Records for a record deal and in 1955 unleashed a series of stunning Rock tracks such as *Rip it Up* (£15 as a 78', £80 as a gold-printed 45'), *Long Tall Sally* (£15 as a 78', £80 as a gold-printed 45'), *The Girl Can't Help It* ★ (£12 for a 78', £100 as a gold-printed 45'),

---

Single Gem – Ron Hargrave co-wrote Jerry Lee Lewis' hit-movie theme High School Confidential *(£50 as a 78') but it's his MGM single* Latch On ★ *that you should look out for. It is worth $40 in the US but, with just six UK copies thought to exist today, they are now worth around £3,000 each.*

Bill Haley
Rock Around the Clock / Shake, Rattle & Roll ★

Little Richard
Here's Little Richard ★

Carl Perkins *The Dance Album of Carl Perkins* ★ / *Whole Lotta Shakin'* ★

Elvis Presley *A Date with Elvis* ★ / *Elvis is Back* ★ / *Elvis Golden Discs* ★ / *Elvis Golden Discs Vol 2* ★ / *Elvis Golden Discs Vol 3* ★ / *Moody Blue* ★

Gene Vincent
Bluejean Bop ★ / *Gene Vincent and The Blue Caps* ★

EPs

Bo Diddley
Rhythm & Blues with Bo Diddley ★

and *Lucille* (£15 as a 78' and £20 as a 45'). Just two years on he renounced everything for Jesus. His *Here's Little Richard* ★ LP is tricky to place – the US Speciality issue is worth $700, a UK flip-backed LP using red gloss is £60 (without red it's worth £40), a small flip back makes £35, and no flip back is £25.

Elvis Presley may not have been the first to adopt the sound of Rock & Roll but he had hundreds of millions of record sales and hundreds of milestone songs. For example, *Don't Be Cruel* sold over six million (worth £20 as a 78', £80 as a 45'; in the US various versions are worth $30–200). He is the icon of Rock and the second most-collected artist in the world with a staggering back catalogue. An early Sun label 78', *That's All Right* ★, is worth over $6,000 today while the classic *Jailhouse Rock* ★ ranges from $30–10,000 for gold vinyl with a gold label. A 1977 experimental RCA LP Picture Disc on gold vinyl, *Moody Blue* ★ , which was never meant for sale, has two known copies still in existence today – each is worth $7,000. A trial format of a 7" Compact 33' (as opposed to 45') picture-sleeved single was also tried – *Good Luck Charm* ★ in this form

> *Christmas Box – Elvis Presley's 1957 Christmas Album* ★ *was available for just two years with a photo booklet (some with gift tags). A later reissue was similar but some copies were made in green vinyl. The famous '57 version was pressed in red vinyl – its owner refused $25,000 for it in 1998.*

is worth a staggering $24,000, while *His Latest Flame* ★ on Compact 33' is $12,000. His very first acetate records, *My Happiness* ★ and *That's When Your Heartaches Begin* ★, were made in July 1953 for his mum. They cost $4 a shot and yet, almost a decade ago, these were valued at £10,000+.

Though always in the shadow of Elvis, others cast their magic too. Gene Vincent and a local DJ wrote *Be-Bop-a-Lula* (£30, $15 as a 45'), which would end up as a million-seller. An unissued demo version of Vincent's *Rip it Up* ★ is worth £225, while the LP *Gene Vincent & the Blue Caps* ★ is $1,000 (the band was named after a member's school hat). Vincent was injured in a car while touring in the UK with Eddie Cochran. Sadly Cochran died within hours, but his short stardom produced glorious singles including *Summertime Blues* (£80 as a 78', £25 as a 45'), *Skinny Jim* ★ ($300), which was a response to Little Richards' *Long Tall Sally*, and his posthumous UK No.1 *Three Steps to Heaven* ★ (worth £500 or £40).

Rock Bands *"MIXED FORTUNES"*

Suggested Strands
Headliners
Splinter Groups
Crowd Pleasers
Power Players

Average Record Cost
★★★☆

Rising Stars
Led Zeppelin
The Rolling Stones
Pretty Things
Uriah Heep

HEADLINERS

Singles
The Grateful Dead *Dark Star* ★

Jimi Hendrix *Hey Joe / Hey Joe* ★ */ Hey Joe* ★ *(Japanese pic sleeve)/ Hey Joe (German pic sleeve) / No Such Animal*

Led Zeppelin
Wearing And Tearing ★ */ Whole Lotta Love* ★ */ Stairway To Heaven* ★

Jimmy Page:
She Just Satisfies ★

The Rolling Stones *Come On* ★ */ Street Fighting Man* ★

The Who *I Can't Explain / My Generation / My Generation* ★ */ Young Man Blues* ★

LPs
The Grateful Dead *Anthem Of The Sun / The Grateful Dead*

Jimi Hendrix
Electric Ladyland ★

Led Zeppelin *Led Zeppelin 1*

The Rolling Stones
Promotional Album ★ */ Rolling Stones* ★

"Rock Group" is a phrase that does little to define its parameters. The talent might be iconic, non-chart tour bands or those that are so hit orientated that they verge on Pop or A.O.R. status. However, they are all at home on stage capturing audiences. The big lesson to remember is that hit singles don't automatically endow acts with collecting status – indeed in Rock terms running after hits can be considered "Selling Out". This was never a danger for those in our first section…

Headliners
Led Zeppelin personified Rock Group power on and off stage. Visionary manager Peter Grant tightly controlled their output – UK singles and TV appearances were simply banned. As a result huge values surround unreleased or promotional 45's. For example, *Good Times, Bad Times* ★ , an unissued one-sided acetate, is worth £400, the unused promo *Communication Breakdown* ★ fetches £500, and the fabled single *Whole Lotta Love* ★, which was almost immediately withdrawn, is worth £450 (beware the large-holed jukebox 45's as these aren't the same thing). LP out-takes were to make up a unique single at a giant Knebworth gig, which was cancelled, but reputedly copies of that *Wearing and Tearing* ★ single have doubled in value up to £1,000 in a decade. For LPs hunt the one-offs – US white-labelled *Houses of the Holy* ★ is worth $1,000, and a late 1970s *Led Zeppelin 4* ★ has been found pressed in swirled gold and black with no production history – the lucky owner found it in a second-hand store and has refused an offer of $2,000 for it.

The Rolling Stones deserve their own book, as they are viewed as giants in the collecting world. Massive attention to detail pays off when collecting this group. For example, a UK favourite like *Come On* ★ is worth £18, but export copies are £100. This is also the case with *Little Red Rooster* ★ (worth £6 and £100 respectively) and *Satisfaction* ★ (again £6 and £100). There are also lots of US prized DJ versions – *Street Fighting Man* ★ with an orange swirl label is worth a massive $10,000, while similarly *Heart of Stone* ★ with the same label fetches $800. The promo for the LP *Their Satanic Majesties Request* ★ had a padded sleeve and is now worth over £1,000, and a famous 1969 *Promotional Album* ★, pressed in very small quantities, was worth £750 a decade ago but is now edging towards £1,000 (beware of the commercially available Australian version, which is worth very little). Many fans have

U2 *Rattle And Hum* ★

The Who *The Who Sell Out* ★

EPs

U2 *Three* ★

SPLINTER GROUPS

Singles

Black Sabbath
Children of the Grave ★ /
Evil Woman

Graham Bonnet *Danny*

Cream *Wrapping Paper*

Deep Purple *Hallelujah* ★ /
Hush ★

Free *All Right Now / Broad
Daylight / I'll Be Creepin*

The Ian Gillan Band
She Tears Me Down

Cozy Powell
Dance with the Devil

Rainbow *I Surrender / Since
You've Been Gone*

Whitesnake *Love an' Affection*

LPs

Bad Company *Bad Co. /
Straight Shooter*

Baker Gurvitz Army
Baker Gurvitz Army

Black Sabbath
*Black Sabbath / Paranoid / We
Sold our Souls for Rock 'n' Roll*

Blind Faith
Blind Faith / Blind Faith ★

Graham Bonnet
Graham Bonnet

Cream *Cream on Top / Disraeli
Gears / Fresh Cream / Goodbye /
Wheels of Fire* ★

Deep Purple *Concerto for
Group and Orchestra* ★ /
Shades of Purple

The Firm *The Firm /
Radioactive*

Free *Tons of Sobs*

the double LP *Rolled Gold*, which is worth £12. This was to have been a three-LP box, *The History of the Rolling Stones* ★ – pink-labelled test pressing versions of this exist and are today worth £800 each.

> *All in the Detail – Research records by the Rolling Stones very carefully as prices vary. For example, a first pressing of their* Rolling Stones ★ *LP, which plays a 2.52min version of* Tell Me *is £100, while the second pressing has a 4.06min version and is £50. A few of the albums have* Mona *listed instead of* I Need You Baby – *examples with this are £80.*

Rock band The Who strangely have more status than value, and more impact than sales. However, there are gems out there. Their landmark song *My Generation* ★ is worth just £10, but picture-sleeved export versions can be worth up to £125, and a US promo white label version fetches $200. The matching LP is worth £100 but is cheaper in the US, where average LPs by The Who go for $30. *The Who Sell Out* ★ in full stereo, stickered, and with poster is worth £250 (up £50 in recent years), but is only worth £50 without these extras. *Who Did It* ★ – a withdrawn mail-order project – is now worth £350.

The Grateful Dead are giants within Rock and among the world's biggest stage bands. However, they hated commerce and encouraged fans ("deadheads") to record their gigs rather than buy records! This is therefore not singles domain but their early *Dark Star* ★ in picture-sleeve form is worth $500, or $30 as a standard disc version. The UK mono LP *The Grateful Dead* ★ is £60 (stereo £30), in the US a mono version is $200 (up from £40 in 1995), in stereo $80 (up from £30). Irish band U2 are really too new to be included in this book, as their singles are now just £3–5. However, early Irish pressings of U2 are beginning to gather value. For example, the EP *Three* ★ in white vinyl is worth £350, while mispressed brown versions also exist that are worth £900. This is a band worth watching.

Legend Jimi Hendrix's records don't fetch what you'd expect. In 1993 *Hey Joe was* worth £8, in 1990 £9, but now it is back to just £8. The mono LP, *Are You Experienced*, fetched £20 in 1990, in '93 £20, and is now worth £60. His image does sell, so picture sleeves help to bump up the value – a German *Hey Joe* ★ is worth £30, a Japanese one £150, and a US one £200. Oddball records again win out – a UK *Electric Ladyland* ★ white test pressing LP is worth £1,000, and a US 1968 mono promo *Electric Ladyland* ★ a staggering $4,000.

Roger Glover *Elements /
The Butterfly Ball*

The Ian Gillan Band
Glory Road

Cozy Powell *Over the Top*

Rainbow *Down to Earth /
Rainbow on Stage*

Whitesnake *Slide it In*

CROWD PLEASERS

Singles

Bachman-Turner Overdrive
My Wheels Won't Turn

Bon Jovi *She Don't Know Me*

ELO *Roll Over Beethoven*

Van Halen *Necromance*

ZZ Top *Francine /
Gimme All Your Lovin'*

LPs

ELO *On The Third Day*

Heart *Little Queen / Magazine*

Van Halen *1984*

ZZ Top *Eliminator*

A very out-of-keeping US DJ medley single featured *The Little Drummer Boy-Silent Night-Auld Lang Syne* ★ – this is worth $150 today.

Splinter Groups

Musicians' fortunes vary between groups. Singer Paul Rogers has sold over 125 million records, yet has just two listed collectables at £6. However, within the band Free he fared much better – eight LPs and four Top 20 singles. The singles *Broad Daylight* and *I'll Be Creepin'* are worth £30, while a rumoured picture-sleeved version would make £100. Rogers and others then formed Bad Company to create still greater success, but as yet there are no real collectors' items among the records – their *Bad Co.* LP is worth £12 and the *Straight Shooter* LP £15 but none is listed in the USA. Rogers and legend Jimmy Page then formed The Firm, which, again, is as yet undiscovered collecting – the *Radioactive* shaped picture disc is only worth £10, as is the LP *The Firm*.

Clapton, Bruce, and Baker formed the powerful group Cream in 1966. Their *Wrapping Paper* single is currently at £12, the mono LP *Fresh Cream* at £45, while mail-order compilation *Cream on Top* is worth £35, and their *Wheels of Fire* ★ mono promo $200. Clapton, Baker, and Steve Winwood then briefly formed Blind Faith – the *Blind Faith* ★ LP is £18, although the US white-label version is worth $200 – before Baker formed Jazz-tinged band Airforce. Its LPs include *Ginger Baker's Airforce* (£20) and *Stratavarious* (£15), but then the band turned into the Baker Gurvitz Army, producing the *Baker Gurvitz Army* LP (£12).

Both Rainbow and Whitesnake came out of Deep Purple, whose *Hush* ★ promo picture-sleeved single is worth £250 (the normal disc version is just £25). The *Hallelujah* ★ promo single, again picture-sleeved, is £250, while the normal disc is £15. Their other 1970s singles are worth about £8. The LP *Shades of Purple*, with a yellow/black label in mono, is worth £85 but in stereo is £50, while most LPs are £15–25. Again, there are discrepancies between countries: the US value for *Concerto for Group and Orchestra* ★ is $300, but in the UK it is worth just £12.

Crowd Pleasers

Not all Rock bands menaced their audiences. Texas group ZZ Top grew from its minor *Francine* hit (worth £15), to the million-selling smash *Gimme All Your Lovin'* (again £15), and LPs like *Eliminator* (the picture disc is £18). One US single on Scat from 1969, *Salt Lick* ★, is now worth $200. Although

POWER PLAYERS

Singles

AC/DC *High Voltage / You Shook Me All Night Long*

Aerosmith *Dude*

Cheap Trick *So Good to See You*

Iron Maiden *Sanctuary / Twilight Zone* ★

Meat Loaf *You Took the Words Right Out of My Mouth*

Nazareth *Dear John / Love Hurts*

REO Speedwagon *157 Riverside Avenue*

Van Der Graaf Generator *People You Were Going To* ★

LPs

AC/DC *Let There Be Rock* ★

Aerosmith *Greatest Hits / Toys in the Attic*

Cheap Trick *At the Budokan / Dream Police*

Meat Loaf *Bat Out of Hell*

Nazareth *Nazareth*

REO Speedwagon *Hi Infidelity / REO Speedwagon*

Van Der Graaf Generator *Godbluff / Last We Can Do is Wave to Each Other*

EPs

Iron Maiden *The Soundhouse Tapes*

beginning to slip out of this particular area, Bon Jovi's 1984 single *She Don't Know Me* is worth £25 and singles are already averaging £30 – this beats Van Halen, whose best list single is *Dreams* at £12, even though it has a car-shaped picture disc with stand. Sisters Nancy and Ann helped elevate female rock bands with Heart's LPs *Little Queen* ($50) and *Magazine* ($20) – (the same release on Mushroom is worth $60 thanks to a "regrets" notice on the back). ELO were borderline Rock but successfully combined high energies and showmanship. They have a big US singles list but few good prices, although a gold vinyl radio promo for *OLE ELO* ★, which has a print line under the title saying "no electric light orchestra", is worth $100 (just $50 without that line).

Power Players

Representing the darker, more powerful side to rock is Van der Graaf Generator, whose single *People You Were Going To* ★ has risen sharply to £300 – it was released for just one week before injunctions were made against the band. Iron Maiden surged in value a few years back and now their *Twilight Zone* ★ mispressed single on brown vinyl is worth £150 (a picture-sleeved version is only £12 and a clear or red vinyl one £25). Their very strong fan base makes the *Holy Smoke* ★ 12" with gold vinyl test pressing promo worth £120, even though it was only created in 1990. Meat Loaf's epic single *You Took the Words Right Out of My Mouth* typifies the fate of mass circulation hit discs as it is worth just $8 (£5). AC/DC hammer out their music on LPs like *Let There Be Rock* ★ (worth £12) but a mispressed Shorewood printed one, which has the same thing on both sides, will fetch around £200. A *Highway to Hell* ★ LP test pressing is now worth £300 and *Live at Atlantic Studios!* is worth around $60 (but watch for counterfeits). Aerosmith had many big hits but virtually all UK singles are now under £10 and their US LPs are worth around $25, though an LP compilation promo *Pure Gold from Rock "n" Roll's Golden Boys* is worth $50. Cheap Trick had to generate an overseas LP success, *At the Budokan* (£12), to get noticed at home. A radio sampler accompanying it, called *From Tokyo to You*, is worth $30.

> *Eating Your Words – A US critic once claimed, "If they make it I'll have to commit suicide." Uriah Heep went on to tour 40 countries and were the first heavy Rock band to play Moscow. There are 12 LPs and singles – their first LP,* Very 'Eavy … Very 'Umble, *has risen from £20 to £30 in a year.*

Glam Rock *"FROTH AND SUBSTANCE"*

Suggested Strands
Pioneers
Entertainers

Average Record Cost
☆☆☆

Rising Stars
David Bowie
Marc Bolan
Slade

PIONEERS

Singles

David Bowie *Can't Help Thinking About Me* ★ / *Do Anything You Say* ★ / *Holy Holy* ★ / *I Dig Everything* ★ / *Jean Genie* / *The Laughing Gnome* ★ / *Space Oddity* ★ / *Time* ★

Alice Cooper *Eighteen* / *Reflected* ★ / *School's Out*

John's Children *Desdemona* ★ / *Go Go Girl* / *Midsummer Night's Scene* ★

New York Dolls *Jet Boys* / *Trash*

Queen *Bicycle Race* ★ / *Keep Yourself Alive* ★

Roxy Music *Virginia Plain*

T. Rex *Christmas Bop* ★ / *Metal Guru* / *Ride A White Swan* ★

LPs

David Bowie *Aladdin Sane* ★ / *David Bowie* ★ / *Low* ★ / *The Man Who Sold the World* ★

Alice Cooper *Easy Action* ★

New York Dolls *New York Dolls*

Queen *Bohemian Rhapsody – Celebration* ★ / *A Kind of Magic*

Roxy Music *For Your Pleasure*

T. Rex *Electric Warrior* ★ / *Hard on Love* ★

Glam Rock was born in the early 1970s while Rock was being pompous, but it still erupts at parties and in boutiques even today. It was not just made up of sparkly costumes, for beneath its simple strong rock rhythms lay social subversion more aligned to Warhol's New York. It was a world that deliberately touted genders and included David Bowie, Marc Bolan, Elton John, and Queen – all Top 5, important acts. The genre didn't last long but it bred numerous copycats and prepared the way for both the New Romantic and Punk eras.

Pioneers

Bowie brought style and theatre to Rock, fascinating public and artists alike and guaranteeing serious collecting. *Space Oddity* ★, an unreleased picture disc, is worth £3,000, and the US picture-sleeved *Time* ★ makes $800. The early singles also fetch substantial amounts – *Can't Help Thinking About Me* ★ is (£110/$400), while *Do Anything You Say* ★ and *I Dig Everything* ★ are each worth £135. Fortunately, his standard releases, such as *Jean Genie* (£5), are still plentiful and cheap.

Tyrannosaurus Rex, John's Children, and T. Rex all mean Marc Bolan to collectors. He had studied early Bowie and was an ambitious Mod looking for stardom. He created a hypnotic mix of Rock and Glitter under various names. His 1965 single *The Wizard* ★ has doubled in value to £300 in a decade, while a rare withdrawn John's Children single, *Midsummer Night's Scene* ★, is now worth £2,000. Two known versions of T. Rex single *Ride A White Swan* ★, with handwritten white labels, fetch £2,500. Cult status and 14 Top 20 hits gave Bolan his fame – incredibly there's a £1,000 price tag on two sets of paper labels for a single, *Christmas Bop* ★, which wasn't even pressed!

Queen, like Bowie, loved attention but also always delivered masterly records for a huge armchair army, although lately collecting has been subdued (£20 gets you most LPs and £10 covers the majority of their singles). However, overseas releases are big business. A Belgian *Bicycle Race* ★ is worth

---

Extreme Queen – The ultimate Bohemian Rhapsody ★ *pack had numbered blue vinyl records, a picture sleeve, an envelope, invite, blue silk scarf, and two EMI goblets within a box. Just 200 were made for guests celebrating Queen's Award for Industry, worth $3,500 each today.*

ENTERTAINERS

Singles

The Bay City Rollers
Keep on Dancing / Saturday Night / Shang-a-lang / We Can Make Music

Gary Glitter *Do You Want to Touch Me / I'm the Leader of the Gang / Rock 'n' Roll Pts 1 & 2*

Elton John *Crocodile Rock / Lady Samantha ★ / Rocket Man / Saturday Night's Alright for Fighting*

KISS *Nothing to Loose*

Suzi Quatro *Can the Can / Devil Gate Drive / 48 Crash*

Slade *Don't Leave Me Now ★ / Know Who You Are / Security ★ / Shape of Things to Come*

Alvin Stardust *Jealous Mind / My Coo-ca-Choo*

LPs

Elton John *Live BBC Concert ★*

KISS *Alive / Kiss*

Suzi Quatro *Greatest Hits*

Slade *Return to Base*

EPs

Gary Glitter *Gary Glitter*

FASHION VICTIMS

Singles

Hello *Another School Day / You Move Me*

Mungo Jerry *In the Summertime*

Mud *Shangri-la / Tiger Feet*

The Rubbettes *Jukebox Jive*

The Sweet
Ballroom Blitz / Blockbuster / Poppa Joe / Slow Motion ★ / Teenage Rampage

LPs

Mungo Jerry *Mungo Jerry*

The Rubbettes *Wear Its 'At*

£150, a Portuguese picture-sleeved *Keep Yourself Alive ★* fetches £800, and a Colombian *A Kind of Magic ★* blue vinyl LP is £1,000. Over 30 overseas Queen records list at £500+.

New York Dolls mixed high heels, feather boas, and Rock to create "Metal Glam", which influenced both KISS and The Sex Pistols (*see* page 91). Still cheap, their *Jet Boys* single is worth £10 and their *New York Dolls* LP £18 – though a promo-only *Trash* single is now $75. Alice Cooper is still affordable too, despite his major influence on Punk. His first hit, *Eighteen*, is now £50 ($20), while his most valued LPs are *Pretties for You ★* ($200) and *Easy Action ★* ($100) – both the white-labelled versions. A Glam anthem like *School's Out* is worth just £8 ($10).

Entertainers

Glam Rock was really all about "good times", and Elton John offered classics like *Rocket Man* (worth £18) and *Saturday Night's Alright for Fighting* (£5), which are largely ignored by collectors at the moment. Gary Glitter's fall from grace is complete but his offerings included songs like *Do You Want to Touch Me* (£6) and *I'm the Leader of the Gang*. KISS were highly successful, even though they were dressed up as Marvel comic figures! Their 17 *Casablanca* LPs are valued from £12 to £50; 50 initial copies of *Alive II ★*, boasting extra tracks later removed, are now worth $400. Also interesting is that the four of them simultaneously produced solo LPs and singles (even releasing them on the same day). Lead guitarist Ace Frehley proved the most successful at this venture.

Ignored now, in her day Suzi Quatro, dressed in black leathers, blasted out great songs like *Devil Gate Drive* and *Can the Can* (£5 each). Early Slade singles such as *Wild Winds are Blowing* and *Shape of Things to Come* are worth £60, while LPs range from £12 to £40 for *Return to Base*. The huge success of The Bay City Rollers helped kill off Glam, shifting the emphasis to teens and commerce, although their UK and US No.1s and costumes confirmed that they were indeed rooted in Glam.

> *Changing Names – Known as The Vendors, Slade cut* Don't Leave Me Now ★ *(worth £500+). Next they became The N'betweens and then The In-betweens. Philips Records suggested yet another change. They wanted Nacky Noo but settled for Ambrose Slade, which was shortened to Slade.*

A.O.R. *"A FUTURE VINTAGE"*

Suggested Strands:
Soft Rock
Studio Born
Grown-Up Rock

Average Record Cost
☆☆☆

Rising Stars
Stevie Nicks
Neil Young
Chicago

SOFT ROCK

Singles
America *A Horse With No Name*

Fleetwood Mac *Rhiannon*

Stevie Nicks *Nightbird*

Boz Scaggs *Lowdown*

LPs
Air Supply *The One That You Love*

The Carpenters *The Singles*

Fleetwood Mac *Rumours*

Stevie Nicks *Bella Donna*

Linda Ronstadt *Hand Sown, Home Grown*

Simon and Garfunkel *Sounds of Silence*

Paul Simon *There Goes Rhymin' Simon*

STUDIO BORN

Singles
Bread *Make It With You / London Bridge*

David Gates *The Happiest Man Alive / Jo-Baby* ★

Toto *Africa*

A child of American radio, A.O.R. (Adult-Orientated Rock), or Soft Rock, is judged more by material than artists. Although it is primarily an American phenomenon, a classic British A.O.R. track would be Gerry Rafferty's *Baker Street*. Hit compilations bulge with A.O.R. rock anthems, but The Carpenters and Simon and Garfunkel also qualify – try to judge the music as though it is coming from a US soft rock radio station. This is a sleeping area of collecting, but with hints of future growth.

Soft Rock
Fleetwood Mac perfectly caught A.O.R., diluting Rock bands' thunder with gentler West Coast sounds and Stevie Nicks' charisma – early picture bag singles fetch £12 today. Their *Fleetwood Mac* and *Rumours* LPs were sold in millions: today white vinyl versions plus lyric sheets go for £18 and the US promo *Fleetwood Mac* ★ white labels are worth $100. Bob Welch left the band in 1974 and Buckingham and Nicks arrived – their own desirable LP is *Buckingham-Nicks*, worth £50 in its original gatefold form. Fleetwood even re-cut its *Crystal* song for use on their hit LP. Later came Stevie Nicks' solo LPs *Bella Donna* and *Wild Heart*, which have risen from £8 to £12 in recent times. Collectors keen on picture bag singles should look out for her *Nightbird* (£18 or $50 in the US).

Linda Ronstadt combined beauty and song: seven of her UK LPs are at £12, while in the US *Simple Dreams* audiophile pressing is now worth $50 but the *Blue Bayou* single is just $4. Boz Scaggs' soulful A.O.R. classic *Silk Degrees* has been largely forgotten, except for the deluxe audio version ($30).

Studio Born
The cream of Los Angles' session players decided to generate a studio LP of their collective skills – thus Toto was born. The band created A.O.R. hits like *Hold The Line*, *Rosanna*, and *Africa* (all worth £6). A deluxe audio version of the LP *Toto IV* is worth $40. Bread was also planned as a studio band –

Late Arrival – Buffalo Springfield *was being manufactured when Stephen Stills witnessed youth riots and wrote* For What It's Worth *in response. The LP was re-pressed to feature it, and early UK copies had the correct sleeves but wrong track* – Baby Don't Scold Me. *These are worth £60.*

GROWN-UP ROCK

Singles

Blood Sweat and Tears
Spinning Wheel

Boston *Don't Look Back*

Jackson Browne *Running on Empty / Somebody's Baby*

The Cars *Drive / Just When I Needed You*

Joe Cocker *Delta Lady*

The Doobie Brothers
Takin' it to the Streets

The Eagles *Take it Easy*

Foreigner *I Want to Know What Love Is / Urgent*

Peter Frampton *Show Me the Way*

Hall and Oates *Maneater*

J Geils Band *Centerfold*

Journey *Don't Stop Believin' / Who's Crying Now*

Steely Dan
Reelin' in the Years

LPs

Boston *Boston*

Jackson Browne *First Album* ★

Chicago *Chicago IV*

Joe Cocker *With a Little Help from My Friends*

The Doobie Brothers
Minute by Minute

The Eagles *Hotel California* ★

Peter Frampton *Frampton Comes Alive*

Hall & Oates *Abandoned Luncheonette*

Journey *Departure*

Little River Band *First Under the Wire*

Steve Miller *Fly like an Eagle*

R.E.O. Speedwagon
Hi Infidelity

Neil Young *Neil Young* ★

Make it with You (£3) was a vast hit and the LP *Bread* is now worth £12. Group member David Gates' solos included singles *The Happiest Man Alive* (£18/$50) and *Jo-Baby* ★ ($150 on Perspective label but £100 on Robbins).

Grown-Up Rock

There just isn't space here to list the army of US bands who provided memorable hits within A.O.R. LPs, but here is a selection. The Cars' *Drive* moved a nation to tears during Live Aid – their LP *Candy-O* is worth $25. The Eagles' picture bag 45' *Take It Easy* is worth £8 and the LPs include *Desperado* (£12) and *One of these Nights* ($20). An audiophile pressing of *Hotel California* ★ fetches $100. In the same vein, The Doobie Brothers' *Takin' it to the Streets* ($40) and *Minute by Minute* ($30) are classic A.O.R. Jackson Browne's US singles are all under $5/£5, but his 1967 *First Album* ★ of song demos in plain wrapper fetches an incredible $2,000.

> *Farm Boy* – Steve Perry was a farm boy and ex-drummer but his mum pressed him to submit demo tapes to record companies. The resulting group, Journey, exploded with his talents – selling 45 million records with LPs like Escape ★ $20 (audiophile version $200).

Using strong singles, Foreigner amassed huge sales but unfortunately still have low collecting values – *Urgent* and *Cold as Ice* are both only £6. Boston created 16 million sales for their LP *Boston* (£12) and R.E.O. Speedwagon enjoyed huge US hits from LPs like their *Hi Infidelity* (worth $30). The J Geils Band went virtual pop for *Centerfold*.

More musically driven was the band Steely Dan. Their *Reelin' in the Years* 45' is worth £5 and the LP *Aja*, with its magnificent artwork, is £50 for the audiophile version. Chicago's promo LP *Chicago* ★ is worth £25, although the first ten gold-stamped copies are $250. Blood, Sweat and Tears' eponymous audiophile LP is $120, as less than 2,000 copies were made.

Neil Young looks good for collectors, having 18 LPs priced between £12 and £60. The 1968 *Neil Young* ★ reprise LP initially had no name on the front cover – if you find one of these it will be worth around $200. There are also various US DJ specials, like the 1977 triple-DJ LP set, *Decades* ★ ($500), or even a DJ test pressing of *Ode to the Wind* ★ – eventually released as *Comes a Time* and worth a staggering $1,000.

Punk *"WELL WORTH UNDERSTANDING"*

Suggested Strands
Proto-Punk
First Generation

Average Record Cost
☆☆

Rising Stars
Captain Beefheart
The Doors
The Sex Pistols

PROTO-PUNK

Singles

Captain Beefheart
Moonchild / Yellow Brick Road

The Doors *Break on Through
(To the Other Side)* ★

Flamin' Groovies *Sneakers* ★

LPs

Captain Beefheart
Bat Chain Puller ★ */ Safe as
Milk* ★ */ Strictly Personal /
Trout Mask Replica* ★

The Doors *Doors* ★ */ Strange
Days* ★ */ Waiting for the Sun* ★

Flamin' Groovies
*Flamin' Groovies Now / Shake
Some Action*

Nico *Chelsea Girl /
The Marble Index*

The Stooges *Fun House /
Raw Power / The Stooges*

Velvet Underground *Velvet
Underground and Nico* ★ */
White Light, White Heat*

EPs

Captain Beefheart
Diddy Wah Diddy ★

The UK and USA both claim to own Punk's roots – the USA actually have it, but in an East Coast, middle-class, arty way. In Britain, fanned by eager tabloids, Punk took on more social tones and Punk tags were applied to almost everything. UK Punk music was serious, with innovators such as T. Rex and Bowie as its flag bearers, but let's first look at the American trailblazers.

Proto-Punk

Punk's heydays were 1975–78 but US homespun Garage bands had existed long before then. This section embraces the various strands of these experimental, non-compliant groups from the late '60s/early '70s – their common denominator was a desire to stretch the current perimeters of Rock and, as such, they were the precursors of the later '70s Punk movement. Velvet Underground influenced many with their primitivism – their *Velvet Underground and Nico* LP is worth £80 in mono, as is the LP *White Light, White Heat*. Nico was a German supermodel with significant friends, such as Lou Reed, Andy Warhol, and Rolling Stones manager Andrew Loog Oldham. Her solo LPs include *The Marble Index* (£35/$25) and the more folky *Chelsea Girl* (£20/$40).

> *Banana Skins* – Velvet Underground and Nico ★ *has three mono versions. The first has a peel-off banana and band photo framed by a male body ($300). On the second the sticker covers the torso ($300). The third is torso-less ($200). A year later an unpeeled banana version appeared ($100).*

Captain Beefheart's output includes the single *Moonchild* (£40/$50) and the *Diddy Wah Diddy* ★ promo (£375). Their album *Trout Mask Replica* ★ is worth $250, and their 1978 LP test pressings of *Bat Chain Puller* ★ are now worth $400.

The Doors introduced many new sounds – their LPs include *Doors* ★ (£40/$200), *Strange Days* ★ (£40/$600), and *Waiting for the Sun* ★ (£40/$1,000). Ex-Bowie collaborator Iggy Pop was influenced by The Doors and as a result created The Stooges. This group produced wild stage shows that included self-mutilation, which The Sex Pistols later copied. *The Stooges* LP is £50 while *Fun House* on an orange label is worth £45 (the reissue is on a red label, worth £20). The

Flamin' Groovies made interesting but unsuccessful US records up until the UK-produced *Shake Some Action*, made waves (£12). Their early 10", *Sneakers* ★, is now worth $100.

First Generation

US Proto turned into actual Punk with records like Patti Smith's *Horses* LP (£12). This was still arty, but The Ramones' 1976 *Blitzkrieg Bop* (£80) began a whole spate of Punk tracks that became increasingly caught up with marketing gimmicks. In the UK pub bands turned Punk, and rafts of variously angry wannabes flooded the market with cheap, poor, but authentic Punk sounds. The Clash powered uncompromising political messages via a major US record company – their *White Riot* single is worth £10, white label copies of *London Calling* are $25, and the *Capital Radio* EP, sold via the magazine *NME*, is worth £40. The Damned played "badly behaved" to the hilt – their best LP *Damned, Damned, Damned* is worth £12, although 2,000 copies had an Eddie and The Hot Rods picture on the rear and these are £50. Their 1976 first punk single,

Showing Off – A porn movie producer created The Plasmatics using the nearly naked Wendy O. Their Punk shows involved exploding cars and sawn-off shotguns. People queued to view these, and Wendy, but not for the records – their New Hope for the Wretched *is worth just £10.*

New Rose, had a push-out centre (£15), and the double A-sided hand-written UK white labels of Euro-only single *White Rabbit* ★ are worth £400+. The Sex Pistols benefitted from a good manager and became the movement's outward figureheads. Their single *God Save the Queen* ★ is now over £2,500. Their *Never Mind the Bollocks* ★ LP picture disc is a more realistic £35, a rarer version had a black back cover, a poster, and a free one-sided single, *Submission* – this has risen from £80 to £125 in just three years. Few of the records from this era charted, and bands came and went, but their impact was powerful on fellow artists. The Jam were post-Mod, attacking gigs like a super-charged version of The Who. Their *Generation* LP included a four-track EP, *Live at Wembley* (£15). The band Wire stripped songs back to basics, fitting 21 into their 40-minute-long first LP *Pink Flag*, worth £15. The same value is given for The Stranglers' LP *Rattus Norvegicus*, and Blondie's early LP *Blondie*. Debbie Harry's sex appeal quickly swept the group away from their Punk roots, although unissued promo copies of their 1977 single *X Offender* ★ are now worth a staggering £750.

New Wave *"PRESENTLY UNLOVED"*

Suggested Strands
New Waves
New Romantics
Synth Pop

Average Record Cost
☆

Rising Stars
The Cure
The Smiths
Joy Division

NEW WAVES

Singles

The Au Pairs *You*

Blondie *Denis / Heart of Glass*

The B-52's *Rock Lobster*

Elvis Costello *Alison ★ / Less Than Zero*

Nick Lowe *I Love the Sound of Breaking Glass*

The Police *Fall Out / Roxanne*

The Pretenders *Brass in Pocket*

Tom Robinson Band *All Right All Night*

Squeeze *Cool for Cats*

Talking Heads *Road to Nowhere*

Pere Ubu *Final Solution / 30 Seconds over Tokyo*

XTC *Making Plans for Nigel / Science Friction ★ / Wrapped in Grey ★*

LPs

The Au Pairs *Playing with a Different Sex / Sense and Sensuality*

Blondie *Parallel Lines*

The B-52's *B-52*

The Police *Ghost in the Machine ★*

The fashion for Punk was short-lived, which left a plethora of bands and styles clamouring for public affection while still trying to be part of a new order. It is really blasphemy to try to categorize them but, loosely, the bands either became Post Punk (challenging and sometimes clever), or modern Pop (as New Wave or keyboard bands). This is still virgin collector's territory but, music taste aside, '80s release gimmickry ensured many, eventually collectable, limited pressings and mistakes.

New Waves

The USA's less anarchical Punk was brought closer to the fresh, edgy, frequently danceable sounds of New Wave. Examples include Blondie's *Heart of Glass* (the export picture bag single fetches £8) or the 1980 LP *Parallel Lines* ($25 in audiophile form). In the UK The Police started in 1977 with the single *Fall Out* (£15), moving on to the hits *Roxanne* (five versions, best £10), and *Can't Stand Losing You* (£5). There is no significant US interest in them except a fascinating 1983 DJ experimental picture-disc LP *Ghost in the Machine ★*, which lights up when played – this is worth $1,000. A single, *Alison ★*, about Elvis Costello's ex-girlfriend, was mispressed on white vinyl and is worth £300, but only £5 without the mistake. The B-52's *Rock Lobster* is £20 and their *B-52's* LP (£15) became a student essential. XTC have a big list: the unreleased picture-bag version of the 1977 single *Science Friction ★* is worth £1,000 (without the bag just £50); the '92 *Wrapped in Grey ★* withdrawn single is worth £100, and the hit *Making Plans for Nigel* (*see* page 109) included a board game and is worth £6 (no US interest).

New Romantics

Born out of Bowie's influence, the New Romantics were perfect fodder for the newly established MTV, as they had flamboyant hairstyles and clothing, cool danceable music, and self-possessed singers. Duran Duran epitomized the style with singles like *Girls on Film* (£8) and *Wild Boys* (£6). There is no

---

Mixed Fortunes – Bassist for Brinsley Schwarz, Nick Lowe made We Love You Bay City Rollers *in 1975 (a hit in Japan). He then become a producer for The Damned and Elvis Costello. His own disc,* So it Goes, *was the first release on legendary Stiff Records in 1976 but its value is just £5.*

Talking Heads *Fear of Music*

The Undertones *Hypnotised / My Perfect Cousin / The Sin of Pride*

NEW ROMANTICS

Singles

Adam and The Ants *Prince Charming / Stand and Deliver*

Duran Duran *Girls on Film / Rio*

Human League *Being Boiled*

Spandau Ballet *Chant No.1 / Communication / Musclebound*

LPs

ABC *The Lexicon of Love*

Spandau Ballet *Diamond*

SYNTH POP

Singles

The Cure *Killing an Arab / The Love Cats*

Depeche Mode *Dreaming of Me*

The Eurythmics *Love is a Stranger / Who's That Girl?*

A Flock of Seagulls *I Ran*

Haircut 100 *Love Plus One*

Joy Division *Love Will Tear Us Apart* ★

New Order *Ceremony*

Gary Numan *Cars / Are 'Friends' Electric*

OMD *Maid of New Orleans*

Rezillos *Can't Stand my Baby*

LPs

The Cure *Lament / The Top*

Depeche Mode *B Sides* ★

The Eurythmics *Sweet Dreams*

Joy Division *Still*

Gary Numan The *Pleasure Principle*

Rezillos *Can't Stand the Rezillos*

The Smiths *Hatful of Hollow / Reel Around the Fountain* ★

real LP interest yet, although a "live in Rotterdam" EP, *Duran Goes Dutch*, is fetching $50. Spandau Ballet typifies the current market – their Top 5 LP *Journeys to Glory* is unlisted despite three Top 20 singles on it, their next LP, *Diamond*, contained the Top 3 *Chant No.1* but also has no listing, and their later singles are just £4 as picture discs. The Human League's early single, *Being Boiled*, is £8. Adam Ant had unsuccessfully tried Punk, but a new manager and style produced *Goody Two Shoes* (£10), *Stand and Deliver*, and *Prince Charming*; copies of his single *Desperate But Not Serious* list at £25.

> *Overexposure – Duran Duran's* Girls on Film *video by award-winning Godley and Crème became a club favourite after bans by the BBC and MTV. By the mid-'80s they had a UK and US No.1 with* The Reflex, *plus the James Bond theme* View to A Kill, *but still the group's value averages at just £5.*

Synth Pop

Guitars were forsaken for electric keyboards, and MTV videos became a new route for short-term group success. Front-runners Depeche Mode had over 30 UK hits. Their red flexi magazine-single, *I Sometimes Wish I Was Dead*, is worth £25 but most of their UK singles are worth around £5, or $3 in the US. A sign that they may be destined for greater things comes from the late-1989 Mute four-LP test pressing, *B Sides* ★, which is worth £1,000. Gothic band Joy Division offer the EP *An Ideal for Living* ★ – the 1,000 copies are each worth £100, while their *Still* double LP is up from £20 to £30 in just a year. The Cure's *Killing an Arab* is £18 (reissue £8), while *The Love Cats* picture-disc with a PVC cover is £25. The band's oddballs are the 1982 *Lament* promo test pressing (£80) and *The Top* – a one-sided 12" three-track LP sampler (£65). Kraftwerk-inspired OMD (Orchestral Manoeuvres in the Dark) issued their *Electricity* single with braille sleeve (£20). Haircut 100's *Blue Hat for a Blue Day* LP was withdrawn – test pressings are now worth £40+. Gary Numan increasingly employed gimmicks to assist record sales: his 1979 single *Cars* (£6) later appeared in the shape of a Grand Prix car, and as a Motorway Mix. The Smiths' record list is scattered with fast-rising mistakes: *Hand in Glove* ★ fetches a modest £15 (later ones, with a London rather than Manchester address on the back, only £10), but a misprinted sleeve with a negative image has jumped from £500 to £600 in a year. Their unreleased white-labelled *Reel Around the Fountain* ★ soared from £600 to £950 in a year, and the unissued live EP *Meat is Murder* ★ from £100 to £1,000.

Prog Rock *"DATED BUT PROMISING"*

Suggested Strands:
Headliners
Eurobands
Backbones

Average Record Cost
☆☆

Rising Stars
Pink Floyd
Genesis
Frank Zappa

HEADLINERS

Singles

Genesis *Happy the Man ★ / The Knife ★ / The Silent Sun ★ / Where the Sour Turns to Sweet ★ / A Winter's Tale ★*

Jethro Tull *Living in the Past / Song for Jeffrey*

Moody Blues *Nights in White Satin*

Pink Floyd *Apples and Oranges ★ / Arnold Layne ★ / See Emily Play ★*

Supertramp *Land Ho*

Yes *Roundabout ★*

Frank Zappa *Big Leg Emma / It Can't Happen Here / Mother People ★*

LPs

Emerson, Lake and Palmer *Emerson, Lake and Palmer / Tarkus*

Genesis *From Genesis to Revelation ★ / Genesis Collection Vol 1*

Jethro Tull *Stand Up / That Was*

Moody Blues *Days of Future Passed ★ / Go Now —The Moody Blues*

Born of a generation thriving upon art schools and modern literature, Progressive Rock (or Prog Rock) had its roots in both psychedelic and more classic cultures. Bands like The Doors and The Yardbirds stretched imaginations, Eastern sounds were cool, but The Beatles and Donovan still had a light, ethereal fantasy approach – all in all it was open season for ideas. From the late '60s a decade of Prog Rock used LPs to tell of legends and concepts, to fuse modern and classical, and to improvise. Fascinating and indulgent, this area is still affordable.

Headliners

Birmingham's Moody Blues topped the charts in 1965 with *Go Now*, but then struggled. Subsequent line-up changes and a new mellotron sound produced the significant LP *Days of Future Past* (£15 mono) and single *Nights in White Satin* (£5). All their UK LPs are worth less than £20, but in the USA a mono *Days of Future Passed ★* is worth $250. Pink Floyd personified "Underground" groups – desirable early singles from 1967, *Arnold Layne ★* and *See Emily Play ★*, are both £30 – but a promo demo version of either in picture-sleeve format fetches £650. Similarly *Apples and Oranges ★* goes for £45 but a demo promo is £650. The important LP, *Pipers at the Gates of Dawn ★*, is worth £165 mono and £70 stereo. Other LPs followed from this band, culminating in the groundbreaking *Dark Side of the Moon ★* (£15 or US ultra hi-fi version $300).

> **Rewriting History** – *Taking 20 days to make, including some old tracks, and with its title temporarily changed to* Eclipse, Dark Side of the Moon ★ *sold over 30 million copies and sat in the charts for 736 weeks – until chart rules banned discs over 10 years old from being included.*

Emerson, Lake and Palmer came out of King Crimson and The Nice. Their *Emerson, Lake & Palmer* debut LP charted the UK and USA (£20), and the *Lucky Man* single was also a hit. They had seven Top 10 LPs, each one increasingly grandiose, and currently sound dated with little collector's movement at the moment, so £15 or $25 should buy you any example.

It was a few years before their LP, *Foxtrot*, put Genesis on the map. Their 1969 *From Genesis to Revelation ★* in mono form with "unboxed" Decca logo is now £175, although a decade

Pink Floyd *Dark Side of the Moon ★ / Pipers at the Gates of Dawn ★ / A Saucerful of Secrets ★*

Supertramp *Breakfast in America ★ / Crime of the Century ★ / Crisis What Crisis / Even in the Quietest Moment / Indelibly Stamped*

Yes *The Yes Album / Time and a Word*

Frank Zappa *Absolutely Free / Freak Out / Lather ★ / Lumpy Gravy / We're Only in it for the Money / Zappa in New York ★*

EUROBANDS

Singles

Focus *Hocas Pocus / Sylvia*

Tangerine Dream *Lady Greengrass / Pheadra*

LPs

Aphrodite's Child *Aphrodite's Child / Rain and Tears / 666 – The Apocalypse of John*

Can *Ege Bamyasi / Cannibalism*

Focus *Focus 3 / Moving Waves*

Kraftwerk *Kraftwerk / Autobahn*

PFM *Photos of Ghosts / The World Became the World*

Tangerine Dream *Atem / Phaedra / Tangerine Dream 70–80*

Vangelis *Chariots of Fire / Heaven and Hell*

ago it was worth just £70 (stereo £60). Generally their LPs are £20– 30, with two LP collections that make £80: *Genesis Collections – Vol 1* includes the *Trespass* and *Nursery Cryme* LPs, while *Vol 2* has *Foxtrot* and *Selling England by the Pound*. The band has a big list of releases – early singles *The Silent Sun ★* and *A Winter's Tale ★* are both worth £225 today, while picture-bagged versions of both *The Knife ★* from 1971 and 1972's *Happy the Man ★* are worth £300 (£50 without the picture bag). A promo-only *Where the Sour Turns to Sweet ★* has doubled to £450 in four years.

> *Better Times – Genesis may have gone mainstream under Phil Collins but Peter Gabriel's reign is much collected – true rarities include an acetate single of* Watcher in the Sky *★, worth £1,250, and a Dutch* Genesis Live *double LP test pressing, complete with unreleased track, worth £2,000.*

All Yes LPs are worth around £20 and contain a fusion of Jon Anderson high vocals and semi-orchestral rock visions. Some odd singles have value: 1969 unreleased demos of *Looking Around ★* are worth £100+ and DJ copies of the 1972 single *Roundabout ★* make $100 in yellow vinyl. Jethro Tull's first record was *Song for Jeffrey* (£25), and their LP *That Was* is worth £60 mono and £35 stereo. Their Top 5 hit *Living in the Past* is worth just £7 today, with the fine *Stand Up* LP making the most at £45. Frank Zappa used over 200 musicians on 50 LPs, most of them alongside his Mothers of Invention. There is a huge collectable list of mid-'60s Verve singles – *It Can't Happen Here* and *Big Leg Emma* are each worth £30 – and The Verve LP *Freak Out* makes £50. There is big US interest in a mono white label version of *Freak Out ★*, which is worth $400 – a yellow label promo fetches $300 in stereo. The 1978 *Zappa in New York ★* test pressing fetches up to $400, and Zappa's *Lather ★* DJ LP test pressing from 1977 fetches $750.

Eurobands

Formative within the Disco and New Wave scenes, Germany's Kraftwerk were also central to Prog Rock – their self-titled LP is now worth £80, and *Autobahn* is £25. Another leading German band, Can, used hypnotic, repetitive sounds, such as on their 1972 LP *Ege Bamyasi* and the 1978 double-LP *Cannibalism* (£30). Experimental German Gothic band Tangerine Dream, named after The Beatles' song *Lucy In The Sky With Diamonds*, prompted the "Kraut Rock" tag. Their LP *Phaedra* was inspired

BACKBONES

Singles

Barclay James Harvest
Brother Thrush

Mike Oldfield *Don Alfonso* ★

Procol Harum
A Whiter Shade of Pale

The Alan Parsons Project
Eye in the Sky

Roxy Music *Love is The Drug /*
Virginia Plain

Soft Machine *Love Makes*
Sweet Music ★

LPs

Caravan *Caravan* ★ */ If I Could*
Do it All Over Again, I'd Do it All
Over You

Curved Air *Air Conditioning /*
Second Album

Egg *Egg / The Polite Force*

Brian Eno *Here Comes the*
Warm Jets / Music for Films ★

Barclay James Harvest
Barclay James Harvest

King Crimson *In the Court*
of the Crimson King

Man *Revelation / 2 ozs of*
Plastic with a Hole in the Middle

Nice *Ars Longa Vita Brevis /*
Thoughts of Emerlist Davjack

Mike Oldfield *Hergest Ridge /*
Platinum / Tubular Bells

The Alan Parsons Project
Complete Audio Guide to The
Alan Parsons Project / Tales of
Mystery and Imagination

Procol Harum *Shine on Brightly /*
A Salty Dog / Procol Harum Lives ★

Roxy Music *Roxy Music*

Pete Sinfield *Still*

Soft Machine *Soft Machine /*
Triple Echo

Rick Wakeman *Journey to*
the Centre of the Earth / Myths
and Legends of King Arthur /
The Six Wives of Henry VIII

by the Greek tragedy of the same name and the single *Phaedra* is worth £20. Their 1973 *Atem* was BBC DJ John Peel's Album of the Year. Greece's Aphrodite's Child had a secret weapon – Vangelis – and during the 1960s and '70s *Rain and Tears* was a hit single (£45) and LP (£20). Their best album was their last, the black-covered *666 – The Apocalypse of John* (£30). Vangelis left to release his stunning *Heaven and Hell* LP (£12) in 1975, and the *Chariots of Fire* movie theme. Italy's top Prog Rock band, PFM, was named after a local sponsoring bakers – Premiata Forneria Marconi. Their 1973 *Photos of Ghosts* and beautiful 1974 LP *The World Became the World* are each £20.

Backbones

The joy of Prog rock is found in its sheer diversity. For example, Rick Wakeman left Yes to stage a trio of highly theatrical concepts: *The Six Wives of Henry VIII* (£20), *Journey to the Centre of the Earth* (£10), and *Myths & Legends of King Arthur* (£10) staged on ice with almost 100 musicians/singers.

Named after William Burrough's novel, Jazz-influenced Soft Machine's debut LP was *Soft Machine*, with a cover that had moving parts (£30). Their single *Love Makes Sweet Music* ★ has gone from £75 to £100 in just four years (a Dutch version is £90). Although quickly forgotten, and never a commercial success, grand art Rock band Egg's 1970 LP *Egg* is going up, from £18 to £30 in a year. Procol Harum's multi-layered keyboards helped the 1967 hit single *A Whiter Shade of Pale* (£6), and they also produced a raft of LPs, such as *A Salty Dog*, all of which fetch around £20. A US 1970s promo box-set of goodies and music, *Procol Harum Lives* ★, is worth $300. Mike Oldfield had his demo of *Tubular Bells* rejected until Virgin finally agreed to take it on, and eventually sold over 10 million copies. King Crimson had Robert Fripp at the helm and had a good live reputation when they launched their debut LP, *In the Court of the Crimson King* (£45). They twice scrapped tapes for the LP, fired the producer, the manager re-mortgaged his house, and the engineer collapsed – but the result was a masterpiece.

Flag Burners – The Nice were intended as P.P. Arnold's backing band but their musicianship propelled them to stardom (LPs include The Thoughts of Emerlist Davjack, *£25). Setting fire to the Stars and Stripes while playing* West Side Story *material got them banned from the Royal Albert Hall.*

RHYTHM & BLUES

R&B is like one of those critical pieces of a jigsaw – once it's in place all manner of things fall into place around it. Like all quality music its roots are firmly seated in human emotions rather than blatant commerce and so many of its key players failed to hog the limelight. The impetus behind it really lay in the birth of more introverted West Coast Cool Jazz and East Coast Bebop, which left the way clear for more exuberant Jump Jazz to entertain. Rhythm & Blues amalgamated highly danceable Jazz material with the infectious repetitive hooks and rhythms of Blues – so its spread to wider audiences was inevitable. By the early 1950s companies like Atlantic Records were actively blending this new phenomenon with existing music from Doo Wop and Country (effectively early Rock & Roll). This temporarily placed stars from those genres within the genuine R&B orbit. Silkier, but still emotional, strands emerged as it matured, clearing the way for the entire Soul movement.

Trad Jazz was the fashion in the UK, and artists such as Chris Barber toured widely, featuring guest bluesmen from the USA and then his wife, Ottilie Patterson. His band fused Trad and Blues. Clubs began changing from Jazz to R&B, with house bands developing a compelling form of music. With so much raw talent jamming together, visiting each other's clubs, listening to and exploring each other's music, change was inevitable. The purists like Long John Baldry and Cyril Davies carried the traditional message, while others created the quintessential Rock formula. The Rolling Stones are a direct result, overshadowing similar band The Downliners Sect. The Yardbirds initially played Chicago Blues material; Eric Clapton, Jeff Beck, and eventually Jimmy Page all became part of the band at various times and each one of them shifted its vision. At its demise Page took control and the New Yardbirds then became Led Zeppelin – another major piece of music's jigsaw.

There are genuinely important records within this section. Many of them were never mass circulation hits, so for collectors the area represents fascinating challenges in finding good examples while still exploring currently neglected artists and recordings.

Compulsive Drifters – Clyde McPhatter formed The Drifters, made changes, and had a few No.1s before he sold his share to the manager. They had various singers before their next No.1., and the whole income from that record went to the manager as the group was on fixed wages. This upset the band and they walked out. The manager acquired a group called "The Crowns", which he renamed "Drifters". Their singer was replaced by one of the original band members until he changed his name to Ben E. King and went solo.

Rhythm & Blues *"FASCINATING CROSSROADS"*

Suggested Strands
American Magic
British Boom

Average Record Cost
☆☆☆☆

Rising Stars
Etta James
The Yardbirds
The Downliners Sect

AMERICAN MAGIC

Singles

Brook Benton
It's Just a Matter of Time

James Brown
Please, Please, Please

Ray Charles *Baby Let Me Hold Your Hand ★ / I Got a Woman*

The Coasters *Besame Mucho ★*

Fats Domino *Ain't That a Shame ★ / Blueberry Hill ★*

The Drifters *Save the Last Dance for Me / There Goes My Baby*

Clyde McPhatter *Seven Days ★*

LPs

James Brown *Please, Please, Please ★ / Try Me ★*

Ray Charles
The Original Ray Charles ★

The Coasters *One by One ★*

Lee Dorsey *Ya Ya ★*

The Drifters *Rockin' and Driftin' ★*

Etta James
At Last / Miss Etta James ★

Louis Jordan
Go Blow Your Horn ★

Clyde McPhatter
Love Ballads ★

Jackie Wilson
Lonely Teardrops ★

This is among the most difficult genres to identify yet it is a pivotal crossroads to Jazz, Blues, Rock, and Soul. Most of the key artists are shared with other sections but R&B casts a powerful shadow over them. In the USA it took Jump Jazz into Rock & Roll and also helped mould Soul. In the UK it operated differently, emerging from Trad Jazz to nurture a generation of important Rock musicians. This is a place where you'll meet many familiar faces and be aghast at their value.

American Magic

The 1940s saxophonist Louis Jordan was a key figure at this time, steering Jump Jazz towards R & B. Between 1942 and '51 he had 57 R&B hits including *Saturday Night Fish Fry* (£12), *Louis Jordan* (this EP had three different covers, each worth £80), and *Go Blow Your Horn ★* ($300). Singer Big Joe Turner furthered the cause with the singles *Chains of Love ★* ($500), *The Chill is On ★* ($800), *Don't You Cry ★* ($100), and the No.1 *Honey Hush ★*, worth $200. Fats Domino's 1949 single *The Fat Man ★* is worth a staggering $2,000; it epitomized R&B's New Orleans roots and sold a million copies. The favourites *Ain't That a Shame* (£50) and *Blueberry Hill ★* ($150 in red vinyl) were just two of 35 Top 40 singles that he had between 1955 and '63. Lee Dorsey's No.1 singles *Ya Ya* ($15) and *Ride Your Pony* ($8), and The Meters' *Look-Ka-Py Py* (£7) and *Chicken Strut* ($10) all carried New Orleans signatures. The Drifters never made a studio album, but a black-labelled 1958 LP, *Rockin' and Driftin' ★*, and a 1960 *Drifters Greatest Hits ★* are worth $600 each in mono.

> *Not Pleasing Mum – The 16-year-old Jamesetta Hawkins left home without her mother's blessing, joined LA's Otis Band, reversed her name to Etta James, and recorded* The Wallflower (Roll with Me Henry). *US radio objected to this so it was renamed* The Wallflower (Dance with Me Henry).

During the mid-'50s the Soul factor increased. Clyde McPhatter left The Drifters to issue more pop-ish singles including his 1956 R&B No.1, *Treasures of Love ★* (£200 as a 78'), and *Love Ballads ★* ($500 in mono). James Brown also has valuable albums. His '58 LP *Please, Please, Please ★* is worth $1,200 ($900 if cover letters are 3in rather than 2in high). The LP's title single is itself worth $400 in a picture bag.

BRITISH BOOM

Singles

Alexis Korner's Blues Incorporated *Blaydon Races* ★

Long John Baldry & The Hoochie Coochie Men *Let the Heartaches Begin*

Georgie Fame & The Blue Flames *Yeh Yeh*

Chris Farlowe & The Thunderbirds *Buzz with the Fuzz* ★

The Groundhogs *Over You Baby*

The Yardbirds *Goodnight Sweet Josephine* ★ / *I Wish You Could* ★ / *Shape of Things to Come*

LPs

Alexis Korner's Blues Incorporated *At the Cavern* ★ / *Sky High* ★

Cyril Davies' All Stars *The Legendary Cyril Davies* ★

The Downliners Sect *The Sect*

Georgie Fame & The Blue Flames *Rhythm & Blues at the Flamingo*

The Graham Bond Organisation *There's a Bond Between Us* ★

The Groundhogs *Scratching the Surface*

Geno Washington and The Ram Jam Band *Shake a Tail Feather!*

The Yardbirds *For Your Love* ★

EPs

Cyril Davies' All Stars *The Sound of Cyril Davies*

The Downliners Sect *Nite in Great Newport Street* ★

The Yardbirds *Over Under Sideways Down* ★

Zoot Money's Big Roll Band *Big Time Operator* ★

Jackie Wilson (who replaced McPhatter in Drifters) had hit singles like *Reet Petite* (£20) and *I'll be Satisfied* (£60 as a 78'). Many Coasters records also present healthy collecting – *One by One* ★ with a yellow harp label is worth $400.

British Boom

The founding father of British R&B was Cyril Davies. With his All Stars he recorded *The Sound of Cyril Davies* (EP £60) and *The Legendary Cyril Davies* ★ (10" £300). With Alexis Korner he made *Red Hot from Alex* (£100) and *Sky High* ★ (£350), and they also opened the Blues Incorporated Club. The Flamingo, Marquee, Crawdaddy, and Eel Pie clubs all followed this example. After Davies died Long John Baldry took over the band, until leaving to form The Streampacket. He went on to employ many future stars in his later Hoochie Coochie Men. This band's hits included *Long John Blues* (£85) and the '67 No.1 single *Let the Heartaches Begin* (£5).

The Graham Bond Organisation was a band that included two-thirds of Rock's "supergroup" Cream – Baker and Bruce. It produced the single *Long Tall Shorty* (£40) and the 1966 LP *There's a Bond Between Us* ★ (£120). Zoot Money's Big Roll Band had the 1964 single *Uncle Willie* (£25) and the '66 EP *Big Time Operator* ★ (£150), while Georgie Fame and The Blue Flames made the *Do the Dog* single (£15) and *Rhythm & Blues*

> *Lost Supergroup – Long John Baldry employed Elton John on keyboards but also toured with The Steampacket using Brian Auger, Julie Driscoll, and Rod Stewart. Each artist had their own hits but contracts prevented them recording together, although a Marquee gig was unofficially recorded.*

at the Flamingo LP, worth £50. The single *Buzz with the Fuzz* ★ by Chris Farlowe and The Thunderbirds is worth £140 (demos are £100); the *Chris Farlowe and The Thunderbirds* LP is £85.

The Downliners Sect are now biting back with sharp value rises – the 1964 EP *Nite in Great Newport Street* ★ has risen from £250 to £275, and *The Sect Sing Sick Songs* ★ EP from £75 to £100. The Yardbirds provide great music for collecting, with many hits such as *Shape of Things to Come* (£6) and the US promo-only single *I Wish You Could* ★ ($800). Their *Over Under Sideways Down* ★ EP is £165, and unreleased acetates of the 1968 single *Goodnight Sweet Josephine* ★ fetch £225.

MOVIES

Roger Daltrey *McVicar*
Staggered releases to tie in with movie launches often generate differing packages of the same single, as illustrated by these UK and US *McVicar* records.

Synchronized keyboard recordings were used in cinemas as far back as 1916. By the 1930s songs from big movies were being released, and in 1942 some of Miklos Rozsa's *Jungle Book* score, complete with storytelling by its star, Sabu, were released on 78's. The arrival of LPs allowed most elements of the film's story to be recorded, which gave the movie valuable advance promotion via radio. By the '60s advanced audio technology tempted studios to re-record old scores and a new breed of composers and arrangers dominated productions. From 1980 the power of hit singles and their artists gave birth to endless soundtracks of movie stories loosely used to exploit chart music; *American Graffiti* ($12) is a quality example of this. Some pop groups skilfully embraced movies, like The Who in *Tommy* or its singer Roger Daltrey's starring role in *McVicar*.

According to *Osborne's Official Movie Price Guide*, eight of the world's Top 10 most valuable soundtrack albums are pivoted around films highlighting major record artists – predominantly Presley. However, by a margin of $4,000, the most prized is one of the two non-musical entries – the 1954 *Caine Mutiny*, worth $10,000. This Humphrey Bogart and José Ferrer film was borne of a successful Broadway play, *The Caine Mutiny Courtmartial*, and the movie company rushed through a music and dialogue soundtrack to borrow status for its forthcoming release. The LP was pressed but the author, Herman Wouk, objected to it and only a few escaped the factory, which is probably why they are so sought after now.

When starting a collection of movie music consider following the career path of a composer, or maybe generic groups like Bond movies or Sci-Fi. Many people collect simply because the music is beautiful, and often overlooked. If browsing, bear in mind that big composer names count, often more than singers. Better still, if the film wasn't a blockbuster it means there are fewer copies in circulation. Good stylized period artwork is another reason to collect a certain record.

You should be very careful to check what you are buying. Soundtracks traditionally contain the key music from the film but by the 1990s more often they were music "inspired by the film", rather than in it. "Original Scores" contain material written specifically for a film, whereas "Movie Themes" are often just general compilations.

Sharing the Limelight – Studio Cast put out 15 albums, all called Co-Star. *They each contain an acting game in which a period heavyweight actor like Vincent Price delivers lines and the listener responds from provided scripts. Most are $12 but Tallulah Bankhead's fetches $25.*

First Beats *"INNOCENT DREAMS"*

EARLY BRITISH

LPs

The Beatles *A Hard Day's Night* ★

Adam Faith *Beat Girl*

Cliff Richard *The Young Ones*

Tommy Steele *Half a Sixpence / The Tommy Steele Story*

EPs

Terry Dene *The Golden Disc*

Billy Fury *Play it Cool* ★

Cliff Richard *Expresso Bongo / Serious Charge*

AMERICAN WAVES

LPs

Chuck Berry, Connie Francis and Frankie Lymon *Rock, Rock, Rock* ★

Eddie Cochran and Ritchie Valens *Go Johnny Go* ★

Elvis Presley *Blue Hawaii* ★ / *GI Blues* ★ / *King Creole* ★ / *Loving You* ★ / *Speedway* ★

EPs

Eddie Cochran and Rickie Valens *Go Johnny Go* ★

Elvis Presley *Jailhouse Rock* ★ / *King Creole* ★ / *Love Me Tender* ★ / *Loving You* ★

Music and movies are natural bedfellows and every nation has contributed to this global archive. In this section the focus is on early contemporary music.

Early British

A very British beginning was the 1957 movie *The Tommy Steele Story* (10" worth £20). Later films such as *The Duke Wore Jeans* (EP £12) and the 1960s *Half a Sixpence* (LP £15) became simple light entertainment. Terry Dene's '58 movie EP *The Golden Disc* fares better at £35. Cliff Richard's 1959 *Serious Charge* film hinted at teen discontentment (EP £30), while *Expresso Bongo* (EP £40) and *The Young Ones* (LP £35) were made of lighter stuff. Adam Faith's 1960 film EP *Beat Girl* is worth £35, the LP £40, and Billy Fury's *Play it Cool* ★ EP is £30 (export versions £100). Compilation soundtracks existed too, such as *It's Trad Dad* with Gene Vincent and Helen Shapiro (£25) and *It's All Happening* with Tommy Steele, Russ Conway, and Shane Fenton (£22). In 1964 The Beatles' *A Hard Day's Night* ★ brought UK musical movies new status (LP early pressings £40–60, US white-label promos $2,000).

> *Manager's Secret – A unique Elvis Presley* Loving You ★ *picture disc LP used a* GI Blues *image on one side. It featured the five* Loving You *songs and five instrumentals. The disc, found in Elvis' manager's office, is worth $6,000.*

American Waves

Early Presley soundtracks are highly collectable. The 1956 *Love Me Tender* ★ EP with a black label but no dog logo is £175, while the orange-labelled *Loving You* ★ EPs are $100 each. One of his best movies, *King Creole* ★, had two EPs – the best version has orange labels and is worth $100. The mono LP *Speedway* ★ is $500, stereo $50, while the 1960 *GI Blues* ★ has ten versions; the mono black label with "Long Play" and a heart-shaped sticker is $300, the regular stereo version is $8.

Other soundtracks include the 1958 *Rock, Rock, Rock* ★ by Berry, Francis, and Lymon ($75, promo version $750) and an EP of *Go Johnny Go* ★ with Ritchie Valens and Eddie Cochran ($300, promo-only version $750). The film *Blackboard Jungle* spawned Bill Haley's '55 hit *Rock Around the Clock* (EP £30).

Big Guns *"INDIVIDUAL PORTFOLIOS"*

Suggested Strands
Europeans
Americans

Average Record Cost
☆☆

Rising Stars
Maurice Jarre
Bernard Herrmann

Unlike most areas of record collecting the film world places the composer/arranger high above the recording artist – particularly in the eras prior to the 1980s. Most were classically trained, and frequently Jazz experts, and they became the main promotion tools for huge motion pictures. Generally inexpensive to collect, the work of a specific composer offers a wealth of one person's musical ideas.

Europeans
Hans Zimmer
German-born Zimmer wrote advertising jingles in London before joining groups like Ultravox and The Buggles. His love for modern sounds perfectly united with movie composer Stanley Myers in their joint film work. By the mid-'80s he was independent and had gained an Oscar, nominations for three more, three Grammies, two Golden Globes, and many other distinctions. His LPs include *The Last Emperor* ($15) from 1987, 1989's *Driving Miss Daisy* ($12), and *Days of Thunder* ($15) from 1990.

Francis Lai
Born in the French Mediterranean, this pianist and Jazz player teamed up with Bernard Dimey. He made his film debut for *La Ronde*, then worked for Jean-Luc Godard on *Masculin/Feminin* before creating his 1966 Oscar-winning soundtrack *A Man and A Woman* (£15). *Love Story* ($15) from 1970 provided another Oscar and a major hit with *Where Do I Begin* (Andy Williams, $5). Other work includes the 1969 LP *Mayerling* ★ ($125).

Maurice Jarre
Jarre had a classical training before going on to win his first Oscar in 1962 for *Lawrence of Arabia* ($45). He was also nominated for *Sundays and Cybele*, and won an Oscar for the 1965 epic *Doctor Zhivago* ($12). Franenheimer's film *Grand Prix* was then followed by *Ryan's Daughter* ($15 or £25) in 1970, and yet another Oscar for *A Passage to India* in 1984.

John Barry
Barry first formed a small band and gained success on early pop TV shows. Chart success brought a movie score for Adam Faith's movie *Beat Girl* (£40). He was invited to complete the unfinished work on *Dr. No* and 20 years of James Bond scores followed, providing numerous Oscars. He also worked on many other fine projects that were overshadowed by the Bond notoriety. His LPs include the 1968 *The Lion in Winter* (£30), *From Russia with Love* (£40) in 1963, and 1969's *Boom* (£90).

EUROPEANS

LPs

John Barry *Born Free / The Lion in Winter / Out of Africa / Dances with Wolves / Beat Girl / From Russia with Love / Goldfinger / Thunderball*

Maurice Jarre *Lawrence of Arabia / Doctor Zhivago / Grand Prix / Ryan's Daughter / A Passage to India / Witness / Gorillas in the Mist*

Francis Lai *A Man and a Woman / Love Story / Mayerling / I'll Never Forget What's 'is name / Life for Life / Rider in the Rain / Marie*

Hans Zimmer *My Beautiful Laundrette / The Last Emperor / Driving Miss Daisy / Backdraft / Thelma & Louise / Days of Thunder / The Lion King / As Good as it Gets*

AMERICANS

LPs

Bernard Herrmann
Citizen Kane / The Devil and Daniel Webster / The Ghost and Mrs Muir / Journey to the Centre of the Earth / Psycho / Taxi Driver / Twisted Nerve ★ / Vertigo ★

Elmer Bernstein
Cat Woman of the Moon / God's Little Acres ★ / The Great Escape / To Kill a Mockingbird / Kings Go Forth / The Magnificent Seven / The Man with the Golden Arm / The Ten Commandments

Henry Mancini
Arabesque / Breakfast at Tiffany's / Days of Wine and Roses / The Glenn Miller Story / The Pink Panther / The Return of the Pink Panther / Romeo and Juliet / Wait until Dark

John Williams
Daddy-O / ET / Jaws / Jurassic Park ★ / Raiders of the Lost Ark / Star Wars / The Towering Inferno / Valley of the Dolls

Earlier Incarnation – John Barry had been rejected by the BBC and then backed pop stars such as Cliff Richard. He had also been Musical Director for TV's Drum Beat and squeezed into the pop charts with singles like the No.10 Hit and Miss (£7) and the No.40 Beat for Beatniks (£6).

Americans

Henry Mancini

Mancini got encouragement from his idol Benny Goodman and gained work with the Glenn Miller Orchestra. His first film score was for Abbot and Costello's *Lost in Alaska*. The *Glenn Miller* and *Benny Goodman* stories followed before he created the 1961 hits *Breakfast at Tiffany's* ($25), *Moon River*, and *Days of Wine and Roses*. He has received more Oscar and Grammy awards than any other pop composer. His LPs include the 1964 *The Pink Panther* ($25) and *The Glenn Miller Story* (£12) from 1954.

John Williams

Williams' first film score was for a modest 1959 crime adventure *Daddy-O* but within a decade he had received an Oscar nomination for music in *Valley of the Dolls* ($30). From there it reads like a Who's Who, with *The Towering Inferno* (£12), *Raiders of the Lost Ark*, ($30), and *Star Wars* (£15). Other LPs include the 1983 *ET* box set (£75), 1993's *Jurassic Park ★* (promo-only picture disc $1,200) and 1975's classic *Jaws* ($20).

Elmer Bernstein

With Aaron Copland as a fan of Bernstein's piano work, recognition by the age of 13 was inevitable. War assignment to arrange Glenn Miller's material led to dozens of broadcasts, then peacetime propelled him through radio to Hollywood and his first movie scores, such as *Cat Woman of the Moon*. His LPs include *The Ten Commandments* (£35) and *Kings Go Forth ★* ($125) from 1958, and 1978's *God's Little Acres ★* ($150).

Bernard Herrmann

This classically trained New Yorker followed similar pathways to Bernstein, moving from radio production work to Hollywood, where he worked with Orson Wells. Within a year he had scored *Citizen Kane* and *The Devil and Daniel Webster* – both of which earned Oscar nominations (*Webster* won). Working with Alfred Hitchcock, Martin Scorsese, Orson Welles, and Brian De Palma he created many brilliant soundtracks. His LPs include the 1958 *Vertigo ★* (£150), *Journey to the Centre of the Earth* ($30) from 1959, and 1969's *Twisted Nerve ★* (with *Les Bicyclettes de Belsize* on the second side, $275).

Blaxploitation *"PRE-SOUL ADVENTURES"*

Suggested Strands
Main Events
Lightweight
Horror Shows

Average Record Cost
☆

Rising Stars
Static Market

MAIN EVENTS – all LPS
Isaac Hayes *Shaft*
Quincy Jones *The Lost Man / They Call Me Mister Tibbs*
Curtis Mayfield *Superfly*
Osibisa *Superfly T.N.T.*

Various Artists *Across 110th Street / Black Caesar / Black Fist / Cleopatra Jones / Coffy / The Final Countdown / Foxy Brown / Gordon's War / Hell up in Harlem / Hit 'em Hard / The Mack / Savage / Shaft's Big Score / Shaft in Africa / Slaughter's Big Rip Off / Three Tough Guys / Three the Hard Way / Trouble Man / Truck Turner / Uptight / Willie Dynamite*

LIGHTWEIGHT – all LPS
Nat Dove and The Devils *Peter Wheatstraw*

Charles Earland *The Dynamite Brothers*

Curtis Mayfield & The Stable Singers *Let's Do it Again*

Michael Tschudin *Honey Baby, Honey Baby*

Various Artists *Dolemite* ★

HORROR SHOWS – all LPS
Gene Page / *Blackula*

Various Artists *Lord Shango / The Thing with Two Heads*

The relatively harmonious music of Motown took second place in the 1970s to a grittier sound personified by James Brown. It was this "Funk", crystallized by Isaac Hayes' milestone *Shaft* soundtrack, which bred a surge in music and action movies featuring black street attitudes, and became known as Blaxploitation. Thanks to constant club exposure such LPs have now become collectable.

Main Events
It all started with Isaac Hayes' 1971 LP *Shaft* (£18), followed in '72 by *Shaft's Big Score* (£18), and a year later *Shaft in Africa* (£25), featuring Johnny Pate's music and vocals by The Four Tops. Italian producer Dino de Laurentis also used Hayes' music for *Uomini Duri* – renamed *Three Tough Guys* (£12). Another essential Blaxploitation LP is *Superfly* – Curtis Mayfield's brilliant 1972 score (£12), with *Superfly T.N.T.* (£15) tempting the star out of crime retirement. The films' stories may have been filled with excesses but good music was critical to their success, and gifted Quincy Jones was teamed up with actor Sidney Poitier in the 1969 film *The Lost Man* (£15) and again in *They Call Me Mister Tibbs* (£60).

Lightweight
Flimsy adventures included *The Dynamite Brothers* (£15) from 1973, which was accompanied by Charles Earland. The 1975 *Dolemite* ★ (£100) film score is a backdrop to Rudy Ray Moore and an all-female kung fu army. He features again in a rather odd romp with more martial arts and the devil in *Peter Wheatstraw* (£50). The score is by Nat Dove & The Devils!

Horror Shows
The 1975 film *Lord Shango* tackled a clash of black faiths with Howard Roberts' co-ordinated score using The Staple Singers and others. *Blackula's* soundtrack was by Gene Page and is now £35. For around £18 you could hunt out the 1972 funk freak movie LP *The Thing with Two Heads*, featuring a variety of artists from Britain's Bonzo Dog Band to Sammy Davis Jnr.

Biding Time – For Isaac Hayes an Oscar, No.1 LP, and single with Shaft *hides a past including gospel, groups like Sir Isaac and The Do-Dads, and a forgotten four-track LP* Hot Buttered Soul *(worth just £15, but its time will come).*

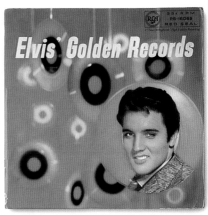

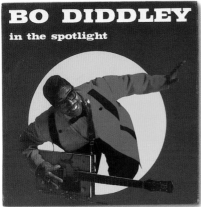

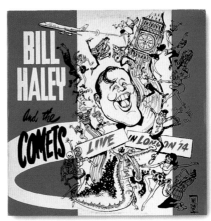

Beyond these classic names, pictured above, are armies of forgotten but highly collectable early Rock & Roll artists. Ivan's *Real Wild Child* single is worth £300 – the sum of all these LPs.

At the moment collectors of Rock Groups are mostly fans, but it will soon become a recognized general genre. The Rolling Stones LP is currently worth £10, Deep Purple less than £20.

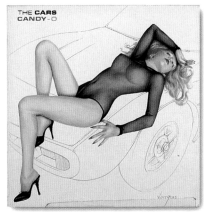

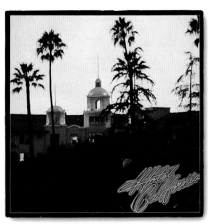

A.O.R., or Soft Rock, is a goldmine of currently under-valued gems. Most of the vinyl pictured here is worth just £10, but Buckingham-Nicks and Buffalo Springfield are fetching £40–50.

Prog Rock is a fascinating, indulgent, and currently cheap genre to collect. The average cost is £12, but early material like this 1967 Pink Floyd LP is starting to reach three-figure sums.

There are dozens and dozens of Punk and New Wave
avenues to explore, although the complexity of styles
means pricing levels are hard to establish.

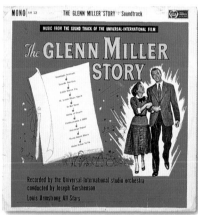

Collectors of Movies vinyl enjoy a phenomenal choice of styles, images, and memories. A dream find would be the soundtrack for *Caine Mutiny* (1954) which was never officially released and is worth $10,000 plus.

above Presentation packs (kits of biographies, photos, and new music), often in limited edition form, are very desirable. They are not easy to find, or to value, but acquire an out of vogue one, such as this Ray Thomas *From Mighty Oaks* solo LP press pack, and wait for the market to change. The LP is currently worth just £10 ($15) but with time this set, complete with very rare, autographed, mounted album artwork, will appreciate well.

right Missing Persons was a curious '80s fusion of an ex-Playboy bunny girl and Frank Zappa musicians. Their producer sent these packs to local radio stations, building up interest until finally they were signed by Capitol Records. The rare packs include two unplayed EPs, sets of press cuttings, and a list of the targeted radio stations. As a cult band they're almost impossible to value – so dependent are they on fans competing for their products.

A single release can give birth to a vast array of collectable versions – foreign ones frequently have different pictures from the original. Extras such as posters can add value.

RADIO

This is an area not often looked into – a treasure chest many collectors aren't even aware is filled with delights. If fans were told there are dozens of live original albums by their favourite star that they have never heard of they just would not believe it. However, radio doesn't just play great collectable records – it creates some of the most desirable ones too.

To appreciate this marketplace it is first necessary to understand American broadcasting. It has more stations and more audiences than any other nation can imagine yet it operates as a patchwork of local radio stations – albeit frequently centrally owned or controlled. In order that record companies and artists can tap into their audiences there is a commercial need to simulate some kind of national network. This is the role of the big syndication houses such as Westwood One, D.I.R. Broadcasting, London Wavelength, Watermark, and Inner View who in the 1970s and '80s nationally canvassed several hundred weekly station outlets to broadcast their shows. These shows featured superstars giving either live performances or music and interviews. The records were beautifully pressed to ensure the best broadcast qualities, and were frequently distributed in plain or company boxes/sleeves with very little label detail and accompanied by stapled or bound script and cue sheet pages. Naturally, artists agreed to these purely for the exposure but such superstars' gems are a haven for bootleggers. The pressings are supposed to be returned each week but of course some aren't, which creates a hungry market for what would have originally been only a few dozen or hundred pressings: so we are talking rare records here. Despite the best efforts, vinyl programming discs are openly advertised and sold in the USA, and from time to time in the UK, where prices range from £30 to nearly £2,000.

In Britain, national radio is centrally controlled and hugely restrictive for artists not suiting corporate visions of fashion. Over the years British DJ Alan Freeman consistently managed to champion major new stars, while fellow DJ John Peel opened door after door for alternative talents. His early radio show, *London Perfumed Garden Show*, inspired many and despite network rules created Dandelion Records, showcasing Bridget St. John's *Ask Me No Questions* (£35), Clifford T. Ward's *Singer Songwriter* (£15), Medicine Head's *Heavy on the Drum* (£30), and Gene Vincent's *I'm Back & Proud* (£30). More recently, 20 years of broadcast archives from his BBC "Peel Live" sessions have started to appear on his Strange Fruit label, including the September 1977 Buzzcocks show, November 1977 Ultravox session, and The Smiths show from April 1983.

Winning Ways – For the 26-week BBC landmark series The Story of Pop, *a fledgling BBC Enterprises department planned an accompanying partwork and LP compilation. But host Alan Freeman wanted a stronger record and so organized an independent double LP,* History of Pop, *which went Gold.* The BBC ended up giving this independent LP as a prize on one of their shows!

Radio *"OLD NAMES, FRESH CHOICES"*

Suggested Strands
Programme
Personality
Stations

Average Record Cost
☆☆☆

Rising Stars
Westwood One
King Biscuit Hour

PROGRAMME – all LPs

D.I.R.

Best of King Biscuit Flower Hour
3 LPs

Bruce Springsteen ★ 2 LPs

David Bowie Concert ★ 2 LPs

King Biscuit Flower Hour 500th Show 2 LPs

King Biscuit Flower Hour 500th Show ★ 4 LPs

The Rolling Stones Concert ★
2 LPs

The Who/Pete Townsend ★
2 LPs

General

Albums Greats ★ 53 LPs

American Top 40 3 LPs

American Top 40 8 LPs

Battle of the Surfing Bands ★
K.P.O.I.

Battle of the Surfing Bands
K.T.L.A.

Battle of the Surfing Bands
K.Y.A.

Continuous History of Rock and Roll ★ 65 LPs within 13
box sets

Elvis Presley Story ★ 13 LPs

Collecting Radio products can prove as varied as the broadcaster's output and many popular souvenirs of a loved series are humorous – for example *Beyond Our Ken* (£20) on Parlophone Records is typical of the price and type explored in the Comedy section (*see* pages 54–57). However, here we are primarily concentrating on music-related strands. The concept of products directly borne of radio exposure emerged in fits and starts for both the organizations and the broadcasters. Collecting this field is a challenge but the investment – and audio interest levels – are high.

Programme

Not surprisingly, this is very much American territory. Britain was late getting into Pop music broadcasting, and even later in realizing its potential commercial powers. The main purveyors of vinyl-based radio shows were the US syndication houses such as Westwood One, Inner View, D.I.R. Broadcasting, Watermark, London Wavelengths, and Global Satellite, and their products were hugely desirable to collectors. They featured major stars with original recordings on extremely limited pressing runs. Frequently a concert recording would be pressed up as different packages. For example, Irish band U2's 1982 Hammersmith Palais gig featured as a BBC series syndication LP *In Concert* ★ (valued now at £350 or $700), yet the same concert appeared as part of a *Superstars Concert Series* ★, which was a 1985 three-LP set from Westwood One (worth £200). London Wavelength also put out a version in the 1990s, valued at £100.

The West Coast syndication house Watermark was responsible for many programmes including the perennial US chart show *TAmerican Top 40* – box sets of three LPs from 1973 onwards are now worth $50–60. There were also many spin-offs, such as *American Top 40 Year End Countdowns* 1973–85. This eight-LP set is worth $75. They also produced

---

Foreign Ambassador – While most US-syndicated shows were hosted by domestic broadcasters such as Casey Kasem, Global Satellite boasted Britain's own Alan Freeman who interviewed major stars like Robert Plant and George Harrison.

Elvis Presley *The Elvis Presley Story* American syndication houses created entire series or specials on a star, including interviews, rare music, and even the advert breaks. Good examples are quite difficult to find so are highly prized. This set of 13 LPs, *The Elvis Presley Story* from Watermark, is still complete with its broadcast script, blank radio station press releases, and PR photo. It is worth in excess of $1,000.

one-offs like their 1975 *California Special*, and the mouth-watering *Elvis Presley Story* ★ (*see* above), which stretched over 13 radio shows and is worth around $1,000 (or $800 if it is without its printed cue sheet, script, and track listings).

D.I.R Broadcasting produced the well-known *King Biscuit Flower Hour*, which had begun in 1973 and reached around 300 stations every week. This "live" concert series chalked up 750 performances, many bootleg versions, and eventually limited commercial releases on CDs. With the US being such a powerful market most artists agreed to the later CD releases, which included The Rolling Stones' May 1986 live concert (the two LPs are $100), David Bowie from 1980, and Bruce Springsteen from '87 (both artists' concerts are found on two LPs, each set selling for $150). The show's 1985 *King Biscuit Flower Hour 500th Show* boasted highlights of 499 shows, including performances by John Lennon and Bruce Springsteen. The two LPs are worth $75. A fuller *King Biscuit Flower Hour 500th Show* ★ has the

Monterey Pop ★ 9 LPs

'60s at The Beeb ★

Multiple Usage

Isle of Dreams ★ Westwood One: 18 LPs

Isle of Dreams ★ Westwood One: 9 LPs

U2: 1 concert's recordings

In Concert ★ BBC

BBC Rock Hour ★ London Wavelength

Superstars Concert Series ★ Westwood One

same highlights but also includes the 500th show. This set comprises four LPs and is worth $125. However, a 1988 TV-advertised three-LP *Best of King Biscuit Flower Hour* is worth just $25.

Naturally, with many radio stations forming part of the same chain, shows also became customized – San Francisco's station issued the K.Y.A. LP *Battle of the Surfing Bands* ($80) in 1964, while in Honolulu it was K.P.O.I.'s *Battle of the Surfing Bands* ★ ($100); in LA the K.T.L.A. version is worth $80.

Elvis Presley apart, highly desirable collectables include *Monterey Pop* ★ – the radio concert of May 1988. This nine-LP set from Radio Express is worth $600. *Album Greats* ★ is an incredible 1979 48-hour radio show highlighting best sellers; the 53 LPs issued by TM Products are now priced at $1,000. Others worth watching out for include *Continuous History of Rock and Roll* ★ – a day-long show from Drake-Chenault at $400, and Westwood One's *'60s at The Beeb* ★ – a live concert featuring The Beatles, The Rolling Stones, and The Who that is worth $190.

> *Dream Event – Westwood One issued a 1983 fantasy festival "Isle of Dreams" ★, an 18-LP box set hosted by Eric Clapton. This is now approaching $300. There was a second version done four years later, worth $200, and a 1989 nine-LP edited set, which is now $125.*

Personalities

American DJs rarely gained a national reputation, but UK national broadcasters eventually saw the opportunities that could be created. At one extreme ex-boxer Jimmy Young twice hit No.1 in 1955 with *Unchained Melody* and *Man From Laramie* (£20 each), while Kenny Everett delivered his Top 10 hit *Snot Rap* in 1983. Terry Wogan offered a certain quaintness with his minor 1978 hit *The Floral Dance*, and Tony Blackburn contributed the single *Chop Chop* (worthy of £6). Ex-wrestler Jimmy Savile staggered through the 1962 single *Ahab the Arab* (£8) backed by the wisely unpublicized Brian Poole and The Tremeloes. Alan Freeman also had his lapse with the 1962 single *Madison Time,* but more than redeemed himself by brokering a unique double Rock LP, *By Invitation Only* ($30), for which he somehow got famous groups like The Rolling Stones, Yes, Emerson, Lake, and Palmer, and Led Zeppelin to share the same vinyl. *Dick Clark's*

PERSONALITIES

Singles

Tony Blackburn *Chop Chop*

Kenny Everett *Snot Rap*

Alan Freeman *Madison Time*

Jimmy Savile *Ahab the Arab / The Bossa Nova*

Terry Wogan *Floral Dance*

Jimmy Young *Unchained Melody*

LPs

Dick Clark *Dick Clark's 20 Years of Rock 'n' Roll*

Kenny Everett *20 Worst Songs Ever Recorded*

Alan Freed *Alan Freed's Memory Lane / Alan Freed's Top 15*

Alan Freeman *By Invitation Only*

David Hamilton *Hamilton Hot Shots*

David Jacobs *Saturday Side of David Jacobs*

Murray the K. *Murray the K's Golden Gassers* ★

Jimmy Young *Presenting Jimmy Young*

Terry Wogan *Terry Wogan*

Familiar Themes – Alan Freeman's radio show theme was At the Sign of the Swinging Cymbal *by Brass Incorporated (£20). Jimmy Young's* Towntalk *was from Ken Woodman's* That's Nice *(£25) while Tony Blackburn's* Beefeaters *(£25) was first used as the theme for TV's* Search for a Star.

---

20 Years of Rock 'n' Roll sold for a good number of years, but only early versions had a booklet and a 7" square record of him looking back at Rock's past; these versions are now worth $30.

Murray the K. made the most of his radio status, producing 21 collectable compilations with modest titles such as the 1964 LP *Murray the K.'s Golden Gassers* ($30), and *Murray the K. Live from Brooklyn Fox in his Record Breaking Show* ($40) from 1963.

Stations

Given radio stations' music power they were embarrassingly slow to market themselves. Early and forgotten gems like Oriole's *Sounds of Time* LP (£10) – an archive of major 1934–49 BBC news events narrated by John Snagge – are fascinating, even important. The Billy Cotton Band Show had their own brand of BBC entertainment – the *Wakey, Wakey* LP, is valued at £25 (*see* page 168 for a colour image of the album cover). Another fascinating LP (also pictured on page 168) is called *The History of Offshore Radio* (£15), which was produced in the UK, Holland, and Germany by the International Broadcasters Society and features extracts from many fabled radio stations such as Caroline and London, including test transmissions and final closures. The album has a dull black and white cover so be sure not to miss it if you ever come across one.

Radio Luxembourg material has recently started to become collectable, and a white gatefold LP, *The Magic Radio* (£20), with artwork of a boy and an old radio, comes complete with a full-page message from the station's general manager persuading advertisers of their power; credits on the LP include "Tea by Ted, Sexy music by Jeff Wayne".

Material from 22 years of the UK radio show *Woman's Hour* was polled by listeners to compile the 1969 BBC LP *Voices from Woman's Hour* (£10). Radio 2's Folk Club offered the *Northumbrian Folk* album (£20), while the *John Peel Presents Top Gear* LP is now worth £30. The 1960 LP

STATION LISTINGS – all LPs

BBC Folk on 2 Presents Northumbrian Folk

BBC Sound Effects

Beyond Our Ken

Cruisin' '55 K.R.A.N.

Cruisin' '56 W.K.M.H.

Cruisin' '57 W.I.B.G .

Cruisin' (5 LPs)

The History of Offshore Radio

John Peel Presents Top Gear

John Peel's Archive Things

The Magic Radio

Saturday Club

The Sounds of Time

Voices from Woman's Hour

Wakey, Wakey The Billy Cotton Band Show

Saturday Club (£40) brings back memories, but is lightweight when compared to the nostalgic US Cruisin' LPs, which each reflect a different station's musical overview of that year. For example, *Cruisin' '56* from W.K.M.H. Detroit and *Cruisin' '57* from W.I.B.G. Philadelphia are each worth $20.

Heavyweight – Rock radio's dream ticket was Led Zeppelin. Fifty American radio shows exist on vinyl from 17 production houses, each boasting interviews and live performances. The best of these is the 1982 album Maxell Presents Led Zeppelin * – the two LPS are worth $1,800.

REGGAE

The Wailers *Burnin'* After a few 1960s UK novelty Ska hits Jamaican music returned to street level and centred on Bob Marley & The Wailers, before splitting into differing forms.

Surprisingly, the roots of Reggae run back to the 18th- and 19th-century society ballrooms of Europe and fashionable formal dances such as the polka and quadrille. These styles travelled across the ocean where plantation owners taught their slaves to play fiddles and fifes. Once skilled, the slaves developed variations for their own entertainment incorporating their traditional West African drums and timekeeping, which was kept alive through usage in their Pocomania churches.

Every birth of a new genre of Caribbean music reflected social change. Jamaican independence from Britain in the early '60s brought about carefree Ska, which introduced black and R&B signatures. By the mid-'60s the economy was suffering badly, and this bred gangs of restless youths who used music as their voice of rage to actively promote violence. This was music being used as a direct emotional outpouring of feelings.

There are a number of issues to consider if you are thinking about starting a Reggae collection. First, unlike other music genres, you'll never know if you have a complete set of any Jamaican releases. A small island race with huge dance discos as its influence naturally bred fast-changing fashions so local records could become hot or cold in a single week. Due to the economy it was a singles market – most LPs came later and were usually collections of those singles. This means that original albums are very collectable, and singles are likely to be quite worn. Jamaica was never awash with Reggae, as its people were as much into the likes of The Beatles or Elvis Presley.

If the adventure of hunting out obscure Caribbean singles doesn't appeal, there are equally authentic UK collections. Melodisc, Blue Beat, Trojan, and Island Records were very real parts of this story. There is so much more here than Bob Marley, and prices are not prohibitive. If you want a collecting challenge then this is ideal.

Raising Funds – Chris Blackwell's fledgling Island Records needed funds so it released Music to Strip By, *which came complete with a free G-string sewn up by an executive's wife; his Surprise Records label produced* That Affair, *which featured David Frost satire over the Profumo/Keeler affair, with Blackwell playing Keeler's Caribbean friend.*

Reggae *"SUNSHINE MUSIC"*

EARLY REGGAE

Singles

The Castle Sisters
Don't Be A Fool

Derrick Harriott *Walk the Streets*

Lord Lebby *Ethiopia*

The Maytals
Never You Change

Keith McCarthy *Everybody Rude Now*

The Melodians *Sweet Rose*

The Skatalites *Guns of Navarone*

Spanish Town Ska Beats
Stop That Train ★

The Wailers *Good Good Rudie (Jailhouse) / Simmer Down / Tell Them Lord ★*

Joe White *Rudies all Around*

LPs

The Gaylads *Rocksteady ★*

EPs

The Blues Busters
Dance the Ska

Ernest Ranglin
Ernest Ranglin & the G Bs ★

Reggae is a very incomplete term used to define the magnificent range of Jamaican music. There are so many style changes that decisions on collecting need to follow the study of a decent Reggae book. Happy, angry, or escapist, Reggae music and its rhythms simply cannot be ignored. One caution though – original Jamaican singles were used to dance to, often, so many might seem to be bargains but could be very tired copies.

Early Reggae

Early Regional Folk, American R&B, and even Swing Jazz had already influenced Jamaican music, but this section begins with the Jamaican Independence of August 1962. Jamaicans celebrated to the sounds of Mento – their version of Trinidadian calypso that included acts like Count Lasher's Calypso Quartet and Lord Messam and The Calypsonians. Suddenly free, they drew on the culture of their American neighbours, adopting tastes, waiting for investments, and celebrating to uplifting Ska styles. Rather than using live gigs, much island music was exposed through massive sound system shows – pulsing base-heavy Caribbean disco. The DJs of the discos would become the stars. Ska enjoyed a decade of growth and even a surprise UK hit with Millie's 1964 *My Boy Lollipop* (£5), plus valuable items like *Stop That Train ★* by Spanish Town Ska Beats (£750).

During 1966's hot summer music tempos were halved in the heat creating the Rocksteady style that had less brass and more bass. Already The Maytals, The Gaylads, and The Wailers were well-known, but now The Melodians and The Ethiopians also grew in stature. Two singles pointed the way for what came next, at least by name – The Maytals' 1968 *Do the Reggay* (£10) and The Tennors' *Reggae Girl* (£10). However, by the mid-'60s darker shadows had fallen as there were no signs of American investment or improved lifestyles. The young converged on towns in the hope of finding work; unhappy and angry, they gave Ska a new emotional signature – the sound of The Rude Boys. This was '60s ghetto-Punk played to a backing track of real violence.

Ska God – Ernest Ranglin was Island Records' first Jamaican record star. Over the decades he's appeared at Glastonbury Festival, Ronnie Scott's Jazz Club, on Bob Marley's early discs, Millie's smash hit, Bond movie soundtracks, and even Halifax television commercials.

Mid-Period

Rudie gangs actually named themselves after movie heroes, and music reflected the moods – The Wailers' *Good, Good Rudie (Jailhouse)* single has gone from £15 to £60 in ten years, and Peter Tosh and The Wailers' single *I'm the Toughest* is now £50. Some asked for restraint – The Wailers' 1963 hit pleaded *Simmer Down* (£60), The Beltones asked for *No More Heartaches* (£7), and Prince Buster's *Judge Dredge* (£12) dammed the Rudie movement. However, it was Larry and Alvin's *Nanny Goat* (£12), with its unheard-of guitar rhythms, and Lynford Anderson's single *Pop a Top*, with its faster tempo, that announced Reggae. Ska and Rocksteady featured just the offbeat rhythms, while Reggae used a second, more rapid, note. Roots Reggae themes played heavily on ethnic origins, such as The Gaylads' repatriation single *Africa* (£15), and African Brothers' *Lead Us Father* (£12).

Jamaican re-mixing was active in the mid-'60s thanks to their huge sound system gigs. From 1970 B-sides were often a voiceless alternative, known as "versions", for DJs to perform to. From 1972 influential producers like King Tubby were delivering complete Dub versions, which raised the drum-and-bass parts up in prominence, as well as losing the voices. DJs tested mixes at clubs with one label, then created another batch with another label if they were successful. Original Dub singles are rare and complex to chronicle. One notable character was U-Roy, who worked for Tubby as a DJ, making *Sound of the Wise*, *Scandal*, and the Jamaican No.1 *Girl I've Got a Date*.

> *Unpredictable – Lee "Scratch" Perry worked on early Bob Marley records. Revered not just in the field of Reggae but by bands like The Clash, many of his productions were issued in small numbers and are therefore rare. In 1978 he burnt down his studios as a political protest.*

The first Dub LPs cost four times the price of a normal one, so few were pressed. Some examples include Lee Perry's *Blackboard Jungle Dub* – mixed by King Tubby – Clive Chin's *Java, Java Dub*, and Herman Chin Loy's *Aquarius Dub*. The first UK Dub LP was Keith Hudson's *Pick a Dub*, from 1974. Dub and Roots Reggae would witness many releases but they had slipped from fashion by the 1980s, and Hip-Hop and Jungle followed on from them.

MID-PERIOD

Singles

African Brothers
Lead Us Father

The Beltones
No More Heartache

Burning Spear *School Days*

Prince Buster *Independence Song / Judge Dread*

Desmond Dekker and The Aces *007 (Shanty Town)*

Devon Irons *Vampire* ★

The Gaylads *Africa*

Ripton Hilton *Creation*

Jammy *Zambia*

Larry and Alvin *Nanny Goat*

The Maytals *Do the Reggay*

Ras Michael
Volunteer Ethiopians

Lee Perry *I am the Upsetter*

The Tennors *Reggae Girl*

Peter Tosh and The Wailers
I'm the Toughest

King Tubby
Tubby at the Control

U-Roy *Girl I've Got a Date / Rule the Nation*

LPs

Clive Chin *Java, Java, Dub*

Keith Hudson *Pick a Dub*

Bunny Lee *Dub from the Roots*

Lee Perry
Blackboard Jungle Dub ★

Commercial

British interest helped fund Reggae artists. The record label Melodisc was recording singles back in the 1940s and '50s, spotted a Jamaican Blues Beat movement, and in 1960 formed Blue Beat Records. Their records include Laurel Aitken's *Boogie Rock* (£20), Keith and Enid's *Send Me (£12)*, and Folkes Brothers' *Oh Carolina (£10)*. The company's most valued LP compilation is *Jamaican Blues ★* (£250).

Chris Blackwell, who already produced local records on the island, saw Blue Beat's success and in 1962 launched Island Records. Melodisc countered this by signing top producer Prince Buster, whose work includes *Al Capone* (£8). Chris Blackwell then delivered a huge UK chart hit with Millie's *My Boy Lollipop* (£5), while The Migil Five's *Mockingbird Hill (£6)* gave Pye a Top 10 in 1964. Trojan then mustered 30 Top 50 singles between 1970 and 1975 – their first was Duke Reid's *Judge Sympathy* (£20) in July '67. Others were Rocksteady classics – The Three Tops' *It's Raining* (£15) and Freddy McKay's *Love is a Treasure* (£10). Their business faltered, then revived with Brother Dan Allstars' *Donkey Returns* (£10) and, later, Jimmy Cliff's *Wonderful World, Beautiful People* (£5). Sanitized lyrics brought commercial success – Desmond Dekker's *Israelites* (£5) had been *Poor Me Israelites* but the BBC rejected it, so it was re-mixed, and became a UK No.1 and US No.9.

> *Island Master – Lynford Anderson was Jamaica's premier sound engineer who worked on vast song lists, from Roberta Flack's haunting* Killing Me Softly *to his own hit* Pop a Top – *an idea taken from a Canada Dry beer advert.*

Island's trump card was Bob Marley and The Wailers. The *Exodus* single is £5, while a double A-side promo 45' fetches £30. Marley's best solo singles are *Judge Not ★* (from £50 to £225 in ten years) and *One Cup of Coffee ★* (£200). The best Wailers single is *It Hurts to be Alone* (£70), while the Bob Marley and The Wailers classic *No Woman, No Cry* is just £3. Marley died in 1981 and the development of Ska slowed down to leave Dancehall – a Ska-like music that reverted to real-life lyrics but with some electronic rhythms and early signs of Rap. An example is Wailing Souls' *Sweetie Come Brush Me* (£5). Dancehall offered wider appeal and was often American in feel; it would eventually lead to acts like Shaggy. The spirit of Ska continued in Coventry at the 2 Tone label, with UK acts like The Specials, Madness, and The Beat.

INTRODUCTION TO JAZZ

There is a triumphalism within Jazz history books that suggests it is the fountainhead of all popular music. This is not strictly true, as centuries of European compositions have fed us many strands of popular music. However, it is fair to state that Jazz is indeed the parent of virtually all popular American music, and its grandparents can be found back in Europe and within Africa. Even so, Jazz books admit to the minefields of attempting to classify aspects of Jazz, and though our guide concerns the world of vinyl collecting, we too are faced with the dilemma of having to try to sectionalize decades of constantly changing styles. What makes matters even worse is that, unlike Pop music where an influential figure might only dominate for a short while, the key Jazz gods like Louis Armstrong, Charlie Parker, Miles Davis, and John Coltrane often remained as influential forces for three, four, even five decades. Such artists often featured within a variety of schools of music. It's in fact easier to view major Jazz talents in the same way as a painter like Pablo Picasso, whose early classical work, Blue Period, and Cubism collectively represent his talent.

If you are approaching Jazz for the first time it can be as bewildering as Classical music. In many ways the best approach is not to track a particular recording artist's work – because he or she is likely to drift through a variety of styles. Instead try and identify a piece of Jazz you really like, whether its an old bit of traditional New Orleans street music, or a catchy, cool Dave Brubeck number, and then use a good book, a helpful record store, or website to build up your knowledge of the era it came from. By doing this you should find more of the music you enjoy, and an unbelievable number of subtle variations that will direct you towards different Jazz styles. You will automatically know when you have reached the border of your tastes, and the more you study and map out an era the more it will reveal itself to you musically.

Warning – As artists and music styles were constantly shifting our listings cannot attempt to lock each recording to fixed categories within the space. They have therefore been selected to represent an artist's work, the extremes of value, and, most of the time, the sound of the category. The aim here has been to raise people's interests rather than trying to create a record history reference.

As you discover more about your favoured Jazz movement it will automatically reveal its close and logical ties with the overall mood of that time. Jazz, like Pop and Rock, constantly reflects its social landscape. For example, the escapism of the 1920s Jazz Age, with its Good Time Dixieland, fell away almost instantly along with the 1929 Great Depression – the wounded and nervous US nation then clutched at more soothing Swing and Dance entertainment. Post-war music intellectuals, sickened by the sugar-coated late Big Bands, invented Bebop, Free, and Avant-Garde Jazz in order to rebel,

Trad and Skiffle are two popular British styles of Jazz that should not be ignored. This 2.19 Skiffle Group EP lists at £45–50, which is more expensive than most Michael Jackson records!

deliberately creating music that didn't invite people to dance. Adopting a style of Jazz is addictive as every recording and every scrap of history that you then discover will become like the pieces of a puzzle you can't put down.

Jazz really began the UK's vinyl-collecting scene due to the exposure in the 1950s to attractive modern pieces. American recordings didn't freely get to Britain's shores, so US servicemen based in the UK were accidental couriers of these new exciting sounds. Specialist suppliers began to feed the market to cities, as "the city" was Jazz's natural domain. Dance band music had already swept the country thanks to regular national radio broadcasts, and really, until the advent of Hit Paraders and the singles charts, Jazz was the hottest ticket around.

The number and choice of Jazz records there is to collect is vast, yet a high proportion of them are worth only £10–20 each, even if they are in perfect condition. However, the top Jazz artists do command $100–300 for their early treasures – unlike Pop and Rock, huge stars' big records weren't numerically large sellers so "hit" records are not as penalized on values. There are mountains of old but not valuable Jazz 78's, but certain album labels, like Prestige, Debut, Dial, and, best of all, Blue Note, are likely to have higher values.

Deep Groove – All mono and stereo Blue Note pressings from 1960 or earlier have "deep grooves". Their factory manufacturing system left this circular groove under the label's surface. Clearly seen or felt, these grooves, which must be on both sides, significantly increase overall values. However, other labels with the same groove are not as valuable.

TRADITIONAL JAZZ

The complex fabrics of Jazz are at their most bewildering in the earliest days and, ironically, in the more recent past. The original music upon which it is all founded was never recorded, and therefore it helps to understand the social environment within which it prospered. Jazz actually grew out of a number of cities but New Orleans gained the historical status of being its birthplace, largely due to its geography. The town was a rich mix of Spanish, French, British, Italian, and German cultures, plus large numbers of blacks from two continents – common languages were a problem but music, at least, was universal. Inevitably, styles were diverse, but more European than African elements would appear – particularly marches and dances. Musically, the black populations were also split – African Americans were free and exuberant, while the French Creoles were more reflective and cultured.

Missing Years – The absence of recorded material from Jazz's first two decades has left purists guessing at its exact qualities. From 1914 cornet-player Freddie Keppard fronted the Original Creole Orchestra, and in 1918 they recorded a test for Victor Records. Legend has it that Keppard refused an earlier opportunity to record in 1916, for fear of plagiarism.

If you enjoy early Jazz then you should initially invest in books about the era, the style, and the records themselves. It wasn't just the dawn of Jazz music but also the record industry itself, so detail counts. Formats were still emerging and artists swapped styles and bands – the latter frequently. Ragtime banjoist Vess Ossman, for instance, has 34 early collectable singles listed, yet the same products on forgotten, earlier labels are much more valuable. One such label is Berliner, which even used 7" records. Some visually identical discs are actually commercially released with different takes from the same recording session. So, as you may have realized, knowledge is paramount to the successful collecting of early Jazz.

New Orleans

The original "New Orleans" style is wrongly perceived as being the first (Ragtime is, in fact, older), but it did embody all the early musical fusions. Marching bands were an important element, often employed for wedding and funeral processions, while "string band" versions were common at dances. Most available New Orleans records were actually recorded later in New York or Chicago, and were therefore rather more polished than the original street bands. If you choose to focus on a single leading New Orleans-style figure then how about locally born cornet master King Oliver? Another might be pianist Jelly Roll Morton, who was central to transforming fixed Ragtime visions into more expressive New Orleans style.

Keyboard Virtuosos

Jelly Roll Morton may have claimed to be the creator of Ragtime but in its pure form it was nearer to 19th-century European piano compositional work than interpretive Jazz – it is in effect the true Classical music of The USA. A very important part of US cultural history, Ragtime existed before New Orleans and is distinctive due to its structure. Syncopation of the right hand offsets other rhythms, which is why it was originally termed "ragging". Initial exponents shone in local bars before its influence stretched to private homes, marching bands, and even to Irving Berlin. Huge sheet music sales prompted armies of talent to arrange popular pieces in a Ragtime form. Other keyboard styles include the powerful Harlem Stride piano recordings, and the remarkably valuable Boogie-Woogie records by Meade "Lux" Lewis or Cow Cow Davenport.

Chicago

This area is fascinating and quite complex to summarize. There was a wholesale migration of New Orleans talent to Chicago after the Prohibition, and so most collectors' New Orleans material was actually recorded in Chicago. Many key talents also followed Louis Armstrong's example of moving on a second time towards New York. Beneath all this transition an identifiable Chicago Jazz was formed, frequently by the very talents passing through. This renders it hard to nominate fixed-style gurus as they proportionately belong in later music styles. The city's 1930s Jump Band phenomena is another fascinating area, with direct links to R&B and Rock music.

Dixieland

This is also Chicago music, but of a subtly differing style. It is Good Time Jazz, loosely based on New Orleans style but without too much emotion or complexity. Dixieland's "sheer entertainment" value has prompted numerous revivals, provided decades of different collectable variants, and frequently been mistreated by amateur bands at summer village fêtes! In the late 1800s there were white Jazz bands playing in the Deep South, and it's generally felt that key figures like "Papa" Jack Laine helped evolve this slightly limited yet enjoyable strand of Jazz. In many ways a style of arrangement rather than composition, Dixieland has provided a vast treasure chest of collectable records.

Trad

This area has an interesting evolution, involving D.I.Y. home groups, huge chart hits, revivalists, gateways to Rock, and even claiming the domain of the world's rarest record – all wrapped within the UK 1950s fad of Trad Jazz. Chart music was aimed at adults (see Hit Paraders, page 40), and British youth had just seen the future with the all-American sensation Bill Haley. This was the transatlantic scent of freedom-filled coffee bars, but the expensive tools needed to make music remained a dream until Skiffle emerged. The fashion was short, but it gifted Jazz a particular hit-parade status. Skiffle clubs opened, filled, and then turned their attention to emerging R&B, offering showcases to then unknown bands like The Rolling Stones and The Yardbirds.

New Orleans *"HISTORIC AMERICAN VINYL"*

Suggested Strands
The Originals

Average Record Cost
★★★☆

Rising Stars
King Oliver
Johnny Dodds

THE ORIGINALS

Singles

Johnny Dodds *Goober Dance* ★ / *Weary Way Blues* ★

Freddie Keppard *Freddie Keppard 1926*

King Oliver's Creole Jazz Band *Krooked Blues* ★

Spike's Seven Pods of Pepper Orchestra *Ory's Creole Trombone* ★

LPs

Johnny Dodds *The King of New Orleans Clarinets* ★

Buck Johnson *Buck Johnson Talking*

George Lewis *Jazz at Ohio Union* ★

Wingy Manone *Trumpet on the Wing Wingy Manone Vol 1*

New Orleans Rhythm Kings *Dixieland Jazz!* ★

King Oliver's Creole Jazz Band *King Oliver* ★ / *King Oliver's Uptown Jazz* ★

Original Dixieland Jazz Band *Historic Records of the First Recorded Jazz* / *Original Dixieland Jazz Band in England*

Kid Ory and his Creole Jazz/ Dixieland Band *Dixieland Marching Songs*

Preservation Hall Jazz Band *New Orleans Vol.1*

This is the original form of Jazz. A New Orleans movement, predominantly ensemble-played, it featured groups of frequently untrained musicians creating inevitably varying renditions of music often used at funerals, parades, and on street corners. No true first-generation material was ever recorded. Collecting is difficult but rewarding – some 78's are highly prized but many others are almost worthless.

The Originals

Buddy Bolden's rightful place as the first Jazz musician is denied him as no recording of his work was ever made. Ironically, it was five white American East Coast musicians – Original Dixieland Jazz Band – who first recorded Jazz; the record, *Livery Stable Blues* ($12), was a hit. In 1919 they also introduced Jazz to the UK. Their LPs include the 1956 10" LP *Historic Records of the First Recorded Jazz* (£20), and the 10" *Original Dixieland Jazz Band in England* (£20). Authentic flag bearers included cornetist Freddie Keppard, whom some contest to be the person who first recorded Jazz. He replaced Boldon and preceded the important cornet player, King Oliver. Oliver's recordings include the 1950 10" LP *King Oliver* ★ ($120) and *King Oliver's Uptown Jazz* ★ ($100). Incredibly, 38 of his 78's have three-figure values – the best being $2,000 for *King Porter* ★.

> *Unexpected Sounds – The French-colonized Louisiana offered great racial fusion, and the emerging music was played with available instruments reworking fashionable European material. This led to very early live Jazz struggling with violins until brass sections took over.*

New Orleans Jazz mainly uses a trumpet or cornet as its strongest voice, and within King Oliver's Creole Jazz Band were the brass players Louis Armstrong and Johnny Dodds, whose most prized 78's include *Goober Dance* ★ ($300) and *Weary Blues* ★ ($200). Dodds' 1951 10" LP *The King of New Orleans Clarinets* ★ is now worth $100. Kid Ory, under the guise of Spike's Seven Pods of Pepper Orchestra, was the first black man to record Jazz. His records include *Ory's Creole Trombone* ★ ($500), the 78' *Dippermouth Blues* (£8), and the 1959 LP *A Kid from New Orleans – Ory, That Is* (£25).

Keyboard Virtuosos *"DECADES OF CHOICE"*

Suggested Strands
Ragtime
Harlem Stride
Boogie-Woogie

Average Record Cost
☆☆☆

Rising Stars
Jelly Roll Morton
James P. Johnson
Meade "Lux" Lewis

RAGTIME

Singles
Jelly Roll Morton
Load of Coal ★ / *London Blues* ★

LPs
Jelly Roll Morton *The Sage of Mr. Jelly Lord* ★ *Vol 1–12*

HARLEM STRIDE

Singles
James P. Johnson *A Porter's Love Song* ★ / *Chicago Blues* ★

LPs
James P. Johnson *Rent Party* ★
Willie "The Lion" Smith *The Lion at the Piano* ★

BOOGIE-WOOGIE

Singles
Cow Cow Davenport *Atlanta Rag* ★ / *Chimes Blues* ★

LPs
Albert Ammons *Boogie Woogie Classics* ★ / *Boogie Woogie Piano* ★
Pete Johnson *Boogie Woogie Blues and Skiffle* ★ / *Pete's Blues* ★
Meade "Lux" Lewis *Boogie-Woogie Classics* ★
Jimmy Yancey *Yancey Special* ★

Aside from marching bands and spirituals, the heartbeat of early American music was the piano. Skilled pianists created three distinct styles of music. The early stars were never recorded but their legacies offer decades of recorded material that is quietly rising in value.

Ragtime

Ragtime isn't just Scott Joplin music from *The Sting*, it is a technique as old as Jazz itself. Joplin's albums *Classic Solos* and the 1970s *Ragtime – Vol 2 & 3* are worth only £10. The same value is put on Zez Confrey's 1920s novelty singles *Charleston Chuckles* and *Kitten on the Keys*. Eubie Blake traded in early Ragtime charms, and then at the ripe old age of 86 made a comeback with *Rags to Classics: Charlestown Rag* ($12), and *The Eighty-Six Years of Eubie Blake* ($20) from 1969. Jelly Roll Morton's record values mirror his importance within Jazz. *Fish Tail Blues* ★, *Weary Blues* ★, and *Wolverine Blues* ★ are worth $1,000; over 40 of his 78's are worth three-figure sums.

> *Camp Entertainment – The emergence of old paper piano rolls in junk shops during the 1950s revealed just how loved Ragtime had been. It was very popular with migrants working in the camps, building American railroads.*

Harlem Stride

Here the left hand acted like a rhythm section and the right created melodies. This was a New York development of Ragtime that influenced masters such as Duke Ellington and Count Basie. The maestro of this was James P. Johnson – his 10" LPs include the 1951 *Stomps, Rags and Blues* ★ ($300), *Jazz Band Ball* ★ ($300), and *The Daddy of the Piano* ★ ($100). New Yorker Willie "The Lion" Smith's work includes *Harlem Memories* ★($250) and the single *Swing, Brother, Swing* ($12).

Boogie-Woogie

This form of piano Jazz became an organized style in the 1920s. It is created by the left hand generating repeated patterns while the right hand deliverers often repeated musical figures. Early practitioners included Meade "Lux" Lewis, whose *Honky-Tonk Train Blues* ★ is worth $200, and Pinetop Smith who recorded *Pinetop's Boogie-Woogie* ★, worth $120.

Dixieland *"FOOT-TAPPING"*

Suggested Strands
First Fruit
Revivalists

Average Record Cost
✫✫✫

Rising Stars
New Orleans Rhythm Kings
Fats Waller

This is an almost disgraced music term, thanks to armies of straw-boatered semi-pros murdering classic Jazz tunes every summer. Yet it's also an umbrella term for a development of original New Orleans Jazz, matured in Chicago and identified by bands' improvisations during choruses, separated by bold solo statements (something New Orleans Jazz lacks). It's more structured, happy music – and fun to collect.

First Fruit

Close to Chicago style, Dixieland is a cheerful sanitizing variant – without the soul but with lots of energy. The band New Orleans Rhythm Kings were an important musical bridge between Traditional and Dixie styles. Their $200 LPs are *Tin Roof Blues* ★, *Angry* ★, *Weary Blues* ★, and *Clarinet Marmalade* ★ while the singles *Mr. Jelly Lord* ★ and *London Blues* ★ are worth $120.

Good-time music naturally tempted many masters to record arrangements: *Kid Ory and his Creole Dixieland* ★ ($100) and *Dixieland Marching Songs* ($50) are both from Kid Ory, while Eddie Condon recorded the 1958 LP *Dixieland Dance Party* ($40), and Fats Waller made *Fats Waller 1934–42* ★ ($150) and *The Young Fats Waller* ★ ($150). Louis Armstrong, Kid Ory, Johnny Dodds, Jelly Roll Morton, Jimmy McPartland, Louis Prima, and Jack Teagarden all made Dixieland records that are worth hunting out.

Revivalists

Officially slumping in 1929 with the Wall Street Crash, Dixieland was kept alive by its main figures, mentioned above. Over six months in 1939 cornetist Muggsy Spanier recorded 16 sides (eight records) defining Dixieland, which were known as *The Great Sixteen* ($50). However, with full revival still around the corner Spanier unfortunately had to disband his musicians. In 1941 Lu Watters founded his Yerba Buena Jazz Band, and carved out a San Francisco variant on Dixie.

Louis Armstrong disbanded his big band in 1947, reverting to his semi-Dixieland All Stars. Red Nichols worked with his Five Pennies, Bunk Johnson came out of retirement, and Eddie Condon regularly gave network-radio Dixie shows – the resulting *Town Hall Concerts: Vols. 1–7* are worth $15 each. Trumpeter Al Hirt and clarinettist Pete Fountain became fashionable, and The Dukes of Dixieland's high profile, through Audio Fidelity label promotion, introduced new fans.

FIRST FRUIT

Singles

Sidney Bechet
Sidney's Blues ★

New Orleans Rhythm Kings
Angry ★ / *Clarinet Marmalade* ★ / *London Blues* ★ / *Mr. Jelly Lord* ★ / *That's a Plenty*

LPs

Sidney Bechet *Classic Jazz* ★ / *Giants of Jazz* ★ / *Sidney Bechet's Blue Note Jazz Men* ★

Kid Ory
Dixieland Marching Songs / *Kid Ory and his Creole Dixieland* ★

Fats Waller
Fats Waller 1934–42 ★ / *The Young Fats Waller* ★

REVIVALISTS

LPS

The Dukes of Dixieland
Up the Mississippi

Pete Fountain *Pete Fountain's Music from Dixie*

New Orleans Rhythm Kings
Dixieland Jazz ★

Muggsy Spanier
The Great Sixteen

Lu Watters
Yerba Buena Jazz Band

Chicago Style *"NEGLECTED TRANSITION PERIOD"*

Suggested Strands
Second Phase
Jump Bands

Average Record Cost
☆☆

Rising Stars
Jimmy McPartland
Bix Beiderbecke
Louis Jordan Tympany Five

SECOND PHASE

LPs

Bix Beiderbecke *Bix Beiderbecke Story / The Great Bix*

Eddie Condon *Dixieland / Jammin' at Condon's / The Roaring Twenties*

Bud Freeman *Comes Jazz ★ / Jazz – Chicago Style / Midnight at Eddie Condon's*

Jimmy McPartland *Meet Me in Chicago / The Middle Road*

Muggsy Spanier *Chicago Jazz / Muggsy Spanier and Frank Teschemacher / Muggsy Spanier and his Bucktown Five*

Frank Teschemacher *Tesch Plays Jazz Classics*

JUMP BANDS

LPs

Harlem Hamfats *Harlem Hamfats*

Louis Jordan Tympany Five *Let the Good Times Roll ★ / Man, We're Wailin' ★ / Somebody Up There Digs Me ★*

Like so much of Jazz's history, definitions of Chicago style are blurred by the constant migration of ideas and musicians. Official closure of New Orleans' French Quarter district caused a general exodus up the Mississippi to Chicago. As a result it was here that "New Orleans" Jazz really matured and recorded, while "Chicago Style" Jazz was itself emerging alongside.

Second Phase

Louis Armstrong remained in New Orleans until 1922, before joining King Oliver's band in Chicago. Their compromised style, united with a musical adventure typified by Armstrong, created Chicago Jazz, which is more structured and has an explosion of solos. Jimmy McPartland mirrored the movement – his 1953 *Shades of Bix* is worth $60, *The Middle Road* $40, and *Meet Me in Chicago* $30. Bud Freeman also developed this style. His 1950 LP *Comes Jazz ★* is worth $100, and his 1955 *Jazz – Chicago Style* $80. Along with Frank Teschemacher they were known as the Austin High Gang. Eddie Condon also prospered, playing on *The Roaring Twenties* ($40), *Dixieland* ($40), and *Jammin' at Condon's* ($50), as well as organizing important recording sessions. Most players would, in time, move towards New York and develop later Jazz movements.

Jump Bands

In the 1930s Chicago also gave birth to small line-up Jump bands. Jump is a fusion of Jazz horns and percussion with Blues guitars, which makes infectious, up-beat music. It was, in effect, the seeds of R&B and Rock Blues championed by the Harlem Hamfats. Their work includes the 1951 *Weed Smoker's Dream* (£15) and *Harlem Hamfats* (£15). Other notable recordings are Stuff Smith's Onyx Club Boys' singles *'Tain't No Use* ($10) and *Sam the Vegetable Man* ($12), as well as the earlier work of Louis Jordan Tympany Five – *Somebody Up There Digs Me ★* ($120), *Man, We're Wailin' ★* ($120), and *Let the Good Times Roll ★* ($100).

> *The Price of Details – Beiderbecke's life is recorded on three 1950 Columbia Masterworks – Bix Beiderbecke Story – worth $70 each. Details matter here: a 1952 black label, silver print version is $50, a 1956 red-and-black label with six "i" logos is $30, while other versions are just $15.*

Trad Jazz *"RESTING, DUE ANOTHER REVIVAL"*

Suggested Strands
Skiffle
Commercial

Average Record Cost
☆☆

Rising Stars
Mick Mulligan
Chris Barber

SKIFFLE

Singles
Ken Colyer's Skiffle Group
Down by the Riverside

Bob Cort's Skiffle Group
6.5 Special

Lonnie Donegan *Rock Island Line*

Chas McDevitt and Nancy
Wilson *Freight Train*

LPs
Johnny Duncan and His Bluegrass Boys *Tennessee Song Bag*

The Vipers *Coffee Bar Session*

COMMERCIAL

Singles
Chris Barber *Petite Fleur*

Kenny Ball *Midnight in Moscow*

Humphrey Lyttleton
Bad Penny Blues

LPs
Acker Bilk *Seven Ages of
Acker / The Veritable Mr Bilk*

Sandy Brown and The
Storyville Jazzmen *Hair at
Its Hairiest / Sandy Brown*

Ken Colyer *Back to the Delta*

Terry Lightfoot
Lightfoot at Lansdowne

Monty Sunshine
Shades of Sunshine

The abbreviation "Trad" is actually a precise term for a British 1950s/early '60s variation of Dixieland revival. Although borne of relative purest bands it lit a fire that would kindle Rock and R&B. By accident it also birthed Skiffle, which helped catapult Trad to the top of the UK charts – and away from its roots. Interesting to collect, there are signs of value rises in this year.

Skiffle

The Ken Colyer Jazz Band created a skiffle spot for its banjo player Lonnie Donegan to perform US Folk Blues. Then trombonist Chris Barber left to form a band, taking Donegan and the skiffle idea with him – it featured on Barber's *New Orleans Joy* (£50). Public interest caused one track, *Rock Island Line* (£20), to be a UK Top 10 and US Top 2 hit single, selling two million copies. Other bands followed suit: Ken Colyer's Skiffle Group's 1955 single, *Down by the Riverside*, is worth £15, and The Vipers covered *Cumberland Gap* (£15 as a 45') and *Don't You Rock Me Daddy-O* (£18 as a 45'). Johnny Duncan and His Bluegrass Boys took Americana to the UK's No.2 spot with *Last Train to San Fernando* (£15 with gold print – silver £7), while BBC TV's first music show theme was *6.5 Special* (named after the show), by Bob Cort's Skiffle Group (£15 as a 45').

Commercial

Ken Colyer's recordings included the 1954 *New Orleans to London* ($50 or £45) and the 1956 *Back to the Delta* ($40 or £35). Humphrey Lyttleton also had fine credentials with *Bad Penny Blues* (export 45' £25), *Triple Exposure* (£80) from 1959, and *Humph in Perspective* (£40). Less known, but worthwhile, are Sandy Brown and The Storyville Jazzmen, who created the 1953 *Sandy Brown* (£20) and *Traditional Jazz Scene 56* EP (£15). Mick Mulligan's Jazz Band are fast appreciating – the 1959 *Meet Mick Mulligan* and '57 *Jazz at the Railway Arms* LPs are each £60 today (£15 two years ago). Commercialism diminished but some figures still profited – Acker Bilk's *Stranger on the Shore* charted for 55 weeks.

Perfect Gift – Lonnie Donegan inspired John Lennon to form skiffle band The Quarry Men. A single 10" acetate was cut, now worth £100,000+ and owned by Paul McCartney; he had 25 replica 78's and 25 45's made for friends (now £10,000+).

BIG BAND JAZZ

Son of a Russian immigrant and a school drop-out, Benny Goodman would eventually become known as "The King of Swing". An idol to millions and subject of fan riots, his musical skills developed and shone through 50 years of performance. He encapsulates the central problem for anyone trying to sectionalize Jazz. Was Goodman a Swing man, a wildly successful Sweet Band member, or the leader of one of the best Big Bands? In fact, like many of his compatriots featured in this book, he was all these things, journeying through musical fashions with an appetite and skill befitting one of the Jazz Greats. So, if you are tempted to collect the works of a single figure, understand you will have to make the same musical journey that they did.

Some collecting is driven by pure nostalgia or evocative artwork, but within Big Band it is truly about enjoying the music and understanding the continuous musical transitions in artists' careers. This may take the form of owning vital products that changed their lives. As a general rule, early mono LPs reflecting the recorded material from the earlier decades are the most desirable. While some of the original 78's are also collectable it is true that, like Pop, the bigger the original hit single the more there are in circulation, which means they are less valuable. Unlike other popular music genres that were driven by a single star ingredient, Jazz (particularly the Big Band eras), witnessed great movement of key soloists within orchestras. This has created a sub-culture of collecting all the best recordings of a specific talent – as a soloist within other bands as well as under his or her own name.

An interesting Jazz subdivision is the output of Kansas City, a railway station stop that many Dixielanders made during their exodus towards Chicago. Gradually the style altered thanks to important local figures like Benny Moten, whose records are now becoming more and more valuable. When he died unexpectedly in hospital during an operation on his tonsils it was Count Basie who took over his band, guaranteeing Moten's ideas would be continued.

Another fascinating cross-collecting route involves vocalists. Most bands had a male and female stand-up singer who were used as an extra focal point to choruses. This added to an evening's show and also helped to promote their shorter radio/record performances. Not treated with the same respect as the star soloists, they would eventually step into the spotlight (*see* page 40). Ella Fitzgerald was with Chick Webb, Sarah Vaughan with Earl Hines, Frank Sinatra with Harry James and then Tommy Dorsey, and Doris Day with Les Brown.

Listen to Mother – Trained by his mother, Dick Haymes' first break was replacing Frank Sinatra in the prestigious Harry James Band. Four years later he replaced Sinatra again in the Tommy Dorsey Orchestra, before joining the fabled Benny Goodman's band. Hollywood movies and two million-selling records followed – the 1943 You'll Never Know *and* Little White Lies *from 1948.*

Swing

Invisible barriers surround Swing: all the ingredients may be in place but if a record is the wrong side of the emotional line then it ain't the real thing. Rising out of the seductive power of Dixieland it may have become more formally arranged, but make no mistake, you'll feel Swing when it's right – when strands of the orchestra weave and answer each other with rhythm pulses that your feet just can't ignore. Contrary to what some commentators believe, Swing grew out of the Jazz Age – the "Roaring Twenties" – and was already established entertainment when the Great Crash of 1929 virtually disposed of Dixieland overnight. Smoother, infectious, and escapist, Swing had everything that a wounded nation needed.

Dance

By 1926 NBC had established a coast-to-coast radio network that instantly filled with bands' performances from their resident hotel ballrooms. It had a meteoric effect on band-leader status and rapidly defined a Dance music-style resting alongside Swing to cater for the millions who literally rolled up their carpets and danced the evening away. Million-selling records, crowd riots, even Hollywood wives descended on the newly famous. In Britain, Jazz and radio also created many success stories, with every major hotel boasting its own prestige band. Hunting down recordings from landmark clubs and hotels presents an interesting challenge, and naturally features occasional vocalists – a 1936 cut, *Moanin' Minnie*, featured a 12-year-old Pat Sibley – years later she was a No.1 chart buster as Anne Shelton.

Sweet Music – Guy Lombardo may have a vast raft of affordable records to collect but his first million-seller was based on an 1894 Dvorak piano piece, Humoresque. *A Canadian, he held residency at New York's Roosevelt Hotel for 33 years, building up a huge following, and had three other million-sellers:* Winter Wonderland, Easter Parade, *and* The Third Man Theme *– each worth under $10 today.*

Big Band

Again this section is tricky to define. Essentially a "Big Band" is a Jazz group of 12 or more players with multiple brass sections. Such bands do naturally exist within Swing and Dance, but these ones are the larger, more rigidly presented line-ups – sometimes virtually Jazz orchestras, who indeed gave theatre concerts (a far cry from the ballroom floors). It was this polishing of Jazz that was the downfall of the entire Swing era, with skilled musicians turning to more challenging modern Jazz as an antidote. A fascinating subdivision, stretching back to Dance bands, are the Sweet Band line-ups, representing both the saccharine Big Bands and a range of Society bands for up-market private events; there was great personal prestige in having big-name musicians playing at your ball.

Swing *"SEEKING A GOOD TIME"*

Average Record Cost
☆☆☆

Rising Stars
Roy Eldridge
Fletcher Henderson
Benny Goodman

Swing – all LPs

Louis Armstrong *A Rare Batch of Satch / Armstrong Classics ★ / Disney Swings the Satchmo Way / Hello Dolly / Satchmo at Symphony Hall*

Count Basie *Count Basie Swings and Joe Williams Sings / The Swinging Count*

Bob Crosby *Bobcats on Parade / Five Feet of Swing / Swinging at the Sugar Bowl*

Roy Eldridge *Little Jazz: Trumpet Fantasy ★ / Rockin' Chair ★ / Roy Eldridge in Sweden ★ / The Roy Eldridge Quintet ★ / Roy's Got Rhythm*

Benny Goodman *An Album of Swing Classics / The Golden Age of Swing ★ / King of Swing ★ / Swing, Swing, Swing*

Coleman Hawkins *Body and Soul / Classics in Jazz ★ / Coleman Hawkins' All Stars ★ / Originals with Hawkins ★*

Fletcher Henderson *Fletcher Henderson ★ / Fletcher Henderson and his Connie's Inn Orchestra ★ / Fletcher Henderson Memorial ★ / Fletcher Henderson: The Swing's the Thing Vol.1 / Fletcher Henderson: The Swing's the Thing Vol.2*

The 1920s Dixieland bands grew larger, using multiple horns, and so necessitated more formal arrangements. This prompted a shift towards musical arrangers and one of these literally orchestrated the switch to Swing Jazz. He was Fletcher Henderson's chief arranger, Don Redman, who, like everyone else, was inspired by the unique approach of band newcomer Louis Armstrong. In Swing some of the band plays hard, driving, musical riffs while front-line instruments like the horns develop the melody line.

Swing Jazz

Louis Armstrong joined Fletcher Henderson in 1924, and his importance in Jazz cannot be overstressed. There are dozens of affordable albums of his – from *Disney Swings the Satchmo Way* ($40) and *Satchmo at Symphony Hall* ($75) through to his 1964 *Hello Dolly* ($15), which knocked The Beatles off the No.1 spot in the charts.

Fletcher Henderson temporarily took on a New York ballroom orchestra that went on to last ten years. Henderson's bands nurtured great talents, such as Coleman Hawkins – *Coleman Hawkins' All Stars ★* ($300), *Classics in Jazz ★* ($250) from 1952, *Originals with Hawkins ★* ($300), and *Body and Soul* ($20) – and Roy Eldridge with *Rockin' Chair ★* ($100), *Roy Eldridge in Sweden ★* ($250), and *Little Jazz: Trumpet Fantasy ★* ($400). Henderson's own works include *Fletcher Henderson and his Connie's Inn Orchestra ★* ($150), *Fletcher Henderson ★* ($150), *Fletcher Henderson: The Swing's the Thing Vol.1* ($30), and *Fletcher Henderson Memorial ★* (the 1952 LP is $150). Sadly he died of a stroke in 1952.

Benny Goodman is important too, and has a fabulous choice of collectables, such as *King of Swing ★* ($150), the 1956 five-LP set *The Golden Age of Swing ★* (bound in white vinyl, $600), and *An Album of Swing Classics* ($50 in mono/$40 in stereo). Another swing god is Count Basie – there are over 150 of his LPs to hunt down.

Swing's Changing Face – While ever-larger bands dominated the 1930s and '40s, passionate players converged on New York's 52nd Street clubs to play what became known as "Swing Street". That was until big revival bands tainted the Swing tag, prompting the groups to switch to "Mainstream".

Dance Bands *"A FORGOTTEN CORNER"*

Virtually all Jazz bands, until the Bebop revolution, catered to recreational aspects like hotel ballrooms, society events – basically anything involving dancing. Some styles, like Dixieland and Swing, were formally recognized, but less obvious was the genre of the Dance Band. Many Swing Bands were dancing bands, and many later Big Bands deliberately targeted dancers, but Dance Bands weren't trying to be anything else. They managed to build up huge dedicated followings for the band leaders, sometimes the key sidemen, and also the vocalists.

Conventional Fare

The 1920s bands, such as Paul Whiteman's, all presented conventional fare: strict tempo for ballrooms with some Jazz flavouring. His offerings include *It's Only a Paper Moon* ($15), *Let 'em Eat Cake* (12" picture disc $150), Victor Records' set of five singles (*Mississippi Mud, San, From Monday On, Louisiana,* and *Changes,* each $12), *Great Whiteman Hits* ($30), and *In Concert 1927–32* ($12). Other bands include the Paul Specht's Society Serenaders – *Hot Lips* ($20), *Roll Up the Carpets* ($12), and *On With the Dance* ($8) – and Roger Wolfe Kahn and Orchestra's *Crazy Rhythm* and *Cheer Up (Good Times are Coming)* ($10). These spelt pure entertainment, even in their titles.

CONVENTIONAL FARE

Singles

Roger Wolfe Kahn and His Orchestra *Cheer Up (Good Times are Coming) / Crazy Rhythm*

Isham Jones and His Orchestra *China Boy / Stompin' at the Savoy*

Ben Selvin and His Orchestra *Happy Days Are Here Again / Morning, Noon and Night / Smile, Darn You, Smile*

Paul Specht's Society Serenaders *Hot Lips / On With the Dance / Roll Up the Carpets*

Paul Whiteman and His Orchestra *It's Only a Paper Moon / Let 'em Eat Cake ★ / Mississippi Mud*

LPs

Paul Whiteman and His Orchestra *Great Whiteman Hits / In Concert 1927–32*

Seeing Double – Society orchestras were often band agencies – leaders like Ben Selvin could have had multiple bands performing under his name. Differing Meyer Davis bands might have been performing in ten different venues on the same night, and at the height of this craze 40 or 50 same-name bands could have been performing.

RADIO WAVES – all singles

The California Ramblers/ Golden Gate Orchestra *Painting the Clouds with Sunshine / Tip-Toe Through the Tulips with Me*

Radio Waves

Dance Band music effectively separated into two categories: protracted live performances to keep the dancers on the ballroom floors, and very clipped, bright versions designed to be squeezed onto 78' singles for the necessary radio exposure. Residences were very important – some bands performed for years in the same hotel or nightclub, building up a fan base. Radio created "studio" orchestras, such as Fred Rich with his Radio/Times Square Orchestras, or the California Ramblers.

Golden Gate Orchestra
*Dirty Hot ★ / Lover Come Back /
For my Baby ★*

Fred Rich Radio/Times
Square Orchestras *Now I'm
in Love / I've Got a Yen for You /
Strike Up the Band!*

BRITISH FEVER

Singles

Bert Ambrose & Orchestra
*Chee Chee-oo Chee / Lilacs
in the Rain*

Nat Gonella and His
Orchestra *Show Me the Way*

Ted Heath and His Music
Swingin' Shepherd Blues

Ray Noble and His Orchestra
*Down by the River /
Let's Swing It*

Edmundo Ros *Sing & Swing
with Edmundo Ros*

LPs

Nat Gonella and His
Orchestra *The Nat Gonella
Story / Salute to Satchmo*

Ted Heath and His Music
*Black and White Magic / Swing
Session / Tempo for Dancers*

The latter's offerings include *Painting the Clouds with Sunshine* ($20) and *Tip-toe Through the Tulips with Me* ($20). They also used the name The Golden Gate Orchestra, under which they boasted a vast, still-affordable record list – although singles *Dirty Hot ★* and *For My Baby ★* are now worth $150 and $100 respectively.

British Fever

In Britain too the dance craze was all-powerful. Each prestige hotel presented a dance orchestra, who in turn presented a vocalist. Band leader Jack Payne had the BBC Dance Orchestra, singer Billy Scott Coomber, and a nightly signature tune of *Say it with Music*. There would be an afternoon-tea dance broadcast between 5.15pm and 6pm, and then at 10.30pm he would broadcast again, inviting listeners to roll back their carpets and dance until midnight.

In 1932 an ex-blacksmith from Peckham replaced Payne, and his catchphrase, "This IS Henry Hall and tonight is my guest night", would ring out of radio for 20 years. His first residency was at the Gleneagles Hotel, and his Gleneagles Orchestra made their first recording at Midland Hotel, Manchester, in 1924; within four years Hall would be director of 32 L.M.S. Railway-hotel bands.

Other familiar London hotel bands include the Jack Jackson Orchestra, and Bert Ambrose and Orchestra. Victor Silvester presented a strict old-fashioned dance setting, while Edmundo Ros introduced sunshine through Latin tempos. The Nat Gonella Orchestra's single *Show Me the Way* (£6) and the LP *The Nat Gonella Story* (£40) reflect British Dance Band values. As post-war years eroded Jazz status, many of these hotel bands embraced great talent who would take a wage from the evening work and then jam in true nightclubs until the early hours. The largest UK Dance band listing is for Ted Heath: the 1959 LP *Swing Session* (£20), 1951 10" LP *Tempo for Dancers* (£20), and many collectable EPs. He also had a surprise Top 3 Chart hit in 1958 with *Swingin' Shepherd Blues* (£6).

*Play Anywhere – Harry Roy toured overseas, had a
residency at London's Café Anglais, and also played
at Leicester Square theatres during movie intervals.
He married the daughter of the last white Ranee of
Sarawak, and under the pseudonym Val Gordon he
composed* Sarawaki *to commemorate the event.*

Big Bands *"PEAK OF THE TREND"*

Suggested Strands
Hot Bands
Sweet Bands

Average Record Cost
★★★

Rising Stars
Bennie Moten
Duke Ellington

Big Bands can be viewed as a collective term, with a distinct parallel identity to Swing, running throughout the 1920s–40s. Many make clear distinctions between the dynamic "Hot" Big Bands and the natural extension of Dance and Swing, known as "Sweet Bands". Line-ups in both grew, as bands discovered that more and more instruments playing the same harmonies spelt out power. This is an era full of popular recordings.

Hot Bands
The mid-'30s rise of Count Basie gave impetus to this movement – his work includes *One O'clock Jump* ($40) and *Count Basie and Duke Ellington* ($10). Ellington himself has over 370 collectors' LPs , such as *Birth of Big Band Jazz* ($60) and *Duke Ellington Vols.1, 2, & 3* ★ ($100 each). Jimmie Lunceford offered entertainment and wonderful arrangements by Sy Oliver, including the 1950 *Lunceford Special* ($80 as 10" and $50 as LP – if it is with a maroon label and gold print, other versions $15). Bennie Moten's Kansas City Orchestra singles include *Baby Dear* ★ ($150), *Small Black* ★ ($250), *The Count* ★ ($300), and Victor-labelled *Professor Hot Stuff* ★ ($400). Andy Kirk made many hits, like *Andy Kirk Souvenir Album Vol 1* ★ ($100), *March 1936* ($12), and the 1956 *A Mellow Bit of Rhythm* ($40).

Sweet Bands
Commercial Swing and Dance led to Sweet Big Bands, which were high-profile and crowd-pleasing. They are epitomized by Glenn Miller – his *Marvellous Miller Moods* is $40 and the *Glenn Miller Limited Edition* ★ (5 LPs with snakeskin covers) is £50 in the UK or $150 in the USA. He had 31 Top 10 hits in 1940 alone, but they remain of little value. Artie Shaw, Benny Goodman, Tommy Dorsey, and Wayne King are all big names, but none were as successful as Guy Lombardo, who has been dubbed the "King of Corn". Over six million danced to his tunes, he sold 100 million records, and there are 300 albums to collect.

HOT BANDS

Singles
Bennie Moten's Kansas City Orchestra *Baby Dear* ★ / *The Count* ★ / *Professor Hot Stuff* ★

Chick Webb and His Orchestra *Heebie Jeebies* ★

LPs
Count Basie *Blues by Basie* / *Basie Big Band* / *Super Chief*

Duke Ellington *Birth of Big Band Jazz*

Chick Webb and His Orchestra *Stompin' at the Savoy 1936* / *Chick Webb 1937–39*

SWEET BANDS

Singles
Harry James and His Orchestra *From the Bottom of my Heart* ★

Guy Lombardo and His Royal Canadians *Cherry Pink and Apple Blossom White*

Glenn Miller *Chattanooga Choo Choo* / *A Blues Serenade* ★

LPs
Tommy Dorsey *In a Sentimental Mood* / *This is Tommy Dorsey*

Glenn Miller *Glenn Miller* / *Glenn Miller Army Air Force Band* ★

Harry James and His Orchestra *Wild about Harry*

College Life – Son of two academics and intended for a career in law, Kay Kyser dressed in academic gowns and led his Sweet Band to 15 years of success. This included the radio series Kyser's Kollege of Musical Knowledge, *and singles* Rainy Weather *($15) and* Collegiate Fanny *($30).*

MODERN JAZZ

Modern Jazz movements have parallels with Rock & Roll or Punk, as they all forged deliberate, reactive ideas to give a jolt and new direction to music. In the Jazz world bands had become so big, so highly arranged, that all sense of spontaneity had been lost. Both young blood and many leading figures craved a return to expressive performances, and another chance to challenge each other on the stage. Modern Jazz strove earnestly to provide this fire and, in becoming radical, effectively arrived at so much "freedom" that the urge for creativity was fulfilled, and Jazz as a main musical force was spent.

From a collector's vantage point Modern Jazz holds a truly fascinating array of talent and ideas. Also, as the movements became more fragmented so the numbers of sales fell, which makes collecting them today a greater challenge. One extraordinary constant was Miles Davis who, as you will discover, remained at the forefront of musical change for over four decades.

Bebop Movement

This was born in New York in the early 1940s, during the overkill of Big Bands. Dizzy Gillespie and Kenny Clarke formed the initial ideas, and Charlie Parker's talent delivered Bebop. During a year-long recording strike, players united in clubs and bred these experimental new ways. World War II had increased the status of black people, and Bebop initially became black elitist – Dizzy even claimed blacks developed Bebop to exclude "lesser" (white) musicians. With its new vocabulary and rise in importance of polyrhythms it did the job of separating itself from the excesses of Popular or Dance music.

Street Styles – Jazz was about nightlife and, inevitably, style. One Jazz festival press release even trailed Miles Davis' specially made Italian suit as being a newsworthy aspect of his stage appearance. Dizzy Gillespie's use of a French beret prompted a rage, as did Gerry Mulligan's crew cut. And Billy Eckstine's collared shirts were actually sold as Mr B. shirts!

West Coast

Cool was Jazz's last real consumer-friendly face, borne of Miles Davis' visions as a reaction to the frantic and abrasive sounds of Bebop. It offered warmer, softer colours, sometimes tinged with melancholy; Miles Davis' trademark sounds were always more intimate, more personally felt, than many of his rivals. The term "Cool", like art's Impressionism, was largely a term christened by critics, but the West Coast was genuinely the base that it first sprang from. Davis brought many to Cool, and others, initially not attracted to Bebop, simply jumped a style straight into Cool. These are interesting, listener-friendly records and, because many are well known, it is an instantly familiar world, even to novice collectors.

Late Bop

Hard Bop and Post-Bop both rest under this umbrella. At the close of an era filled with multiplying Jazz fractions, Post-Bop was more a musical shelter for those who'd made the journey, being a temporary point from which they could think and then launch into fresh visions. The exciting freedoms brought by new styles so divided players and enthusiasts that never again would Jazz have the strengths of being a real collective. Rock, Funk, and Soul would become more comfortable zones to many fans than the distant forms of Jazz. Hard Bop hinted at this switch of tastes, with Soul and Blues elements creeping into the material.

Experimental

As the harbingers of death to Jazz, or simply pure fascination, Free Jazz and Avant-Garde naturally deliver controversy. View them like you would abstract art forms: traditionally trained artists stepping outside the standard compositional forms to present new ideas. Inevitably it was hit or miss, but this does mean there are thousands of highly individual LPs, often sold in small numbers so not transferred to CD, inviting open-minded listeners. Journey with a single leading figure, or take the time to absorb the Experimental movement's credentials, and let your collection expand just as the original '60s music did.

Art on Covers – Three record labels placed huge importance on art covers and all these are now highly collectable. Blue Note used Reid Miles for over 500 wonderful cropped portraits and breathtaking typographical covers, Contemporary used the camera skills of William Claxton, and David Stone Martin created 200 masterpieces for Clef – one Japanese fan even privately commissioned him to do 60 portraits of Jazz stars.

Fusion

The twin influences of Hard Bop and Avant-Garde had both enjoyed their moments of high fashion and left a creative lull, while in the Rock world the 1970s "supergroups" were cramming their pockets, and vast stadiums, trying to become "arty". If the Jazz rule book really had been torn up then why not musically borrow from Rock? The world of Fusion is complex as it applies to any marriage of Jazz with outside styles such as Funk, World Music, Dance, and Latin. What Jazz Fusion created was a modern stylistic variation that could be collected under Jazz or any of the other banners.

Bebop Movement *"THE MODERN JAZZ CROSSROADS"*

Average Record Cost
☆☆☆☆

Rising Stars
Charlie Parker
Jackie McLean

BEBOP – all LPs
Kenny Clarke *Kenny Clarke Vol. 1* ★ / *Paris Bebop Sessions*

Dizzy Gillespie
Dizzy Gillespie ★ / *Dizzy in Paris* ★ / *Horn of Plenty* ★ / *Modern Trumpets* ★

Jackie McLean *The Jackie McLean Quintet* ★ / *McLean's Scene* / *Swing, Swang, Swingin'* ★

Charlie Mingus
Mingus at Monterey ★ / *Special Music Written for (But Not Performed at) Monterey* ★ / *Strings and Keys* ★

Thelonious Monk
Genius of Modern Jazz Vol. 1 ★ / *Thelonious Monk Plays Duke Ellington* ★ / *Thelonious Monk Trio* ★

Charlie Parker *Charlie Parker Quintet* ★ / *Charlie Parker* ★ / *Bird & Diz* ★ / *Charlie Parker Sextet* ★ / *Charlie Parker With Strings* ★

Bud Powell *Bud Powell Trio* ★ / *Bud Powell Piano* ★ / *Bud Powell Piano Solos* ★ / *Jazz at Massey Hall Vol. 2* ★

Max Roach *Max Roach Plus Four* ★ / *Max Roach Plus Four Plays Charlie Parker*

Bebop, Bop, or indeed in early times Rebop, are all the same thing – a movement that is virtually a blueprint for all modern Jazz styles. People either celebrate its freedoms or turn away because it unsettles convention. It is really an artistic extension of Swing, with more complex performances woven together. For example, a song may include a drummer just marking time on cymbals, or solo players exploring chordal but not melodic improvisations.

Dizzy Gillespie's and Kenny Clarke's visions in the early 1940s were really launched by Charlie Parker. His work of this style includes the 1954 Clef label *Charlie Parker* ★ ($400), *Charlie Parker with Strings* ★ ($400), the 1949 *Charlie Parker Quintet* ★ ($800) on the tiny LA label Dial, *Charlie Parker Sextet* ★ ($800), and the Savoy label *Charlie Parker Vols. 1, 2, 3, & 4* ★ (each $500). Dizzy Gillespie also has records on the LA Dial, label including the 1952 *Modern Trumpets* ★ ($400), *Dizzy in Paris* ★ ($200), and *Horn of Plenty* ★ ($300) on Blue Note.

> *In the Groove – The Blue Note label is highly collectable today. For example, Bud Powell's 1963 mono* Bud *has a "New York, USA" address on it and is $25, while the 1957 version has "Lexington Avenue" and is $150. However, if a 1957 record has Blue Note's "deep groove" it is worth $200.*

The keyboard skills of Bud Powell can be heard on the 1950 Roost LP *Bud Powell Trio* ★ ($400), and Mercury label's *Bud Powell Piano* ★ ($250). Thelonious Monk's records include *Genius of Modern Jazz Vols. 1 & 2* ★ ($400 each on the 1952 Blue Note version, but later ones are cheaper). His Prestige label list is very good – *Thelonious Monk Trio* ★, worth $200, is just one example. Despite his early vision, Kenny Clarke's prices remain steady today – *Kenny Clarke Vols. 1 & 2* ★ are each $150, and the 1969 *Paris Bebop Sessions* just $15. However, Jackie McLean shows strongly – his 1955 Adlib label LP *The Jackie McLean Quintet* ★ is worth $1,000, while his Blue Note label list has 12 three-figure LPs. Charlie Mingus offers many LPs around $30, as well as some rare items. His own-labelled products include the 1966 *Mingus at Monterey* ★. This is worth $700 with a sepia picture and single sleeve, but $300 with a colour and gatefold sleeve marked "by mail order". However, if it was distributed by Fantasy it is worth just $60!

West Coast *"COLLECTABLE, EASY ON THE EARS"*

Suggested Strands
Cool

Average Record Cost
★★★

Rising Stars
Gerry Mulligan
Stan Getz
Chet Baker

COOL – all LPs

Chet Baker *Chet Baker Ensemble ★ / Chet Baker Sextet ★ / Chet Baker Sings ★*

Dave Brubeck *Jazz Goes to College / Time Out*

Miles Davis *Birth of the Cool ★ / Kind of Blue ★ / Miles Ahead*

Paul Desmond *Desmond Blue / Take Ten*

Gil Evans *Out of the Cool*

Stan Getz *Cool Velvet – Stan Getz and Strings / More West Coast Jazz with Stan Getz ★ / New Sounds in Modern Music ★ / West Coast Jazz ★*

John Lewis *Grand Encounter: 2° East, 3° West ★*

The Modern Jazz Quartet *Django / The Modern Jazz Quartet with Milt Jackson ★*

Gerry Mulligan *Gerry Mulligan and his Ten-Tette ★ / Mulligan Too Blows ★ / Paris Concert ★*

Shorty Rogers *Cool and Crazy ★ / Modern Sounds ★*

Howard Rumsey *Howard Rumsey's Lighthouse All-Stars ★ / Sunday Jazz à la Lighthouse ★*

Lester Young *Blue Lester / Lester Young ★ / Lester Young Trio ★*

West Coast Jazz has grown into a category almost as a consequence of certain Miles Davis recordings, but in fact Kid Ory recorded in Los Angeles way back in 1922. Its roots stem from Miles Davis' live performance in September 1948 at New York's Royal Roost (recorded by Capitol in 1949/1950), and by Lennie Tristano's "New School of Music" formed in New York in 1951. The emphasis then shifted back to the West Coast.

Cool

This was the growth of modern, small line-up Jazz with clean sounds, nestling between Bebop and Hard Bop. A consumer-friendly counter to Bebop – just as Trad Jazz was in the UK – Cool prompted a commercial fight between demanding East Coast styles and the more melodic West Coast ones. For Miles Davis' first recording chance outside Charlie Parker's work, he gathered Cool-toned soloists and played a two-week gig as an interval group for Count Basie, before recording the influential 1956 album *Birth of the Cool ★*, worth $150. Davis' *Miles Ahead* LP ($90) has a cover showing a woman and her child on a sailboat, but the same record is worth just $50 if the cover features him performing.

Another high-profile modern Jazz figure was Dave Brubeck, who made the cover of *Time* Magazine in 1954 – long before his huge hit with *Take Five*. He produced lean, infectious material with fresh, digestible timing, and toured the student circuits extensively, often recording shows. Some of these can be found on the 1954 *Jazz Goes to College* LP (worth $80 if the label is dark red with gold print, but other versions are much less). His *Time Out* album is worth $60 if the label is red/black with an eye logo. His original issues on Fantasy are all worth $150 apiece. Stan Getz also built a high profile, with clean modern arrangements – his 1955 *West Coast Jazz ★* LP is worth $150, *More West Coast Jazz with Stan Getz ★* $100, and *New Sounds in Modern Music ★* $300: His Norgran label material is $100–200 and initial releases on Roost label are $150 or more.

> *Chartless Hit – Miles Davis' famous 1959* Kind of Blue *album is worth $120 stereo ($60 mono) if it has six "i" label logos. It ranks 14th in a UK book by Colin Larkin,* The All-Time Top 1,000 Albums, *beating U2 and Bruce Springsteen, yet it never actually entered the LP charts.*

Late Bop *"GATHERING TALENTS & MOODS"*

Suggested Strands
Hard Bop
Post-Bop

Average Record Cost
☆☆☆

Rising Stars
Horace Silver
Jimmy Smith
Max Roach

Evacuees from Bop's increasingly technical foundations either pursued Cool Jazz or switched to Hard or Post-Bop, which mixed all the challenges of freedom with more melodic, soulful feelings. Even briefly referred to as Funk, Late Pop would eventually lead to Soul Jazz. It claimed the high ground from the mid-'50s until 1970, when Avant-Garde and then Fusion encroached on it. It was also affected by the growth in Rock music and the subsequent loss of many independent labels.

Hard Bop
The birth of Hard Bop cannot be pinpointed exactly, but Miles Davis placed a marker with his 1952–54 Blue Note recordings *Miles Davis Vol.I* ★ ($200) and the 1957 *Cookin' with The Miles Davis Quintet* ★ ($100). One of his session men, Sonny Rollins, also contributed his own work – *A Night at the Village Vanguard* ★ and *Newks Time* ★ (both with "deep groove" labels they are $120 each), and *The Sound of Sonny* ★ (the 1967 white label/blue print version is $100). Detail is again important: for example, the 1954 *Max Roach Quartet featuring Hank Mobley* ★ is worth $300 on Debut, but just $10 if it's on Fantasy. A rare 10" shared LP, *Max Roach Quintet/Art Blakey and his Band* ★, from 1952, is worth $600. For sheer collectors' choice the Horace Silver Quintet offers 21 albums valued in three figures, mostly "deep groove" – *Horice Silver Quintet* ★ ($250), *Spotlight on Drums* ★ ($200), and *Horace Silver and The Jazz Messengers* ★ ($200). Another key figure was Art Blakey – his *At the Café Bohemia Vols.1 & 2* ★ are each worth $150, and *Art Blakey and The Jazz Messengers* ★ is $150. He and Horice Silver founded The Jazz Messengers in 1955, which was a loose union of developing Hard Bop talents. Prolific Jimmy Smith offers over 200 collectables, including many Blue Note discs, such as *Jimmy Smith at the Organ Vols.1, 2, & 3* ★ (with "deep groove" they are each $150) and *Groovin' at Small's Paradise Vol.1* ★ ("deep groove" $120).

HARD BOP – all LPs
Cannonball Adderley *Know What I Mean? / Things are Getting Better*

Art Blakey *Art Blakey and The Jazz Messengers* ★ */ At the Café Bohemia Vols. 1 & 2* ★ */ Hard Bop*

Miles Davis *Cookin' with The Miles Davis Quintet* ★ */ Miles Davis Vol. 1* ★

The Benny Golson Jazztet *Gettin' With It / The Other Side of Benny Golson*

Thad Jones *The Magnificent Thad Jones* ★ */ Motor City Scene / Thad Jones* ★

Yusef Lateef *Live at Peps / Lost in Sound*

Wes Montgomery *Easy Groove / Full House / Montgomeryland*

Lee Morgan *Candy* ★ */ City Lights* ★ */ The Sidewinder*

Max Roach *Max / Max Roach Plus Four* ★ */ Max Roach Quintet / Art Blakey and His Band* ★ */ The Max Roach Quartet Featuring Hank Mobley* ★

> *Blue Heaven – The sale, in 1967, of Bebop's main record label Blue Note hurt the whole industry. Founded in 1939, it championed artists with beautifully packaged albums. The label was latterly revitalized under EMI. Any Blue Note record is worth checking as rare ones are collectors' gems.*

Sonny Rollins *A Night at the Village Vanguard ★ / Newks Time ★ / Tour De Force / The Sound of Sonny ★*

The Horace Silver Quintet *Horace Silver and The Jazz Messengers ★ / The Horace Silver Quintet ★ / Six Pieces of Silver ★ / Spotlight on Drums ★*

Jimmy Smith *Groovin' at Small's Paradise Vol 1 ★ / House Party / Jimmy Smith at the Organ Vols. 1, 2, & 3 ★*

POST-BOP – all LPs

Miles Davis *E.S.P. / Nefertiti*

Eric Dolphy *Out to Lunch*

Herbie Hancock *Crossings / Fat Albert Rotunda / Mwandishi / Treasure Chest*

Bobby Hutcherson *Dialogue / Happenings*

Ahmad Jamal *Alhambra / But Not for Me / Ahmad Jamal at the Pershing*

Keith Jarrett *Death and The Flower / Mourning of a Star*

Elvin Jones *Live at The Lighthouse*

Clifford Jordan *Blowing in from Chicago ★ / Cliff Craft*

Steve Lacy *The Straight Horn of Steve Lacy*

Booker Little *Booker Little and Friends / Out Front*

Wynton Marsalis *Carnival / Hot House Flowers / Wynton Marsalis with Art Blakey and His Jazz Messengers*

Woody Shaw *The Complete CBS Studio Recordings of Woody Shaw*

Wayne Shorter *Ju Ju / Schizophrenia*

McCoy Tyner *Extensions / Inception*

Post-Bop

Over the era Jazz camps of many differing designs had been pitched, each gathering its own specialist armies. Those remaining followed a general blueprint, set yet again by Miles Davis and important mid-'60s recordings, including his 1965 *E.S.P.* ($25) and 1968 *Nefertiti* ($50). Davis created a "No time changes" concept, using composed themes with soloists picking their own unrestricted voices. This expanded small line-up improvisation and led to longer compositions and new sound palettes – namely Fusion. As this was really a transitional period, many familiar names feature, such as Charlie Mingus, Thelonious Monk, Max Roach, and Pat Metheny. Young Memphis trumpeter Booker Little joined the prestigious Max Roach Band, and performed with both Eric Dolphy and John Coltrane before dying at the age of 23 from blood poisoning. For others, such as Herbie Hancock, Post-Bop was just a brief moment in four decades of creativity – his 1972 LPs *Fat Albert Rotunda* and *Crossings* are each worth $15. Higher valued are Clifford Jordan's LPs *Cliff Craft ★* and *Blowing in from Chicago ★* – each $120 if "deep groove" labelled.

> *A Lone Voice – An earlier element of Bop was Vocalese, which involved singing to existing instrumental compositions. Lambert, Hendricks, and Ross (Dave, John, and Annie respectively) made this fashionable in the early '60s, but Ross carried on long after Bop's demise.*

Based on Hard Bop, the process began of integrating the feel of R&B, Funk, and World Music, to which were applied more opened-ended harmonies and complex chordal work. Wynton Marsalis personified this new blood in his 1981 *Wynton Marsalis with Art Blakey and His Jazz Messengers* ($15), and the later *Carnival* and *Hot House Flowers* (each worth $10). A collective of ideas in the 1980s was termed *The Young Lions*. Another "Lion" was Wayne Shorter – his *Schizophrenia* LP is worth $20 and the 1965 *Ju Ju* $30 (if it has a "New York, USA" label address – other versions are $10). Bobby Hutcherson's 1965 LP *Dialogue* is worth $30 with a "New York, USA" address, but if it says "Liberty Records" or "Finest Jazz since 1939" on it then the value is cut by a half or two-thirds. Hutcherson also featured on Eric Dolphy's 1964 album, *Out to Lunch*, which is worth $80.

Experimental Jazz *"A COLLECTORS' SAFARI"*

Suggested Strands
Free Jazz
Avant-Garde

Average Record Cost
☆☆☆

Rising Stars
Lennie Tristano
Sun Ra
Eric Dolphy

Experimental Jazz was the healthy outcome of Sweet Big Bands reducing Jazz creative challenges to simplistic dance tunes, and then Bebop imposing forms and harmonic frameworks. The very essence of Jazz was personal expression, and an underground movement built up that questioned the traditional compositional rules of engagement. It would yield extraordinary music that was fascinating and challenging – sometimes even musicians questioned if it was strictly music. Collect these forms of Jazz to take a musical safari; expect the unexpected and thrill at new visions.

Free Jazz

Here there are no rules on musical pitch or speed. Soloists were literally free to take the performance wherever it felt right at that moment – an understandable adrenaline rush for musicians in the band. This was largely American East Coast bred and it existed in ever more fragmented forms from the 1960s until the 1990s. However, a much-neglected pianist, Lennie Tristano, actually began the movement in 1949. His work includes the 1950 *Lennie Tristano with Lee Konitz* ★ ($250), *On New Jazz* ★ ($200), and *Holiday on Piano* ★ ($150). The movement's "Godfather" was Ornette Coleman, whose 1958 album *Something Else* ★ is $120, the 1961 *Free Jazz* $50, and the 1959 LP *The Shape of Jazz to Come* $50 or $40 mono (both with bull's-eye labels – early '60s versions with differing labels are worth less money).

Another formative figure was John Coltrane, who redefined the tonal platform of Jazz. Minimalist yet complex, his LPs include *Giant Steps* – with the 1959 black label it is $50, the 1960 orange/purple label and white fan logo $25, and the 1962 version with a black fan just $15. His respected 1965 LP *A Love Supreme* is $40, and the 1957 Blue Note recording *Blue Train* ★ is $150, although the '80s pressing is worth just $10. The Prestige label LP *Coltrane* ★, from 1957, is worth $150 if the label is yellow, and yet fetches just $30 if it has a blue label.

FREE JAZZ – all LPs

Muhal Richard Abrams
Young at Heart/Wise in Time

Albert Ayler
Virgo Vibes / West Coast Vibes

Ornette Coleman *Free Jazz / The Music of Ornette Coleman – Something Else* ★ */ The Shape of Jazz to Come*

John Coltrane
Blue Train ★ */ Coltrane* ★ */ Giant Steps / A Love Supreme*

Bill Dixon *The Bill Dixon 7-Tette / Intents and Purposes*

Joseph Jarman *Song For*

Roscoe Mitchell *Roscoe Mitchell Sextet / Sound and Space Ensembles*

Sun Ra *Cosmic Tones for Mental Therapy* ★ */ Super-Sonic Jazz* ★ */ When the Sun Comes Out* ★

Cecil Taylor *Jazz Advance* ★ */ Looking Ahead*

Lennie Tristano *Holiday on Piano* ★ */ Lennie Tristano with Lee Konitz* ★ */ On New Jazz* ★

> *Black View – New York pianist Cecil Taylor was the son of a dancer. He powered his keyboard with breathtaking skills, saying, "I try to imitate on the piano the leaps in space a dancer makes".*

Cecil Taylor was a trailblazer lost in the shadows of Coleman's career – his 1959 *Looking Ahead* is $50, and the 1956 Transition label *Jazz Advance ★* is $200 ($150 if the booklet is missing). But he did find audiences in Europe, as did Albert Ayler. The latter's 1964 *West Coast Vibes* is $25, and *Virgo Vibes* $20. Watch out for Sun Ra recordings as they are rare and often sell for higher prices than the guide figures. For example, the 1963 *When the Sun Comes Out ★* is $300 (but only if it has a black figure on the cover), and *Super-Sonic Jazz ★* is $300 with a silk-screened cover.

Avant-Garde

Avant-Garde shares the common pioneers of Lennie Tristano and Ornette Coleman and is therefore often simply bundled together with Free Jazz. Though most of the musicians explored both strands, Avant-Garde is in fact a semi-free Jazz form that reaches beyond Bebop. Rising during the 1960s it offered more structured ensemble solos, using some conventional forms. By the mid-'60s many Free musicians had feasted enough on formless compositions and, as with many other times in Jazz history, Miles Davis pointed the way to something new. Between 1964 and '69 he performed awesome, emotional music, often set over a repetitive rhythm section. Recordings include 1963's *The Original Quintet* ($20), *Diggin'* ($50), and *Miles Davis at Carnegie Hall* ($50 with "Guaranteed High Fidelity" on the label, other variants worth less). This was Avant-Garde at its best – free from conventions but generally providing a set tempo or sequential tones.

Somewhere Else – Influential Jazz figure and a collector's delight, Herman Blount has many rare discs to hunt out. He had a personal obsession with outer space, writing poetry about it, naming himself Sun Ra, and creating bands based on that theme.

The Art Ensemble of Chicago, an influential quintet including Lester Bowie and Roscoe Mitchell, offered *Fanfare for the Warriors* ($15) and the 1973 *Bap-Tizum* ($15). Eric Dolphy had been associated with Ornette Coleman, but in the '60s he progressed to more narrative records of his own under the Avant-Garde umbrella. His 1963 *Conversations* is worth $50, *Outward Bound ★* and *Out There ★* from 1960 are each worth $120 with purple labels, and the 1961 *Eric Dolphy at The Five Spots ★* fetches $100 if purple-labelled.

Jazz Fusion *"NO MAN'S LAND"*

JAZZ-ROCK – all LPs

Blood Sweat and Tears
Blood Sweat and Tears ★

Chicago *Chicago* ★ / *Chicago Transit Authority*

Parliament *Osmium* ★ / *Up For the Down Stroke*

Sly Stone *Sly and The Family Stone's Greatest Hits* ★

ORIGINAL FUSION – all LPs

Brecker Brothers *Heavy Metal Be-Bop / The Brecker Brothers*

Larry Carlton *Larry Carlton / Singing/Playing*

Billy Cobham *Spectrum*

Chick Corea *Inner Space*

Miles Davis *Bitches Brew / Live-Evil / On the Corner*

Herbie Hancock *Succotash / Thrust*

Mahavishnu Orchestra *Apocalypse / Birds of Fire*

Return to Forever *Musicmagic*

Weather Report *Tale Spinnin'*

SECOND WAVE – all LPs

Stanley Clarke *School Days*

Pat Metheny *Bright Size Life / Song X / Watercolors*

Jazz Fusion is a very overused title that includes M-Base/Avant-Fusion (Funk Dance-tinged), Jazz-Rock Fusion (singers with a Jazz feel), Original Fusion (Jazz, R&B, and World), and World Fusion (Ethnic inspirations). There is also Second Wave Fusion (soulful, Latin-tinged), and Light Fusion (softer, Easy Listening). In essence, Fusion is a set of Jazz improvisation cocktails to which differing quantities of Rock's energies are added.

Jazz-Rock

US chart bands like Blood Sweat and Tears can be placed under this umbrella. Their *Blood Sweat and Tears* ★ audiophile version is $120 (but just $20 if standard). Chicago's 1976 LP was self-named *Chicago* ★; the promo-only version had its first ten copies stamped with gold on the packaging – these are worth $250. Even Jimi Hendrix's band, The Jimi Hendrix Experience, produced recordings that saw the more skilful Rock musicians leaning towards the approachable edges of Jazz. Largely frowned on by Jazz enthusiasts, and marginalized by traditional Rock fans, such records are generally easy to find.

Original Fusion

This cluster is the centrepiece of the Jazz migration to Fusion. Miles Davis explored the style, which can be heard in his 1972 LP *Bitches Brew* ($40), and *Live-Evil* ($30). His former sideman Chick Corea made *Inner Space* ($15), before creating the band Return to Forever, whose 1977 LP *Musicmagic* is worth $20. John McLaughlin and Billy Cobham created The Mahavishnu Orchestra, but Cobham also offered fine solo LPs such as the 1973 *Spectrum* ($15). High respect for these quality talents has so far failed to lift collectors' enthusiasm, simply because the music itself is largely out of fashion.

Second Wave

This was a place for the talent who were drawn to Jazz's creativity, yet were tempted to inject more of their musical roots into it. Stanley Clarke moved from Stan Getz and Return to Forever, before entering Second Wave and bringing Rock and Latin into his style, as can be heard on the 1976 LP *School Days* ($12). Steely Dan were highly respected Rock figures with quality hits like the Top 10 *Reelin' In the Years*, but in 1977 they released the beautiful Jazz-tinged album, *Aja*, which went Top 5 and Platinum. The Jazz world approved, and Woody Herman even recorded an album of their material.

FOLK MUSIC

Folk covers a huge range of traditions. Its precursors were the troubadours who toured European communities, often performing topical material about events happening elsewhere, but it also covers isolated native American Indians living high in the mountains who celebrated seasonal changes. Then there's New York Folk, which was active with left-wing thinkers from the 1940s but hijacked in the '60s by becoming fashionable. Earnest desires to crusade worthy issues forged working groups such as The Composer's Collective and People's Song Organization – committed to "create, promote and distribute songs of labour and the American People". As it turned out, East Coast Folk was adopted not by the workers but by middle-class romantics.

It comes as something of a surprise that such a backwater of music yields valuable records, given that the majority of the recording artists over the next few pages will probably be unknown to you. Within Folk, initial markets were not perceived as being big, and so pressing-runs of 500 or 1,000 were not unusual, which makes for collectable records today. It is ironic that the one exception is Bob Dylan, who boasts some of the collecting world's most desirable items. He caused a revolution within Folk, and then conspicuously deserted it for the trappings of Rock. Undeniably, he spearheaded the move away from recording traditional material by injecting strong modern lyrics relevant to a period of social unrest. The actual number of Folk-tinged albums he released was quite small and naturally they sold well, which makes the process of collecting them quite unchallenging. It's therefore in the test pressings, artworks, and oddities that the values surge for Dylan's work.

One of the World's Most Wanted – Always look carefully at copies of Bob Dylan's 1960s LP The Freewheelin' ★: humble mono copies are just $30, but various label/track deviations can pitch it up to $12,000; there's even a version with a guide price of $30,000. It is best, therefore, to research this item using collectors' magazines.

One of the exciting aspects of delving into Folk is its authenticity. Unlike virtually all other music strands, Folk genuinely records moods and events. It's too easy to dismiss the '60s movement as merely a hippy gathering with a grudge about an unwanted war, as the American "Establishment" had been equally unstable since the 1950s. An example of this is a resolution extract from the Los Angeles Fire and Police Research Association:

"WHEREAS, it is becoming more and more evident that certain of the 'Hootenannies' and other similar youth gatherings and festivals, both in this country and in Europe, have been used to brainwash and subvert, in a seemingly innocuous but actually covert and deceptive manner, vast segments of young people's groups…

PHIL OCHS: CHORDS OF FAME

Phil Ochs *Chords of Fame*
Unlike rival Bob Dylan, this man remained true to his cause, using his singer-songwriter credentials to protest and lobby; he called himself a "Singing Journalist".

WE CONCLUDE, there is much evidence indicating an accelerated drive in the Folk Music Field is being made on or near the campuses of a number of high schools and colleges by certain individuals of questionable motivation, including members of the Communist Conspiracy."

To such backdrops came the healthy and powerful voice of protest songs – entirely consistent with Folk's tradition. By contrast UK Folk remained a gloriously eclectic mix of whims and missions, from the novelty hit *My Last Cigarette* by actress Sheila Hancock (with Sydney Carter), through to Loudest Whisper's haunting Irish story of *Children of Lir*, or the ethereal *Synanthesia* – a solitary masterpiece from a Scottish trio of the same name. Many extreme Folk albums were privately pressed, which adds greatly to their value today. For example, copies of Caedmon's 1978 album *Caedmon* ★ with an extra single, *Beyond the Second Mile,* included on them are now worth an impressive £500.

Strong musical traditions survive detailing adventures at sea, drinking songs, the hardships of mining, shipbuilding, and working the land. There are strands of children's Folk and plenty revolving around the rural community's dances – jigs and reels. This world is not unlike traditional American Folk as it is centred on universal sentiments rather than personal statements. What the UK did bring uniquely to Folk was a fusion with the gentler side of Rock. Spearheaded by Fairport Convention and Steeleye Span, this movement much-expanded the basic concepts of Folk, and introduced further strands such as Celtic Rock through bands like Horslips, and more electric Blues-tinged work from artists such as John Martyn.

What is wonderful for the record collector is that, unlike the over-publicized Rock and Pop records, many second-hand shops and car boot sales will never have heard of some of the collectable records, such as an old LP by Mushroom called *Early One Morning* ★ (£350). The British Folk world is filled with obscure but valuable items just waiting to be found.

A Different Crusade – Canadian Cree-Indian Buffy Sainte-Marie used Folk to champion the Native American's cause, but she succeeded in the mainstream too, co-writing Up Where We Belong *for Jennifer Warnes in the film* An Officer and a Gentleman. *Her own song,* Until It's Time for You to Go, *was also separately recorded by both Elvis Presley and Bobby Darin.*

Folk Music *"A LOT TO SAY FOR ITSELF"*

Suggested Strands

Traditions
New Voices
British Scene
Folk Rock

Average Record Cost

★★★☆

Rising Stars

Bob Dylan
The Carter Family
Loudest Whisper

TRADITIONS

Singles

Ramblin' Jack Elliott
Talking Minor Blues

The Kingston Trio
Greenback Dollar / Tom Dooley

The Limeliters
Cabin Hideaway ★

Peter, Paul and Mary
Lemon Tree / Puff (The Magic Dragon)

The Weavers
On Top of Old Smokey

LPs

The Carter Family
All Time Favorites ★ */ Gold Watch and Chain* ★ */ In Memory of A.P. Carter* ★ */ On the Sea of Galilee* ★

Ramblin' Jack Elliott *Jack Takes the Floor / Ramblin' / Woody Guthrie's Blues*

Woody Guthrie *Dust Bowl Ballads* ★ */ Songs to Grow on for Mother and Child* ★

Tommy Jackson *Do-Si-Do / Popular Square Dance Music / Square Dance Fiddle Hits*

Folk music intrigues collectors. Its image of well-meaning amateur musicians, its sheer earnestness to convey political messages, its near encounters with hippie movements, and its metamorphoses into the gentler aspects of later Rock all tend to marginalize this genre of music. In fact, it is rather like Jazz in that it is a collection of individual groups with separate visions, all sheltering under the one umbrella. This can be seen as a fringe subject for collecting – until you realize just how central Folk has been to hundreds of years of popular music.

Traditions

Grass roots Folk music can mean various different things around the world. In Europe it represents a century-old tradition of storytelling, while in 19th-century America it stemmed from the isolation of the Appalachian Mountain communities, which were often made up of immigrants from the UK. These remote communities created fragmented styles but largely universal themes of working the mines or logging, of emotions and retributions – *The Ballad of Tom Dooley* stemmed from this tradition. Folk group The Carter Family produced a large body of this sort of work – their single *Gold Watch and Chain* ★ is $150, seven of their other singles are currently worth three-figure values, and plenty more fetch around $60–80.

Folk music in the first half of the 20th century was very subservient to tradition, using classic old sea shanties, prospectors' songs, and square dances. Tommy Jackson's 1957 LP *Popular Square Dance Music* ($30) used material typically popular before World War II that reflected the amateur nature of traditional Folk cultures. Afterwards came groups like The Weavers – their 1951 LP *Folk Songs of America and Other Lands* ★ is worth $100, and singles like *On Top of Old Smokey* just $20. Peter, Paul, and Mary's 1965 LP *A Song Will Rise* is $25 and the single *Puff (The Magic Dragon)* £5, while The Limeliters' EP *Fun Folk* is £8 and the US single *Cabin Hideaway* ★ worth $150. These groups popularized Folk but still sometimes used traditional material. At times they reworked the songs of artists such as Folk/Country star Woody Guthrie. His work includes the 1950 10" *Dust Bowl Ballads* ★ ($600 – reissues are $500 and use the prefix FA, not FP), and *Songs to Grow on for Mother and Child* ★ ($600, but reissues are less).

This epitomized the sharp divide that Folk would suffer. Groups like The Weavers were perfectly happy recording others' work,

The Kingston Trio *Number Sixteen / The Kingston Trio / Sold Out / The Folk Era* 3 LPs

The Limeliters *The Limeliters / The Slightly Famous Limeliters*

Peter, Paul and Mary *In the Wind / A Song Will Rise*

Pete Seeger *Folk Songs of Four Continents ★ / Frontier Ballads Vols. 1 and 2 / Lincoln Brigade*

The Weavers *At The Carnegie Hall / At Home / Folk Songs of America and Other Lands ★*

EPs

The Carter Family *Mountain Music Vol. 2 / Original and Great Carter Family Vols. 1–6*

The Limeliters *Fun Folk*

NEW VOICES

Singles

Joan Baez *We Shall Overcome*

Bob Dylan *Mixed-up Confusion ★*

The Highwayman *The Gypsy Rover*

Burl Ives *A Little Bitty Tear*

The New Christy Minstrels *Green, Green / Three Wheels on My Wagon*

Buffy Sainte-Marie *Soldier Blue / The Universal Soldier / Until It's Time for You to Go*

LPs

Joan Baez *Diamonds and Rust / Joan Baez / Joan Baez in Concert / Joan Baez 5*

Bob Dylan *Blonde on Blonde ★ / Blood on the Tracks ★ / The Freewheelin'*

The Highwayman *The Highwayman / March On, Brother*

Burl Ives *Ballads and Folk*

concentrating on style and presentation, while individuals like Guthrie were hungry to express topical personal views rather than traditional stories. Pete Seeger's *Folk Songs of Four Continents ★* is $100 and *Lincoln Brigade ★* also $100, but in the UK nothing of his is worth over £15. Although a founding member of The Weavers, his emphasis was on delivering a message through his lyrics; one of his inspirations was Ramblin' Jack Elliott – a much revered figure in Folk for five decades.

> *Even with the Record Missing!* – Ceremonies of the Horseman ★ *was the original title of the 1974 Bob Dylan album* Planet Waves *($50) but no pressings were actually made with this title. However, three or four known sets of never-glued covers exist, and these are worth $3,000 each.*

New Voices

Having been with land workers, Woody Guthrie had already set the tone for Folk's social protesting by creating poignant songs for them, such as *This is your Land*. His admirer Bob Dylan would change the face of Folk with his highly personal vinyl crusades. Due to the Vietnam War, Civil Rights, and political witch-hunting, there was plenty to engage the new fans whose love affair with festivals gave perfect mass platforms for messages. Dylan's 1964 album savaging conflicts, racism, and social inequalities – *Times They Are A-Changin' ★* (white promo copies $400, regular mono $30) – caught the mood, as did his famous single *Blowin' In The Wind ★* ($500 in promo form). For a brief spell he was the master of all before him and collectors' interest still reflects that status. His 1966 LP *Blonde on Blonde ★* is worth $100 (white label version $1,000). DJ copies of *Blood on the Tracks ★* include five songs that differ to the regular 1976 album and these are worth $5,000 each. The 1962 single *Mixed-up Confusion ★*, with an orange label, is $1,500. Ironically, Rock and Roll would blunt Dylan's blade, but his recordings launched others who were less well-known but had similarly strong views.

Joan Baez, with her beautiful clear voice, had built a strong middle-class popularity before Dylan's emergence. Her first two albums, *Joan Baez* in 1960 and 1961's *Joan Baez Vol. 2* (both £12), remained in the US charts for two years. However, she was another of the artists influenced by Dylan's creative material, which can be seen in the anthemic protest single *We Shall Overcome* ($8) and LPs like *Joan Baez 5* ($20) and *Joan Baez in Concert* ($25). Her single *There But for*

Songs / Down to the Sea in
Ships / The Wayfaring Stranger /
Women: Folk Songs about the
Fair Sex

The New Christy Minstrels
Land of Giants / The New
Christy Minstrels

Phil Ochs All the News That's
Fit to Sing / I Ain't Marching
Any More

Tom Paxton Outward Bound /
Ramblin' Boy

Buffy Sainte-Marie
Many a Mile / Sweet America

EPs

Joan Baez
With God on our Side

Bob Dylan Dylan /
Mr Tambourine Man

BRITISH SCENE

Singles

Vashti Bunyan Some Things
Just Stick in Your Mind

Sandy Denny
Candle in the Wind

Donovan The Music Maker /
Sunshine Superman

**Sheila Hancock and Sydney
Carter** My Last Cigarette

Ewan MacColl Streets of Song

Ralph McTell Streets of London

Mellow Candle Dan the Wing

Mushroom Devil Among
the Tailors

The Spinners On Ilkley Moor
Baht'at

LPs

Back Alley Choir Back Alley
Choir ★ / A Single Smile Born
of Courtesy

Bread, Love and Dreams
Amaryllis ★

Anne Briggs
The Time has Come ★

Fortune made No.8 in the UK Charts (a US picture-sleeved version is $30). It was written by Phil Ochs who was the authentic face of political Folk but lacked Dylan's skills of self-promotion. Calling himself a "Singing Journalist", he created albums like the 1964 *All the News That's Fit to Sing* and, a year later, *I Ain't Marching Any More*, filled with anti-war sentiments (both LPs, with gold labels and guitar logo, are $40). Tragically, he committed suicide at the age of 36.

It's easy to view Folk as a lightweight genre, but start researching and you'll soon discover that this isn't true. Woody Guthrie's guitar was actually inscribed with "This machine kills fascists" and his lyrics were peppered with lines like "Some rob you with a six gun, some with a fountain pen" (from *Pretty Boy Floyd*). Folk protesters were campaigning with all the zeal of a political party. Naturally, the leading figures fell under the harsh searchlights of McCarthy's Un-American Activities Committee, as did right-wing counter recordings like John Wayne's 1973 album *America Why I Love Her* ($25).

> *Expensive Mistake – Buffy Sainte-Marie's* Universal Soldier *was a No.1 for Donovan ($12) and subsequently parodied by the famous surf duo Jan and Dean as* The Universal Coward. *She had signed away the publishing rights for $1 and it cost her $25,000 to retrieve them a decade later.*

Someone was needed to cater for the vast majority who loved Folk's style of music but not all the political angst. The Kingston Trio and Peter, Paul and Mary delivered the goods, but the giant among such groups was the much-maligned New Christy Minstrels. Viewed as the devil by purists, they sold huge numbers of folk records including *Green, Green* (£6) and *Three Wheels on My Wagon* (£6). These songs took folk onto network television. The band's large line-up created great vocal power and their frequently changing personnel included Kim Carnes, two members of the cult West Coast group The Byrds, and even Country superstar Kenny Rogers.

British Scene

The British Folk world is immensely complex and awash with different strands, such as Irish, Scottish, Welsh, North Country, and even Cornish traditions. The Skiffle of the 1960s created lots of small music venues, and many became Folk clubs for a rapidly expanding army of baggy sweatered, coffee-bar-loving students. Naturally the Joan Baez-style of Folk star was much

Vashti Bunyan
Just Another Diamond Day ★

Callinan-Flynn
Freedom's Lament ★

The Ian Cambell Folk Group
Across the Hills

The Chieftains
The Chieftains

C.O.B. *Moyshe McStiff &
the Tartan Lancers of the
Sacred Heart* ★

Sandy Denny *Sandy*

Donovan *A Gift from a
Flower in the Garden /
HMS Donovan*

Robin Hall and Jimmy
MacGregor
Wee Magic Stane

Loudest Whisper
Children of Lir ★ / *Hard Times* ★ /
Loudest Whisper ★

Ewan MacColl
Jacobite Songs

Fresh Maggots
Fresh Maggots ★

Ralph McTell
*Eight Frames a Second /
My Side of the Window*

Mellow Candle
Swaddling Songs ★

Mushroom
Early One Morning ★

Pentangle *Basket of Light /
Sweet Child*

John Renbourn *Another
Monday / The Lady and the
Unicorn* ★

The Spinners *The Spinners*

Meic Stevens
Canaeon Cynnar ★ / *Outlander*

Synanthesia *Synanthesia*

Westwind *Love is …*

Wooden Horse *Wooden
Horse* ★ / *Wooden Horse II* ★

admired, but few actively related directly to all the American social angst. Instead, a wide variety of Folk acts grew. Those with public status were helped by their regular TV exposure, such as Ralph McTell – *My Side of the Window* LP (£15) and *Streets of London* single (£5) in 1969, The Spinners – *On Ilkley Moor Baht'at* (£5) and *The Spinners* (£12), and even Robin Hall and Jimmie MacGregor – *Wee Magic Stane* (£8) or *Glasgow Street Songs* (£8). All their values are low today due to success at the time, while a 1971 LP by forgotten midlands duo Fresh Maggots, *Fresh Maggots* ★, is now worth £160.

> Lost – Harbouring an absolute fear of performing, and pin-sharp honesty over his haunting melancholy, Nick Drake created chillingly beautiful personal albums. He died at the age of 26 leaving LPs such as Pink Moon, which was his last and most bleak (£30).

Because of Folk's credibility it attracted adventurers. For example, The Rolling Stones' manager Andrew Moog Oldham tried recording the Jagger/Richards song *Some Things Just Stick in Your Mind* with Vashti Bunyan; the record, and eventually Oldham, disappeared but Bunyan later recorded *Just Another Diamond Day* ★, which sold few copies – hence its hefty £250 value today. Yorkshire TV took a look at Folk, but an offshoot operation selected the Back Alley Choir, a studio-based group, and released the *Back Alley Choir* ★ LP in 1972. As touring was not possible and only 500 copies circulated it disappeared, leaving collectors with a record that's jumped from £175 to £275 in a handful of years. Such rises are not automatic – the Penny Farthing label, who generally issued Pop records, released Westwind's 1970 *Love is….* Because of its scarcity it was valued at £180 a decade ago but is now valued at just £75.

A more successful crossover artist was Donovan, who delivered Pop singles like *Sunshine Superman* (£15), plus interesting LPs such as *A Gift from a Flower in the Garden* (£50), or *The Music Maker* (£50). Pentangle also crossed the barriers between Folk and Jazz with great success – the 1968 *Sweet Child* double album is £20 and *Basket of Light* also £20.

The Irish culture offered many gems both famed and forgotten now. One of the latter is Loudest Whisper with their *Children of Lir* ★ based on a national mythological story. Only 500 were pressed for Southern Ireland distribution – it was worth £400

A Good Year – In 1970 The Brethren played the Marquee Club and were spotted by the boss of Charisma label. Their name was changed to Lindisfarne and an LP followed, plus a tour with Genesis and a collaboration with Bob Dylan's producer. This resulted in the No. 1 album Fog on the Tyne.

in 1994 and has now reached a staggering £600. Their other locally distributed albums, *Loudest Whisper* ★ from 1981 and *Hard Times* ★ from 1983, are each £200. Utterly forgotten Irish talents Mellow Candle released a really beautiful, interesting 1972 album *Swaddling Songs* ★, which is now worth £400, and its original single *Dan the Wing* is valued at £35. Others worth watching for are Mushroom's *Early One Morning* ★ (£350), Scottish couple Bread, Love and Dreams with album *Amaryllis* ★ (£220,), Welsh folk talent Meic Stevens' *Outlander* ★ (£140) or his privately pressed Tic Toc LP *Canaeon Cynnar* ★ (£200), and beautiful Scottish trio Synanthesia's one LP *Synanthesia* – if you can find one.

Banking Loss – An Irish bank strike in the 1960s led one clerk, Christy Moore, to look for English employment. His musical skills produced the LP Paddy on the Road ★ *(£175), which is now so rare that many believe it doesn't exist.*

Folk Rock

Folk Rock is a fusion of styles inspired by a single track on Fairport Convention's first LP, *Unhalfbricking*, called *A Sailor's Life,* in which fiddler Dave Swarbrick duelled with band member Richard Thompson. This group and their individual efforts were the hub of Folk Rock. Their work includes the 1968 LP *Fairport Convention* (£80), seminal LP *Liege and Lief* (first pressing with pink label and "i" logo £20), or the rare *Full House* (white-label test pressings including tracks *Poor Will* and *The Jolly Hangman* – missing on later records – fetch £22). Group members included Sandy Denny, who then formed Fotheringay, Ian Matthews, and Ashley Hutchings who was first with Steeleye Span and then later with the Albion Band.

Bert Jansch and John Renbourn had success on their own and then united with others to create Pentangle. The band's LPs include *Solomon's Seal* (£30) and *Basket of Light* (£20),

Pentangle *Basket of Light / Solomon's Seal / Sweet Child*

John Renbourn *Another Monday / The Hermit*

Spyro Gyra *Bells, Boots and Shambles* ★

Steeleye Span *Hark! The Village Wait / Now We are Six*

The Strawbs *Dragonfly / Grave New World* 3 LPs

EPs

Bert Jansch *Needle of Death*

while Scotsman John Martyn's atmospheric solo albums included *The Tumbler* (first pressing with black circle logo £25) and *London Conversation* (£35 with the same logo). The other main Folk Rock family tree revolves around the Incredible String Band – their work includes *Incredible String Band* (first pressing with white label, green logo, black lettering £80) and *Wee Tam/The Big Huge* (double LP with red label £45). This group would sire others such as Amazing Blondel and Spyrogyra (not the Jazz group). Some individuals also emerged within this movement, particularly Roy Harper – his 1969 LP *Folkjokeopus* is £30 and *Harper 1970–1975* ★ is a six-LP set worth £125. There is also a rare 1977 LP, *Commercial Break* ★, which was never released but test pressings exist that are worth £200. Highly independent Irish band Horslips offered the *Happy to Meet – Sorry to Part* LP (£20) while The Strawbs produced *Grave New World* (three LPs with a booklet, £15) and *Dragonfly* (£20 with mustard labels). Newcastle band Lindisfarne earned high reputations with records like *Nicely Out of Tune* (with pink label £15, or Mad Hatter label £12).

Extended Playing – Groups often quickly disappear but the Albion Band boast 18 albums, theatre and TV projects, and 100 band members since 1971. Leader Ashley Hutchings was there from the start, and found time for more than a dozen solo LPs including Rattle and Roughneck *(£20).*

Fairport Convention *Liege & Lief*, **Joan Baez** *Joan Baez*,
Muddy Waters *The London Sessions*, **John Mayall** *The
Turning Point* The 1950s and 1960s witnessed great
adventures in both Folk and Blues, often splitting the
traditionalists from the new young blood.

BLUES

Now we enter one of the most perfect arenas of collecting, in which music truly reflects its time, and the passing decades have only served to raise interest and values. Along with Jazz it's probably the only genre in which you can genuinely collect artists and material with a direct lineage. For example, Willie Dixon, a one-time boxer born in Mississippi who was central to the Chicago Blues sound, recorded *Spoonful*, as did Rock "supergroup" Cream in 1966 – both were based on the original by Papa Charlie Jackson – *All I Want is a Spoonful*, from 1925. Blues' core persona is a solitary figure shedding his or her pains in life, not in a defeatist manner but with passion and resolve – decades later this became the absolute blueprint to Rock music. Blues is more about feelings than definitive performances – the only perfect Blues recording is one that pushes buttons in your own psyche.

Inevitably all the early gems were singles, which presented considerable challenges for raw performers who were suddenly required not only to record live but to savage their six- or eight-minute Blues number to fit onto a three- or four-minute disc. Albums were another matter – central Chicago figure Tampa Red recorded 300 songs from 1927 until 1953 before he was asked to do an LP. He offers over 100 discs to collect, 22 valued in three figures including the singles *Through Train Blues* ★ ($200) and *Jelly Whippin' Blues* ★ ($150).

Blues actually started out as banjo music, and early guitars themselves were often hybrids – for example, "Big" Joe Williams had a nine-string model, "Papa" Charlie Jackson used a six-string with a banjo-type body, and Leadbelly played a 12-string Stella. Then there were steel-bodied National Dobro guitars, with built-in resonator cones to give them power – Dire Straits' Mark Knopfler used one of these. Blues survived a suspect mid-life crisis and, as you will see in the Disciples section, became adopted by Rock's elite – coincidentally raising the fortunes for early artists and material. No praise is more cherished than from your own peer group, and ageing figures like Muddy Waters suddenly found themselves recording or touring with Rock millionaire fans like Eric Clapton and The Rolling Stones.

In this collecting genre the challenge might be to try and assemble all the works of one figure, or perhaps one song, as a single Blues copyright was often recorded dozens and dozens of times by wildly different artists. One word of warning – be careful when judging one of the great men's work by using an LP or CD set; try and remember that these were almost certainly recorded over decades of changing styles and mood and the songs were never meant to be heard together.

Elusive – Only two pictures exist of Robert Johnson – one he took himself in a booth – but even so the British Sunday Times *newspaper put him ninth in the World's Top 100 cult figures, and the USA issued a commemorative postage stamp of him. There are few of his records in existence, and subsequently a copy of* Love in Vain *recently went at auction for $9,900.*

Blues *"BLUE-RIBBON COLLECTING"*

This is one of the least corrupted strands of music and therefore its pedigree can be traced easily over the decades. It began as a loose union of styles developed under the Blues banner, but was ultimately neglected in favour of Rock, which chose to adopt the essence of Blues and deify its early heroes. This has subsequently catapulted original Blues vinyl into an ultra-rare status.

Lone Voices

Blues was started at the turn of the last century in the United States' "deep south" by travelling minstrels at fairs and at medicine shows, which toured the small black communities. These tough times were expressed in the music, which was tinged with determination. The Dinwiddie Colored Quartet made six gospel recordings in 1902, but the first real Blues record was cut on Valentine's Day, 1920 by Mamie Smith – *That Thing Called Love* ($20). This prompted numbers of female singers, such as Ma Rainey – *Baby No No* ($80), Bessie Smith – *Safety Mama* ★ ($150) and *Hot Spring Blues* ★ ($120), and Alberta Hunter – *Experience Blues* ★ and *Miss Anna Brown* ★ ($150 each). The first Country Blues artist to record was "Papa" Charlie Jackson, who created *Skoodle-Um-Skoo* ($75) and *Forgotten Blues* ★ ($100).

The music produced within poor communities was mostly released on vinyl in the single form, but some artists were eventually put onto albums. Leadbelly had a modest white following for his Folk/Blues – he boasts ten three-figure singles including *Pig Meat Papa* ★ and *Packin' Trunk Blues* ★ (each worth £100). Pink Anderson was more Jazz-based, aiming at a sophisticated market. In the 1960s her LPs included *Carolina Blues Man* ★ ($120 with blue label and silver print)

> *Meeting Demand – In the 1920s "Blind" Lemon Jefferson sold so many records (up to 750,000 of some titles) that he had to record them again to replace worn masters. There are now 40 singles valued in three figures including* How Long, How Long *★ ($200) and* Cat Man Blues *★ ($150).*

and *Medicine Show Man* ★ ($100 with the same label details). Piano Red's 1956 LP *Piano Red In Concert* ★ ($600) includes both a live performance and collected singles.

LONE VOICES

Singles

"Big" Bill Broonzy
Station Blues ★

Willie Dixon
Crazy for Me Baby ★

Alberta Hunter *Empty Cellar Blues* ★ / *Experience Blues* ★ / *Miss Anna Brown* ★

"Papa" Charlie Jackson *Forgotten Blues* ★ / *Skoodle-Um-Skoo*

"Blind" Lemon Jefferson *Cat Man Blues* ★ / *How Long, How Long* ★ / *Weary Dog Blues* ★

Leadbelly *Packin' Trunk Blues* ★ / *Pig Meat Papa* ★

"Blind" Willie McTell *Dark Night Blues* ★ / *Writin' Paper Blues* ★

Ma Rainey *Baby No No*

Bessie Smith *Hot Spring Blues* ★ / *Safety Mama*

Mamie Smith *Crazy Blues* / *Golfing Papa* / *Kansas City Man Blues* / *That Thing Called Love*

Tampa Red *Through Train Blues* ★ */ Jelly Whippin' Blues* ★

Bukka White *Black Train Blues / Sleepy Man Blues*

LPs

Pink Anderson *Carolina Blues Man* ★ */ Medicine Show Man* ★

Leadbelly *Blues Songs* ★ */ Sinful Songs* ★

Piano Red *Piano Red In Concert* ★

BOOM YEARS – all Singles

Charlie Burse's Memphis Jug Band *I Got Good 'Taters* ★ */Tapping that Thing* ★

Eddie "Son" House *Clarksdale Moan* ★ */ My Black Mama* ★ */ Preaching the Blues* ★

Robert Johnson *Cross Road Blues* ★ */ Love in Vain* ★ */ Milkcow's Calf Blues* ★ */ Terraplane Blues* ★ */ 32-20 Blues* ★

Jack Kelly's South Memphis Jug Band *Highway No. 61 Blues* ★ */ Ko-Ko Mo Blues* ★

"Memphis" Minnie *Garage Fire Blues* ★ */ Good Girl Blues* ★ */ My Butcher Man* ★

Charley Patton *Frankie and Albert* ★ */ Hammer Blues* ★ */ Joe Kirby* ★ */ Rattlesnake Blues* ★

"Sleepy" John Estes *Black Mattie Blues* ★ */ Hobo Jungle Blues*

MELTING POT

Singles

B.B. King *Three O'Clock Blues* ★

Sonny Terry *Harmonica Hop*

'Big' Jo Turner *Goin' Away Blues*

T. Bone Walker *Street Walkin' Woman* ★

Boom Years

Commercial success sent record company talent scouts south with cumbersome equipment to make field recordings. Memphis proved to be bountiful in Jug Bands (made up of guitar, harmonica, fiddle, and a booming empty whisky jug blowing a bass line). Charlie Burse's Memphis Jug Band mixed Blues with light entertainment material, which can be heard on *I Got Good 'Taters* ★ and *Tapping that Thing* ★ (both $300). Jack Kelly's South Memphis Jug Band produced *Ko-Ko Mo Blues* ★ and their hit *Highway No. 61 Blues* ★ (each worth $100). "Memphis" Minnie was another find – particularly desirable are the records she made with her second husband "Kansas" Joe McCoy. Her outgoing style makes her big list worth collecting – examples include *My Butcher Man* ★ ($150), *Hole in the Wall* ($75), and *Garage Fire Blues* ★ ($200). Deeper south, in Mississippi, Charley Patton delivered masterful Blues recordings, celebrating everything from faith to women and drugs, and he is hugely collectable today. His *Joe Kirby* ★ and *Some Summer Day* ★ are both worth $1,000 and *Green River Blues* ★ $800; his

> *Personal Stuff – Sleepy John Estes from Tennessee themed his material around his own life – a neighbour whose house burned down, a tough boss, his own car accident, and even his hoboing to Chicago to record. Singles include* Hobo Jungle Blues *($20) and* Black Mattie Blues ★ *($150).*

cheapest record is $500. Another gem in that circle was the unrefined talents of Eddie "Son" House – his *Preaching the Blues* ★ is $800, and *Clarksdale Moan* ★ is worth $1,000.

Hazelhurst's most celebrated music son, Robert Johnson, died in 1938 – a talent so revered he would be the subject of tribute books, records, and movies 50 years later. Rock giants Jimmy Page, Robert Plant, and Mick Jagger all competed to pay one million dollars for a rumoured 40-second archive performance film of his in 1998. His guitar work was the blueprint for all – from Muddy Waters to Eric Clapton – though Johnson's undisputed talent was drawn partly from studying others like Charley Patton and Eddie "Son" House. Only his first record, *Terraplane Blues* ★ (now worth £3,500), sold well at the time, and he made just 29 recordings in five sessions in less than one year. His turbulent lifestyle reflected his music, and caused his end – he was poisoned by a jealous husband.

Melting Pot

The financial melt down of the Great Depression in 1929 pitched the USA progressively into despair. The poorer southern states suffered the most, driving huge numbers of people north to the big cities in search of work. Hostility prevented talent scouts roaming south, and the migrant blacks found no place in more racist cities like New York to celebrate their musical roots. Many of the small Blues and R&B labels were also victims of the crisis. Acoustic hometown Blues dived, while a mutation occurred in the form of late Swing Jazz Blues.

The war years were also damaging, due to the Union recording strike, followed by raw material shortages. However, new ideas had been steadily growing. For example, T. Bone Walker began using an electric guitar, and his early 1940s solo recordings set a standard for others. John Lee Hooker reduced Blues to its essence by making records accompanied only by his electric guitar and a tapping foot, which can be heard on the 1960 album *The Blues* ★ ($100 if silver crown on black label) and *John Lee Hooker Sings the Blues* ★ ($500). This is more sophisticated than it sounds, and he grew into the elder statesman of Blues – a UK Top 5 chart star at the age of 74.

"Lightnin'" Hopkins had also traded in an intimate recording sound, this time for a Country Blues style. He was loved by campus circuits and many Rock stars. His 1965 album *Lightnin' and the Blues* ★ is $800 if yellow labelled, and the rare *Lightnin' Hopkins Strums the Blues* ★ is $1,200. Howlin' Wolf had migrated north and mixed his strong southern sounds with Chicago's grit to generate landmarks such as *Smoke Stack Lighting* (£15), the '62 *Howlin' Wolf* ★ ($600), and *Big City Blues* ($40). Rival Muddy Waters also shone in Chicago, his biting guitar work moulding classics such as *I've Got My Mojo Working* ($50), and collectors' joys like *All Night Long* ★ ($2,500), *She's all Right* ★ ($400), and *Walking Blues* (£60) – all singles.

> *Suspect Trading – Paramount Records and others deliberately issued really poor pressings so that they would wear out quickly and require a second purchase. This unfortunately resulted in few records by acts like Blind Lemon Jefferson surviving, which has also made digital transfers and CD reissues difficult.*

Muddy Waters *All Night Long* ★ / *She's All Right* ★ / *Walking Blues*

LPs

Bo Diddley with Muddy Waters *The Super Super Blues Band*

Buddy Guy *A Man and the Blues / First Time I Met the Blues*

John Lee Hooker *The Blues* ★ / *How Long Blues* ★ / *John Lee Hooker Sings the Blues* ★

"Lightnin'" Hopkins *Last Night Blues* ★ / *Lightnin' and the Blues* ★ / *Lightnin' Hopkins Strums the Blues* ★

B.B. King *Blues is King / King of the Blues* ★ / *Mr. Blues*

Jimmy Reed *Blues for Twelve Strings* ★

Sonny Terry *City Blues* ★ / *Folk Blues* ★

"Big" Jo Turner *The Boss of the Blues* ★ / *Rockin' the Blues* ★

T. Bone Walker *T. Bone Blues* ★ / *T. Bone Walker Sings the Blues* ★

"Sonny Boy" Williams *Down & Out Blues* ★ / *The Real Folk Blues*

Howlin' Wolf *Big City Blues / Howlin' Wolf* ★ / *Real Folk Blues*

EPs

John Lee Hooker *The Blues of John Lee Hooker*

Jimmy Reed *Blues of Jimmy Reed*

T. Bone Walker *Travellin' Blues*

Muddy Waters *Mississippi Blues* ★

DISCIPLES

Singles

Jack Bruce *I'm Getting Tired*

Eric Clapton *After Midnight / Lonely Years* ★

"Champion" Jack Dupree
Get Your Head Happy ★

Fleetwood Mac
Albatross / I Believe My Time Ain't Long

Mick Fleetwood's Zoo
I Want You Back

John Mayall
Crawling Up a Hill

Mick Taylor *London Town*

"Sonny Boy" Williams
From the Bottom

LPs

Mike Bloomfield
It's Not Killing Me

Jack Bruce *Songs for a Tailor / Things We Like*

Paul Butterfield
Paul Butterfield's Blues Band

Cream *Disraeli Gears / Fresh Cream / Goodbye / Wheels of Fire*

Willie Dixon *The Chess Box: Willie Dixon* 3 LPs / *Willie's Blues* ★

"Champion" Jack Dupree
Blues From the Gutter ★ / *Low Down Blues* ★

Fleetwood Mac
Peter Green's Fleetwood Mac / Mr Wonderful

Peter Green
The End of the Game

Eddie "Son" House
Father of the Folk Blues

Albert King *Big Blues* ★ / *Born Under a Bad Sign / Live Wire Blues Power*

John Mayall
Bluesbreakers with Eric Clapton / Blues from Laurel Canyon / The Turning Point

"Sonny Boy" Williams
Don't Send Me No Flowers

The Yardbirds (with "Sonny Boy" Williams) *Sonny Boy Williams and The Yardbirds*

Disciples

In 1958 Muddy Waters played his first UK tour to astonishingly big white audiences. "The Blues had a baby," he declared, "and they called it Rock and Roll". Immediate beneficiaries included B.B. King and Howlin' Wolf, and record companies started exhuming anybody old and authentic, such as Bukka White. Albums were made with Eddie "Son" House – *Father of the Folk Blues* ($25) and Willie Dixon – *Willie's Blues* ★ ($150 with silver-printed blue label).

Blues preservation necessitated a switch over to modern artists. In 1964 The Rolling Stones cut tracks in Chicago like *It's All Over Now* and *Confessin' the Blues*. Blues elder statesmen suddenly got big concert fees, and giants like Cream, The Yardbirds, Led Zeppelin, and The Rolling Stones recorded their songs – these are now unimaginable nest eggs. In the '70s these bands, along with The Allman Brothers, Eric Clapton, Ten Years After, and The Marshall Tucker Band, created a new worldwide Blues appreciation – for instance, an elderly B.B. King, was honoured at the Kennedy Centre, played the 1996 Atlanta Olympics, and had a 3m- (10ft-) high statue erected in his honour in Memphis.

UK's Blues master is Macclesfield's own John Mayall, whose bands have contained most Rock luminaries. His first album, in 1965, was *John Mayall Plays John Mayall* (£35), while his *Bluesbreakers with Eric Clapton* (£25) is now a classic, and *Bare Wires* (£18) may be his best. In 1997 he dropped The Bluesbreakers and went drumless to create *The Turning Point* (£18), which entered the UK charts.

Ex-Bluesbreakers include Peter Green – *The End of the Game* (£18) and Mick Fleetwood – *I Want You Back* (£8, as Mick Fleetwood's Zoo). They then created Fleetwood Mac's *I Believe My Time Ain't Long* (single £65 with picture sleeve), *Albatross* (single £6), and the 1968 LP *Peter Green's Fleetwood Mac* (£40). Other Bluesbreakers were Eric Clapton and Jack Bruce, who together formed Cream. Their LPs included *Fresh Cream* (£45) and *Disraeli Gears* (£45) – both with laminated covers, plus *Wheels of Fire* (£45) – the *In the Studio* and *Live at Fillmore* versions of this are £25.

The Yardbirds – This important Blues band never recorded as its original line-up but later boasted Jeff Beck and Eric Clapton. The Yardbirds played Chicago Blues style and toured with their hero "Sonny Boy" Williams. The 1965 LP Sonny Boy Williams and The Yardbirds *is worth $80.*

Jazz, the Godfather of record collecting, is rewarding, intricate,
and often stunning. Most records can be bought for between
£20 and £50, but 78's are rarely a good investment in this genre.

New Age records are calming, minimalist, and future collectables. Long before Enya's quiet, quality recordings were released, through the 1970s husband-and-wife label Windham Hill were making records that were so good they were bought out by the mighty BMG, but can still be bought for under £10 today. Independent labels also offer great choice – for example the self-titled *Iona*, on Celtic Music, is more valuable than most Enya records.

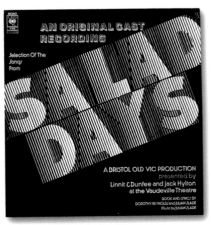

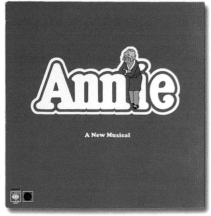

The genre of Musicals is a specialist collecting area, but there is a long tradition of cast recordings from which to choose, mostly £10–20. Many collections are themed around a specific composer.

Quality vinyl covers can be collected purely for their fine artwork,
at a fraction of the price of a gallery poster print – South American
artist Kim Poor's fascinating Steve Hackett image is around £5.

above This extremely rare brass DMM (Direct Metal Master) is the original master copy cut at Abbey Road for dispatch to the pressing factory to generate the vinyl edition of Russ Ballard's *Once a Rebel*.

above There are a fascinating number of records from major songwriters and publishers that are not for public sale but that cram in huge numbers of titles in order to promote their skills to those in the industry. This Bee Gees disc features 50 samples of their classic songs and is valued at around $60.

above Major records often go through a number of pressings. First Pressings, as shown with the top one of these Lennon *Imagine* LPs, often benefit from booklets, posters, printed inner bags, and better-quality printing, making them generally more valuable.

above An industry joke answer to the Sex Pistols' single *God Save the Queen*, which was distributed as an acetate pressing, is this single *God Save the Sex Pistols* by Elizabeth. The value of Pistols releases range from £2,000 to just £5; the Elizabeth single is so rare that it is yet to record a sales price.

above The LP by the Chanter Sisters, two respected session singers, is typical of a limited-sale "sleeper". Gogmagog was a stillborn '70s "supergroup" project as just three demos eventually appeared; expect to pay £50–70 for these rare collectables.

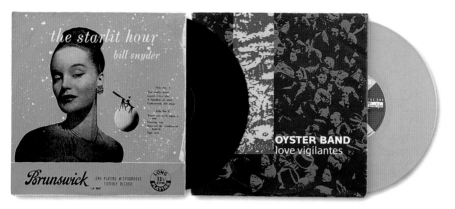

above This 1954 Bill Snyder 10" LP, worth around £15, is a typical '40s/'50s release. The 10" format lost out to 12" LPs and 7" 45's, until a revival in the 1990s when Indie groups such as Oyster Band made them trendy again. Their four-track record, pictured above right, is wrapped in a special fold-out poster.

above One of the last highly desirable Island Records "Pink" labels, this fully lamented Quintessence LP (£30–40) boasted extraordinary packaging with its legendary "Altar Cover" opening out to provide a meditation triptych.

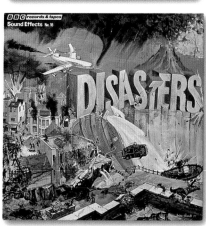

Radio is an Aladdin's cave of comedy, music, drama, and history. The LP for a modest light entertainment show such as Billy Cotton is now worth around £20.

POP

The diversity of Pop provides huge scope for collectors. Chiefly singles dominated, the genre is a split world of fanciful figures who passed by with changing fashions, and pivotal artists who became the fabric of popular music. If you have the appetite, explore beyond the obvious headliners and discover individuals and centres of influence. The Brill Building, for instance, was an entire New York block housing publishing companies that employed young writers to create songs. They paired up Gerry Goffin and Carole King, Jerry Leiber and Mike Stoller, Burt Bacharach and Hal David, for example, all names you will have seen on many hits for Pop groups – which is itself a collectors' dream section.

Pop Stars

Almost by definition this is a world filled with fabrication and crammed with more self-belief than talent yet, as with classic TV soaps, we eagerly accept the limitations in return for the entertainment. More than anywhere else in the book, Pop underlines the collecting anomaly that the big records we all loved are sadly uncollectable, while piles of failed efforts are rapidly rising in value. For example, the '60s British regional singer Mal Ryder recorded a handful of unsuccessful singles with The Spirits and then The Primitives. The latter's records are now approaching £200 each, despite never getting on radio, simply because of an unnamed hired session guitarist who would later become famous – Jimmy Page.

Big stars' records do count but generally only if they are offbeat. Elvis Presley gigs were very special – at a concert in Las Vegas guests were each given *International Hotel, Las Vegas, Nevada Presents Elvis 1970* boxes, packed with 2 LPs, a press release, the 1970 catalogue, a photo, a booklet, and the dinner menu. Surprisingly, the box on its own at around $1,200 is worth more than all its contents put together ($1,800 for the complete set)! These are strange preoccupations perhaps, but Elvis Presley is one of the Pop world's two most collectable acts – the other being The Beatles.

Brit Invasion – This is a frequently used American phrase loosely defining UK Pop output from the mid-'50s to the mid-'60s. It embraces anything from Trad Jazz to The Beatles, and from Dr Who to Vince Hill. They all reflected British youth culture and its US impact and therefore "Brit Invasion" creates an umbrella heading for transatlantic collectors.

Pop Girls

Not only is this section filled with unexpected stories but it paints a curiously familiar picture. When girl groups first broke into fashion they were highly polished youngsters in a virtually equal partnership with producers and songwriters. The ensuing years witnessed the emergence of the same arrogance that blights so many male stars, and frequently places image above songs. The story of girls in Pop reveals many parallel strands of high-profile stars and

Splinter *The Place I Love*
This is a perfect example of a
collector's dream find – a George
Harrison-produced white label
record, completely forgotten
by the collectors' bibles.

forgotten artists who often outpriced their more famous rivals. Glamorous record
covers command premiums, and sometimes even become the sole reason for
collecting. Any serious collection based on aspects of Pop Girls will in time do well
if it combines its visual appeal with the music. If you choose to collect certain
individuals, such as Brenda Lee, then you will take a voyage beyond Pop into
other genres. Brenda moved from Pop into Country, where she succeeded to the
point of becoming the head of The Country Music Association in Nashville.

Pop Groups
Aside from huge status bands like The Beatles and The Rolling Stones, Pop
groups such as The Hollies delivered a steady list of quality hits that remain
sensibly priced, while other once-status names, such as The Spencer Davis
Group, now command little attention. Some supporting groups independently
have eclipsed their former star employers: a rare album by The Roulettes
is worth £450 – far in excess of material by their old boss, Adam Faith;
likewise for The Tremeloes after leaving Brian Poole. Another Pop Group
strand is Bubblegum – largely stimulated by TV series such as The Monkees,
The Partridge Family, and The Archies – all affordable and amusing to
collect. Not all groups relied on vocalists, and there's a wealth of diverse
instrumental collectables from Winnie Atwell to Duane Eddy, and from Link
Wray to Mike Oldfield. We also expose a more challenging strand with bands
seldom heard of but worth perhaps £2,000 a disc, as they turn out to be a
superstar's first group.

Regional Pop
This isn't quite as geographic as it appears because a "Sound" born of a
particular region always attracts copycats from elsewhere. Nothing could be
more specific than Californian Surf, yet chart records in that style were appearing
from Minneapolis (The Trashmen with the Top 5 *Surfin' Bird*), The Astronauts
from Colorado, or even The Atlantics – who were, in fact, from Australia.
Because only a handful of key bands were involved choices are limited, but
collecting the "Surf Sound" gives you plenty of challenges. Towards the end
it created a subgroup, "Hot Rod" music, which themed cars and sometimes
drag racing – for example look out for the Rip Chords' *Hey Little Cobra*.

Clearly the British Merseybeat had a much larger impact, creating what is viewed as the "British Invasion" of America. This culminated in The Beatles' dominance. However, it is just as interesting to collect the other Liverpool bands that simply couldn't survive in The Beatles' slipstream. Liverpool might initially appear to be a strange musical birthplace, but it was an important sea terminal constantly touched by American seamen. They took early Rock & Roll to the Liverpool youth who were not wedded to Trad Jazz and were equipped with cheap Skiffle gear. The results changed the world of Pop music forever.

The Godfathers

One of the main frustrations of entering the world of vinyl collecting is that most of the records you know well are hits and so are not – at least for the time being – very collectable. Conversely, all the tantalizingly rare records are so unknown it's hard to know where to start. In Godfathers we give you a fascinating insight into the careers of four critical figures in Pop's commercial development. Within each one are many famous records, as well as plenty of forgotten ones with rising values. Of the four it is currently Joe Meek, with his stable of neglected singles artists, who has, on average, doubled in value in the last few years. A 1965 Syndicat single doesn't sound as exciting a find as a good copy of The Ronettes *Be My Baby* for £6 – that is until you discover The Syndicat's *On the Horizon* was listed at $25 in a 1997 American price guide and now UK listings place its value at £400.

Pop Composers

This area is really the powerhouse for all Pop music. Having the talent to craft their own material has helped everyone from Bob Dylan to ABBA, but with Dylan his courage to compose personal sentiments rather than generalities about love and life impacted musicians around the globe. Singer-Songwriters (excluding Dylan) is a highly affordable area of collecting, as the compositions are frequently covered by other artists.

With The Beatles, collecting takes on a different meaning and, with global competition for anything rare, prices are the highest for any artist, living or dead. As time passes it is most likely their songwriting skills that will be most revered, although it's hard to imagine just how high the values of their rare records will reach. Research is critical, as things as tiny as a publisher's credit can impact on the value. Also look out for songs that never meant much in your own country, as they may be highly valued singles elsewhere. The Beatles, for instance, had *Mr. Moonlight* as a Japanese single, *Boys* in Canada, France, and South Africa, and *Honey Pie* in Venezuela.

Seeing Red –The first two Beatles singles Love Me Do *(£50) from Oct 1962 and* Please Please Me *(£60) from Jan '63 were issued on Parlophone red labels. These were replaced by black from March '63, which makes the original ones desirable. An '80s* Love Me Do *reissue also had red labels, but the originals have an Ardmore & Beechwood song credit to differentiate them.*

Pop Stars *"BOTH EXTREMES OF TALENT"*

Suggested Strands

Teen Idols
Headliners
Pack Animals

Average Record Cost

☆☆☆☆

Rising Stars

Ricky Nelson
Cliff Richard
Johnny Burnette

These were the chosen role models for youth, who studied everything from the stars' lyrics to their hairstyles. Some truly are undisputed stars, with talent, charisma, and musical ideas aplenty, while others are clones that have less natural skill, but plenty of business force behind them, as well as blind ambition or simply gimmicks to assist their sales. These "stars" make interesting collecting as their enviable status means that most of their records were mass circulated and are therefore not excessively expensive to pick up today.

Teen Idols

The USA naturally paved the way for Pop stars – with TV as the main cultural diet, a handsome teenager who was seen regularly by 18 million in the sitcom *Ozzie and Harriet* was a natural candidate. Ricky Nelson sold a million copies of his first record in seven days – *A Teenage Romance* ★ is $50 in the USA with orange/yellow label, but in the UK gold or silver lettering means £125 or £75. Nelson has strong EP lists – the US red vinyl single *A Long Vacation* ★ is worth $300 and *Lonesome Town* ★ $600. A mixed 1957 Verve LP *Teen Time* ★ includes three Nelson tracks and is worth $500. Paul Anka had cut a record by the time he reached the age of ten, and also recorded his own song, *Diana* (UK mauve label is £7 while the re-pressings with green or black labels are worth surprisingly more at £12). In four years he'd sold over 30 million discs, including the 1959 single *Lonely Boy* and the LP *Paul Anka* (both $50 today). Still with the looks, but much less talent, was Fabian – his 1962 *What Did They Do Before Rock & Roll* ★ is $400, the 1959 LP *Hold That Tiger* ★ $500 with a pink label, and the single *Johnny Angel* ★ $500 with picture sleeve, but just $20 without. Frankie Avalon's 1978 single *Why* is worth £50 as a 78' and the 1959 single *Bobby Sox to Stockings* is $40. Both of these characters drifted towards more stable careers in television.

Like Avalon, Bobby Rydell stemmed from Philadelphia. He has a big US list, including the 1959 LP *We Got Love* ($60), the

TEEN IDOLS

Singles

Paul Anka *Diana / It's Time to Cry / Lonely Boy / Put Your Head on My Shoulder*

Frankie Avalon *Bobby Sox to Stockings / Why*

Freddy Cannon *Tallahassee Lassie*

Chubby Checker *The Class / The Twist / You Just Don't Know*

Dion *Runaround Sue / The Wanderer*

Fabian *I'm a Man / Johnny Angel ★ / Turn Me Loose / What Did They Do Before Rock & Roll ★*

Brian Hyland *Ginny Come Lately / Itsy Bitsy Teeny Weeny Yellow Polka Dot Bikini*

Laurie London *He's Got the Whole World in His Hands*

Chris Montez *Let's Dance*

Ricky Nelson *Alone / Lonesome Town ★ / A Long Vacation ★ / A Teenager's Romance / Yes, Sir, That's My Baby ★ / You Are the Only One*

Ray Peterson *Corrina, Corrina / Shirley Purley / Tell Laura I Love Her*

Copycat– *A fat ex-chicken plucker, Chubby Checker's stage name was a deliberate parody of the existing star Fats Domino. Checker's first record* The Class *saw him mimic both Domino and Elvis Presley, and gain a Top 40 debut.*

Gene Pitney *Twenty Four Hours from Tulsa*

Cliff Richard *Fall in Love With You ★ / Living Doll ★ / Mean Streak ★ / What'd I Say ★*

Bobby Rydell *Dream Age ★ / Please Don't be Mad / Wild One*

Tommy Sands *Old Oaken Bucket / Teenage Crush*

Tommy Steele *Doomsday Rock / Rock with the Caveman*

Johnny Tillotson *Jimmy's Girl / Poetry in Motion / True True Happiness ★*

Bobby Vee *How Many Tears*

Marty Wilde *Donna / Endless Sleep / Teenager in Love*

LPs

Paul Anka *Paul Anka*

Frankie Avalon *The Young Frankie Avalon*

Freddy Cannon *Bang On / The Explosive Freddie Cannon ★*

Chubby Checker *It's Pony Time*

Dion *Lovers Who Wander / Presenting Dion and The Belmonts ★ / Runaround Sue ★*

Fabian *Hold That Tiger ★ / Rockin' Hot / Young & Wonderful*

Brian Hyland *Sealed with a Kiss / The Bashful Blonde ★*

Chris Montez *Let's Dance & Have Some Kinda Fun*

Ricky Nelson *Ricky ★*

Ray Peterson *Tell Laura I Love Her ★*

Gene Pitney *The Many Sides of Gene Pitney*

Bobby Rydell *All The Hits ★ / We Got Love*

Tommy Steele *The Tommy Steele Stage Show*

Johnny Tillotson *It Keeps Right on Hurtin'*

Bobby Vee *Take Good Care of My Baby*

Marty Wilde *Wilde About Marty*

red vinyl LP *All the Hits ★* ($150), and the 1960 million-selling single *Wild One* (£6). Dion also has a huge list, with UK 78's ranging from £50 to £75, while in the US the 1959 LP *Presenting Dion and The Belmonts ★* is now £275. His hit *Runaround Sue* is worth $50 and the 1961 album *Runaround Sue ★* is $800 with gold-, green-, or blue-coloured vinyl.

Gene Pitney sustained a career long after his hit single *Twenty-Four Hours from Tulsa* (£5) and EP *Town without Pity* (£60). Chris Montez's success hinged on one huge 1960 dance hit *Let's Dance* ($5) – the *Let's Dance* EP is £49 and the LP *Let's Dance & Have Some Kinda Fun* is £4. Chubby Checker scored a 10-million sale by covering Hank Ballard's *The Twist ★* (worth $15, or up to $200 for DJ copies on a white label with blue print). Others also traded in teenage dreams: Johnny Tillotson's 1960 single *Poetry in Motion* is $20, Brian Hyland's *Sealed With a Kiss* LP $40, Tommy Sands' single *Teenage Crush* £18, and Bobby Vee's LP *Take Good Care of My Baby* is $30.

The UK had Billy Fury (*see* Merseybeat, page 187), as well as rival Marty Wilde, who enjoyed success with covers of the US hits *Endless Sleep* (£12) and *Donna* (£30 as a 78'). The EP *Presenting Marty Wilde* is now worth £45. Tommy Steele began his varied career by playing at being young and cute, producing the 1956 singles *Rock with the Caveman* (£35) and *Doomsday Rock* (£30). Cliff Richard's long career has created a huge collectors' list, although there is little US interest. His EPs average at £50 each now, while LPs are slightly less. The 1959 single *Living Doll ★* is worth £100 as a 78', the 1963 single *What'd I Say ★* £300 (export issue), the EP *Cinderella ★* £100, and the single *Fall in Love with You ★* £150+.

> *One-Hit Wonders – Laurie London was just 14 when* He's Got the Whole World in his Hands *(£6) sold a million copies. He was huge in the US but only a minor hit in the UK, and later became a croupier at a London casino. Ray Peterson also had one major hit,* Tell Laura I Love Her, *in 1960 ($25).*

Headliners

This section looks at the dominant talent that had worldwide fan bases. This does of course include David Bowie, whose 1980 LP *Scary Monsters (and Super Creeps) ★* is worth £600 as the semi-official factory special in purple vinyl, but we have dealt with him within Glam Rock (*see* page 86). Elvis Presley is likewise discussed within Rock Roots, although as the second most collectable artist in the world the collecting

EPs

Paul Anka *Diana*

Freddy Cannon *Four Direct Hits*

Laurie London *Laurie London / Little Laurie London No.2*

Chris Montez *Let's Dance*

Gene Pitney *Town without Pity*

Cliff Richard *Cinderella* ★

Tommy Sands *Steady Date with Tommy Sands*

Bobby Vee *Sincerely*

Marty Wilde *Presenting Marty Wilde*

HEADLINERS

Singles

Johnny Burnette *Bigger Man* ★ / *Dreamin'* / *Drinkin' Wine Spo-Dee-Dee* ★ / *Eager Beaver* ★ / *Lonesome Train* ★ / *Midnight Train* ★ / *Rock Billy Boogie* ★ / *Tear it Up* ★ / *The Train Kept a-Rollin'* ★ / *You're Undecided* ★

Buddy Holly *Blue Days* ★ / *Peggy Sue Got Married* ★

Michael Jackson *Got to Be There / Someone in the Dark / Thriller*

Roy Orbison *Crying / Devil Doll* ★ / *I'm Hurtin'* ★

Elvis Presley *Can't Help Falling in Love* ★ / *Jailhouse Rock* ★ / *Milkcow Blues Boogie* ★ / *Old Shep* ★

LPs

David Bowie *Scary Monsters (and Super Creeps)* ★

Johnny Burnette *Johnny Burnette & The Rock n' Roll Trio* ★ / *Johnny Burnette Sings*

Buddy Holly *Buddy Holly* ★

EPs

Buddy Holly *Listen to Me* ★ / *That'll Be the Day* ★

Roy Orbison *Hillybilly Rock* ★

choice is huge, and US prices terrifying. For example, the 1957 single *Jailhouse Rock* ★ is $10,000 if with gold label and gold vinyl, a picture-sleeved single *Can't Help Falling in Love* ★ is $4,000 and the 1955 single *Milkcow Blues Boogie* ★ $5,000. Beware of the single *Tell Me Pretty Baby*, which has the same song on both sides. It claims to be Elvis' first studio recording but it's not and is worth just $2.50.

Roy Orbison offers a haunting catalogue of classic singles, like the 1960 *I'm Hurtin'* ★ $120, *Crying* $40 with picture sleeve, and *Devil Doll* ★ $250, while his 1957 EP *Hillybilly Rock* ★ is £125 if picture sleeved with a mauve/silver label and tri-centre. Buddy Holly is another globally revered figure who offers plenty to collectors – his 1956 single *Blue Days* ★ is £650 as a 45' or £220 as a 78', and the 1978 *Peggy Sue Got Married* ★ is £200. Desirable EPs include 1958's *Listen to Me*, which is worth £350 if the cover shows him without glasses but just £40 with them, and *That'll Be the Day* ★, which is $2,000 if the liner notes are on the back, but if it shows mini record adverts then the price is $600. His 1958 LP *Buddy Holly* ★ fetches $400 if it features a maroon label.

Early Warning – According to a leading UK dealer, Buddy Holly's 1960 EP The Late Great Buddy Holly *is reputedly one of the very last to use the collectable tri-centres, and so this will probably rise in value to several hundred pounds as a result – currently it is worth just £50.*

Michael Jackson's status naturally places him here, but due to mass sales he has relatively muted modern prices – $3 on average for US singles – which makes him borderline. However, the 1983 single *Thriller* is £50, with an LP and remix versions on a 12" calendar picture disc, and a 1997 withdrawn CD, *Smiles* ★, is £500, which all suggests that in time values will rise.

If you want to get serious, then try collecting the work of a Memphis ex-tug boat deck hand who played guitar by the age of five and co-wrote three Ricky Nelson million-sellers – this is, of course, Johnny Burnette. In the same mould as Presley, his work is highly prized by collectors. Singles from 1956 include *Tear it Up* ★ ($300), *Midnight Train* ★ ($300), *The Train Kept a-Rollin'* ★ ($250), and *Lonesome Train* ★ (£550). A year later came *Eager Beaver* ★ (£250), *Drinkin' Wine Spo-Dee-Dee* ★ ($300), and *Rock Billy Boogie* ★ ($300).

PACK ANIMALS

Singles

Terry Dene
A White Sports Coat

Craig Douglas *Nothin'
Shakin' / Teenager in Love*

David Essex *And the Tears
Came Tumbling Down / Can't
Nobody Love You / This Little
Girl of Mine*

Adam Faith *(Got a) Heartsick
Feeling / A Message to Martha /
High School Confidential*

Frank Ifield *I Remember You*

Tom Jones *Chills and Fever*

Mike Sarne *Just like Eddie*

Rod Stewart *The Day Will
Come ★ / Shake ★*

LPs

Dave Berry *The Special Sound
of Dave Berry / Dave Berry '68*

Craig Douglas *Craig Douglas*

Adam Faith
England's Top Singer

Heinz *Tribute to Eddie*

Tom Jones *A-Tom-ic Jones*

Eden Kane *It's Eden*

Mike Sarne *Come Outside*

Rod Stewart *Reason to Believe*

EPs

Terry Dene *The Golden Disc /
Terry Dene No 1*

Heinz *Heinz*

Frank Ifield
Just One More Chance

Eden Kane *Well I Ask You*

Mike Sarne
Mike Sarne Hit Parade

If you still have savings left then there are LPs such as the 1956 *Johnny Burnette & The Rock 'n' Roll Trio ★*, which is worth $6,000 with a maroon label reading "made in USA".

Pack Animals

Lesser mortals attempted to emulate the biggest stars, and this has generated yet another collecting layer. Terry Dene struggled to be the UK's Elvis with his 1957 single *A White Sports Coat* (£30), and the EPs *The Golden Disc* (£35) and *Terry Dene No 1* (£50), but unfortunately he succumbed to a breakdown. Sheffield's Dave Berry tried to emulate Gene Vincent – LPs include *The Special Sound of Dave Berry* (£45) and the 1968 *Dave Berry* (£30) – but failed in his vision of reincarnation as a snake. Adam Faith was at one time a singer and at other times a manager, actor, and journalist. Only his first singles are worthwhile, such as *(Got a) Heartsick Feeling* (£90) and *High School Confidential* (£70), while a typically humble US LP *England's Top Singer* is now $40. Other figures included Eden Kane, who made the 1962 EP *Well I Ask You* (£25), or Heinz who produced *Tribute to Eddie* (£60) – the Eddie in the title being Eddie Cochran.

David Essex delivered theatrical good looks and credible records like *Hold Me Close*, although only his early singles carry value today. The 1965 singles *And the Tears Came Tumbling Down* and *Can't Nobody Love You* are both worth £35. Isle of Wight milkman Craig Douglas also delivered loads of hits, including *Teenager in Love* (£6) and the LP *Craig Douglas* (£45). Tom Jones released many records, but the highest valued is the 1965 LP *A-Tom-ic Jones*, which is still just £15. Rod Stewart did muster two worthwhile singles in 1965 – *The Day Will Come ★* and *Shake ★*, which are each £100 – but again his best LP, *Reason to Believe*, is just £30 (originally it was only available via Marks & Spencer) – not really the stuff of pop idols.

Multi-talents – Mike Sarne may have delivered only lighthearted hits, such as Will I What *with Billie Davis (£6) and the EP* Mike Sarne Hit Parade *(£50), but he was multilingual and provided phonetic foreign translations for artists such as Billy Fury and John Leyton.*

Pop Girls *"PUTTING GLAMOUR INTO POP"*

Suggested Strands
Groups
Traditional
Independent Women
Adventurers
Mainstays

Average Record Cost
☆☆☆

Rising Stars
Brenda Lee
The Ronettes
The Chiffons
Kate Bush

GROUPS
Singles

The Bangles *Manic Monday*

Blondie *In the Flesh/XOffender / X Offender/In the Sun* ★

The Crystals *He Hit Me (It Felt Like a Kiss) / (Let's Dance) The Screw* ★

The Go-Gos *The Wild One*

The Nolans *Blackpool*

The Pointer Sisters
Don't Try to Take the Fifth / Fire

The Ronettes *I Want a Boy* ★ *My Darling Angel* ★ */ Walkin' in the Rain* ★

The Shangri-Las *Leader of the Pack / Simon Says / Wishing Well*

The Shirelles *I Met Him on a Sunday* ★ */ Will You Love Me Tomorrow*

The Slits *Typical Girls*

The Supremes
Your Heart Belongs to Me ★

The Three Degrees
Maybe Yours

With today's Pop charts filled with talented females it's hard for new generations to appreciate how the early chart era was so dominated by male performers. Rock & Roll was male territory – that is until in the early '60s when classic girl groups began to appear. Emerging in the brief gap between Rock & Roll's initial thrust and the invasion of The Beatles, these girl groups may have looked wimpish by modern standards, but they certainly paved the way for modern female chart presence.

Groups

The first real girl-group success story was The Shirelles, with their classic 1960 No.1 *Will You Love Me Tomorrow* (£10), although their single from two years earlier, *I Met Him on a Sunday*, is more prized at £60. The pattern they set was of polished appearances and performances – often with good harmonies (born of Doo Wop), and classic songs with mostly optimistic yet vulnerable lyrics. Most companies spotted the potential of such groups, but it was the Philles label and its owner Phil Spector who acted first. He culled baskets of good songs, grandiose productions, and teams of girl groups. When The Crystals' 1962 single *He Hit Me (It Felt Like a Kiss)* ★ ($100) was withdrawn and replaced with *He's a Rebel*, the lead singer wasn't around so Darlene Love sang it instead. The Ronettes increasingly gained Spector's favour – indeed, he married one of the girls. *Presenting the Fabulous Ronettes Featuring Veronica* ★ is rare and sought after – if the LP has a plum-coloured label it is £100, while a black label is £50 (five different versions exist altogether).

> *Label Conscious – The high school group The Poquelles became The Shirelles and made a record for the tiny Tiara label. The label was then licensed to Decca and the hit became* I Met Him on a Sunday ★. *Various pressings are worth £6 to £45, but the original Tiara copies fetch $800.*

In the UK in the 1960s there were less glamorous groups like The Vernon Girls – *We Love The Beatles* (single $30), and the 1970s group The Nolans – *The Nolan Sisters*, which was sold only at a London Club, is £25. In the '70s the US Pointer Sisters added slick style, while Blondie brought Debbie Harry's

The Vernon Girls
We Love The Beatles

LPs

Blondie *Parallel Lines*

The Chiffons *The Chiffons / My Secret Love ★ / One Fine Day ★*

The Crystals *He's a Rebel ★*

The Go-Gos *Swim With the Go-Gos*

The Vernon Girls *The Vernon Girls*

The Nolans *The Nolan Sisters*

The Ronettes *Presenting The Fabulous Ronettes Featuring Veronica ★*

The Slits *Cut / The Return of the Giant Slits*

The Supremes *Meet The Supremes ★*

EPs

The Chiffons *He's So Fine*

The Shangri-Las *The Shangri-Las*

TRADITIONAL

Singles

Petula Clark *First You Are My True Love*

Alma Cogan *Bell Bottom Blues / Blue Again*

Connie Francis *Lipstick on Your Collar / My First Real Love ★*

Anita Harris *Just Loving You / The Playground*

Lulu *Shout*

Susan Maughan *Bobby's Girl*

LPs

Petula Clark *Pet Clark / Petula Clark Sings / Petula Clark Swings in the Jungle ★ / Prends Mon Coeur*

Alma Cogan *Alma Sings With You in Mind*

charms to the world – watch out for *X Offender/In the Sun* – a 1977 unissued promo-only single worth £750 in the UK, but just $30 in the USA. Another rare LP, *Meet the Supremes ★*, by The Supremes is worth $900 if the cover shows the group sitting on stools, while close-up portrait versions are $30–40.

Traditional

The clean-cut female singer also had her place in the charts. Domestic UK entertainer Susan Maughan's single *Bobby's Girl* (£6) reached No.3 in October 1962. Likewise, Anita Harris' *Just Loving You* (£6) made the UK's No.6, although the follow up *The Playground* (£15) only made it to No.46. Alma Cogan dominated the '50s with 18 chart appearances, as well as films and TV – her LP *Alma Sings With You in Mind* is £80, and the 1957 EP *She Loves to Sing* £30. Petula Clark offers a huge range of vinyl covering 40 years. Surrey-born, she was in movies by the age of 12 and moved to France in 1959, establishing record and TV fame there. She returned to the UK in 1962 to do a BBC series and then went on to Hollywood. Not just a talent and a shrewd businesswoman, her multilingual skills created a substantial French catalogue that is worth collecting. Her 1959 LP *Prends Mon Coeur* was already worth £75 over a decade ago. Also watch for a 1966 Coca-Cola-labelled US promo LP, *Petula Clark Swings in the Jungle ★*, as it's now worth $150. Glasgow's Marie Lawrie (Lulu) won her first singing contest aged five, had a group (The Gleneagles) while still at school, was invited to audition, made the 1964 Top 10 single *Shout* (£7), and has remained a star ever since. Subsequent singles struggled, until a two-year patch with producer Mickie Most created seven straight hit singles and two albums. Such success affords great foreign-release collections including picture sleeves from Malaysia, Argentina, and New Zealand. Lulu is an easy collectable as her records are not expensive.

> *Secret Love – Born in London, Alma Cogan was a true '50s star, loved by all; Paul McCartney even played on one of her B-sides. A big fan of TV's* The Man From UNCLE, *she actually recorded a tribute record,* We Love Ya Illya, *under the pseudonym Angela and The Fans.*

As discussed in the Hit Paraders section, Connie Francis is a wise collecting subject (*see* pages 39–40). Her single *Lipstick on Your Collar* has gone from £10 to £40 in a decade, and

Connie Francis
Who's Sorry Now

Lulu *Something to Shout About*

Susan Maughan
I Wanna Be Bobby's Girl But …

EPs

Anita Harris *Anita Harris*

Lulu *Lulu*

Alma Cogan *She Loves to Sing*

INDEPENDENT WOMEN

Singles

Kate Bush *Eat the Music* ★ /
Moving/Them Heavy People ★ /
Wuthering Heights

Madonna *Borderline /
Keep It Together*

Marianne Faithfull *Sister
Morphine* ★ / *Something Better*

LPs

Laurie Anderson
The United States Live 5 LPs

Celine Dion
La Voix du Bon Dieu

Madonna *Like a Virgin*

Marianne Faithfull *Broken
English / Loveinamist /
Marianne Faithfull*

ADVENTURERS

Singles

Julie Driscoll
Take Me by the Hand

Maureen Evans *Like I Do*

Sam Fox *Aim to Win*

Dana Gillespie *Donna, Donna*

Lesley Gore *It's My Party*

Françoise Hardy *Catch a
Falling Star / The "Yeh Yeh"
Girl from Paris*

Melanie *My Beautiful People /
Ruby Tuesday*

Hayley Mills *Johnny Jingo*

My First Real Love ★ from £80 to £175. However, not all is logical – the 1958 album *Who's Sorry Now* has dropped from £70 to £60 in the same period!

Independent Women

The 1980s produced considerable polarization of gender power bases, which threw up excesses of expectation that anything female would succeed, irrespective of talent. However, truly gifted women were already recording fascinating records. For example, Marianne Faithfull had been a '60s media "doll", yet she delivered a wrenching personal audio statement with the 1979 LP *Broken English* (the later '95 audiophile copies are worth $25). Also watch for her single *Sister Morphine* ★ (now $100) or the withdrawn *Something Better* (£35).

Laurie Anderson revels in live performance art, and she had a massive hit by accident – an 8-minute single, *O, Superman*, that was made for the tiny New York 110 Records. Other avant-garde Pop albums followed, which included collaborations with Lou Reed, Peter Gabriel, and Brian Eno. Her major seven-hour multi-media show makes fascinating listening – *The United States Live* 5-LP box set fetches $30 today. Kate Bush stunned with her initial single *Wuthering Heights* (£40 with picture sleeve), and went on to create volumes of haunting records and images. Her cancelled single *Eat the Music* ★ fetches £1,500 today as only 17 exist.

> *Making the Most of Time – Kate Bush's rarest record was a Seiko-sponsored promo disc* Moving/Them Heavy People *, to coincide with her first Japanese visit. The 25 with sleeves, including watch advert, are currently £500, while the 200 lesser ones without the advert are £300.*

Madonna was, relatively speaking, a newcomer at this time, but by the end of the '80s she'd already sold 30 million records and had six UK and US No.1s. Her commercial adventures and self-styling naturally produced quantities of future collectables, although their high sales are currently tempering values. The most expensive today include a *Like a Virgin* album in white vinyl with silver spine, which is $60 (normal ones $3), and her 1984 *Borderline* single with fold-out poster sleeve, which is $80. However, you shouldn't buy everything that you find – she has become such big business that it will take time to identify what is truly collectable.

Adrienne Posta *When a Girl Really Loves You / Only Fifteen / Shang a Doo Lang*

Twiggy *Over and Over / When I Think of You*

Twinkle *Terry*

LPs

Julie Driscoll *Julie Driscoll – 1969*

Maureen Evans *Like I Do*

Sam Fox *Touch Me*

Dana Gillespie *Book of Surprises / Foolish Season*

Lesley Gore *It's My Party and I'll Cry If I Want To*

Melanie *Candles in the Rain*

Hayley Mills *Let's Get Together*

EPs

Maureen Evans *Melancholy Me*

Twinkle *Twinkle – a Lonely Singing Doll*

Lesley Gore *Lesley Gore*

MAINSTAYS

Singles

Pat Benatar *Day Gig*

Cilla Black *Anyone Who Had a Heart / Is It Love?*

Skeeter Davis *Time Seller*

Kiki Dee *I Dig You Baby / Now the Flowers Cry*

Brenda Lee *Ain't That Love ★ / Dynamite ★ / I'm Gonna Lassoo Santa Claus ★ / Ring-a-Phone ★ / Sweet Nothin's ★*

Olivia Newton-John *If Not for You / Take Me Home Country Road /Till You Say You'll be Mine ★*

Linda Ronstadt *Living in the USA / Silk Purse / Simple Dreams*

Diana Ross *Reach Out and Touch / Top of the World*

Decried in fashionable circles, Celine Dion is well worth watching from a collecting point of view. She has a substantial French-Canadian catalogue – one 1981 album, *La Voix du Bon Dieu*, is already £75. The rich French-language list is currently worth around £25–50 each, which is substantially more than her international fare fetches.

Adventurers

Career paths aren't always obvious. Twiggy could never have expected the legacy of her modelling work to be collectors' records such as *When I Think of You* (£15), likewise Sam Fox, whose *Aim to Win* 12" picture disc is £12. Melanie attended acting school, but just for two months. Reputedly she went to a play audition but ended up in a music business office, played, and joined Buddah records; *Ruby Tuesday* ($5) was her biggest record. Twinkle had an upper-class background and promised to attend finishing school if her first record failed – this became the cult 1964 bikers' anthem *Terry* (£6).

Actresses had a public platform to help them embrace the record industry. Hayley Mills' screen debut was in the 1959 *Tiger Bay*, then 14 movies followed in the next decade, along with stray vinyl releases such as *Let's Get Together* (£12 or $40) and *Johnny Jingo* (picture-sleeved single $25). Adrienne Posta started out in Pop music aged 15, then in 1966 appeared in the movies *To Sir With Love* and *Here We Go Round the Mulberry Bush*, both of which had Pop music in them. Her records include the 1964 *Shang a Doo Lang* (£15) and the 1966 *When a Girl Really Loves You* ($10). Françoise Hardy added sex appeal to the mix of movie star and pop star – her single *The "Yeh Yeh" Girl from Paris* is worth $25.

> *Going for It – The 17-year-old Lesley Gore made a record, only to discover that Phil Spector and The Crystals were doing the same one. So she recorded extra acetates and rushed them to the local radio. On air within the week, her first-ever record,* It's My Party, *became the American No.1.*

A music business secretary and organizer of The Yardbirds fan club, Julie Driscoll joined The Long John Baldrey Steampacket alongside Rod Stewart and Brian Auger and The Trinity. In 1965 the group dissolved, but the remnants, who included Jools, had a Top 5 hit with *This Wheel's on Fire* (£7) – the composition that was used for TV's *Absolutely Fabulous*. Maureen Evans

Sandie Shaw
As Long as You're Happy Baby

Dusty Springfield   *Losing You*

Tina Turner
Same Old Feeling / Tarzan

Bonnie Tyler   *Lost in France /
Total Eclipse of the Heart*

LPs

Pat Benatar
In the Heat of the Night

Cilla Black   *Cilla*

Skeeter Davis   *End of the World*

Kiki Dee   *Great Expectations*

Brenda Lee   *Grandma What
Great Songs You Sang*

Olivia Newton-John
Music Makes My Day

Stevie Nicks   *Bella Donna /
The Other Side of the Mirror*

Helen Shapiro   *Helen's
Sixteen / A Teenager in Love*

Sandie Shaw   *Me*

Dusty Springfield   *Dusty /
A Girl Called Dusty / Stay Awhile*

Tina Turner   *Private Dancer*

EPs

Skeeter Davis   *Silver Threads
and Golden Needles*

Cilla Black   *Time for Cilla*

Kiki Dee   *Kiki Dee*

Helen Shapiro
A Teenager Sings the Blues

Sandie Shaw   *Sandie Shaw in
French / Sandy Shaw in Italian*

Dusty Springfield
Mademoiselle Dusty

sang in the shadows, recording cheap covers of American hits for the Woolworths label until she broke loose with her own '63 single, *Like I Do* (£12), and matching album *Like I Do* (£40).

Mainstays

These artists may lack excitement, but from a collector's vantage point they frequently produce large bodies of work, and many foreign-country releases that are great collectable targets. Brenda Lee is a good example – she was broadcasting Country songs at the age of seven and had a gold disc award by the age of 15. Her debut album in 1960 was *Grandma What Great Songs You Sang* ($50). However, earlier singles like the 1957 *Dynamite* ★ and 1958 *Ring-a-Phone* ★, which are both tri-centred, are each worth £125. *Sweet Nothin's* ★ raised her chart profile – the US picture-sleeved version is $120, while UK 78's fetch £150. The hits continued into the '60s, before Lee returned to Country; she was still recording in the 1990s.

Dusty Springfield sang with The Lana Sisters, followed by The Springfields with brother Tom – this group had the hits *Island of Dreams* and *Silver Threads and Golden Needles* (each £5). She then developed an impressive solo career, although the resulting records are currently static in value – *A Girl Called Dusty* LP is £20 and the *Mademoiselle Dusty* EP £25.

> *One-Hit Wonder – Take a Troggs song, session musicians, and an ex-Penthouse Pet singer and call them Fancy. Their* Wild Thing *became a huge US hit. Unprepared, the group tried another song without success, changed their line-up to offer* Something to Remember *(£12), and ultimately failed.*

Many of the big stars are still too recent, with too many hit records to show collectors' prices yet, but rest assured that they will. Bonnie Tyler's single *Total Eclipse of the Heart* is £6, but the much earlier *Lost in France* is also just $6 right now. Stevie Nicks' LP *The Other Side of the Mirror* is £15 – the early copies, which are worth grabbing, had holograms. Pat Benatar's hit LP *In the Heat of the Night* is $25 for audiophile copies – everything else is under $5 except *Day Gig*, an earlier Mace label single worth $40. Tina Turner's huge hit-LP *Private Dancer* is still common, but her 1951 single *Same Old Feeling* is now worth $30. Diana Ross' DJ copies of *Top of the World* are worth $50 each, and Linda Ronstadt's top-selling album *Living in the USA* had limited numbers in red vinyl, which are now worth £12.

Pop Groups *"FAVOURITES & SECRETS"*

Suggested Strands

General Groups
Status Bands
Hidden Talents
Bubblegum
Instrumentals

Average Record Cost

☆☆☆☆

Rising Stars

The Kinks
The Rolling Stones
Duane Eddy (& The Rebels)

GENERAL GROUPS

Singles

The Dave Clark Five *Bits and Pieces / Chaquita / Glad All Over / Over and Over* ★

The Spencer Davis Group *Dimples / Keep on Running*

The Hollies *(Ain't That) Just Like Me / The Baby*

Johnny Kidd and The Pirates *Please Don't Touch*

Manfred Mann *5-4-3-2-1 / Hubble Bubble* ★ */ Why Should We Not*

Brian Poole and The Tremeloes *Twist and Shout*

The Roulettes *I Can't Stop* ★

The Small Faces *All or Nothing / Small Faces* ★

Traffic *Paper Sun*

The Tremeloes *Here Comes My Baby / Silence is Golden*

The Zombies *She's Not There*

LPs

Badfinger *Magic Christian Music / Straight Up / Wish You Were Here*

Over the years the very definition of Pop has drifted from being a precise term to an umbrella phrase, used to describe any record of three or four minutes' duration that attracts reasonable audiences. It's artistically bizarre to embrace, for example, The Rolling Stones and The Monkees in the same section, and yet both have pursued mass sales through the singles charts. It is this that is the essential definition of a Pop record. Collecting this style of music is primarily driven by fans of a specific group or star, whose supporting group has often been ignored, dropped, or succeeded separately.

General Groups

Here we take a brief look at the general group marketplace. One of the most quintessential British Pop groups was The Hollies. Hailing from Manchester, they were initially a duo and then briefly became The Deltas. As The Hollies they created a vast and affordable collectors' list – their UK EPs are generally more valued than their LPs. The 1964 *Here I Go Again* is worth £40 and 1966 *I Can't Let Go* is £45 (both EPs). In the USA the picture-sleeved single *The Baby* is worth $50, and the LP *Here I Go Again* ★ $150, if black-labelled with stars.

The Spencer Davis Group draws very little collecting today in the UK or the USA – their most tempting item is the unissued LP *Letters from Edith* ★, as the 50 white label test pressings are worth £200 each. By contrast, Adam Faith's group The Roulettes has had far more success – the 1966 one-sided single *I Can't Stop* ★ fetches £120 with picture sleeve, and the 1965 album *Steak and Chips* ★ is worth £450.

At the height of the Merseybeat explosion Brian Poole and The Tremeloes, from Barking, were the only southerners impacting the charts. *Do You Love Me* made No.1 and *Twist & Shout* No.4 – each is under £5 today. However, the 1964 EP *Brian Poole & The Tremeloes* is £30. Poole dropped The Tremeloes, and they promptly enjoyed twice as many hits – the 1967 singles *Here Comes My Baby* and *Silence is Golden* are both £5.

> *Overlooked – Virtually unknown in their native UK, Chad and Jeremy enjoyed 11 American chart hits in 1964. After moving to Hollywood, they made frequent TV appearances on series like* Batman. *Rival record companies Columbia and Capitol both issued releases from them in 1965.*

The Dave Clark Five
The Dave Clark Five ★

The Spencer Davis Group
Letters from Edith ★

The Hollies *Here I Go Again* ★

The Rockin' Berries *In Town / Life is a Bowl of Berries*

The Roulettes *Steak and Chips* ★

The Small Faces *Ogden's Nut Gone Flake / Small Faces*

Traffic *Mr Fantasy*

The Tremeloes *It's About Time*

The Zombies *Begin Here* ★ / *Odyssey and Oracle*

EPs

The Hollies
Here I Go Again / I Can't Let Go

Johnny Kidd and The Pirates
Shakin' All Over

Manfred Mann *Mann Made*

Brian Poole and The Tremeloes
Brian Poole & The Tremeloes

The Rockin' Berries
Happy to be Blue

The Tremeloes *My Little Lady*

STATUS BANDS

Singles

ABBA *Anniversary Boxed Set* ★ / *Ring Ring / Under Attack / The Winner Takes it All*

The Everly Brothers
Bye Bye Love / Keep A Lovin' Me ★ / *Wake up Little Susie* ★

The Fairies *Don't Mind / Don't Think Twice / Get Yourself Home* ★

The Kinks *Long Tall Sally / One of the Survivors* ★ / *You Still Want Me*

Queen *Bohemian Rhapsody / Bohemian Rhapsody* ★ / *Man on the Prowl* ★ / *The Show Must Go On*

The Rolling Stones
Come On / Heart of Stone ★ / *Not Fade Away* ★ / *Poison Ivy* ★

Status Bands

The Rolling Stones' Pop credentials are clearly visible in their early '60s singles. *Poison Ivy* ★ is worth a huge £400 – it is a cancelled export version, but there are some record club copies around. *Not Fade Away* ★ fetches $1,000 if it is the rare version with a white label, black print, and "*London*" in script type on top. Even rarer still is the 1964 LP *Let it Bleed* ★. It's worth a massive $10,000 in one-off form – this is a semi-official pressing using red/blue and green vinyl mixed with a huge yellow star.

The Kinks look worthwhile for collectors. The 1964 singles *Long Tall Sally* (£60) and *You Still Want Me* (£90) fetch reasonable prices while the 1966 EP *The Kinks* ★ is now £200, and the LP *The Kinks Kontroversy* is £175 in export form. An unissued 12-track LP, *The Kinks Are the Village Green Preservation Society* ★, is worth £600+, but only two test pressings are known to exist; the regular LP had 15 tracks and is £70 in mono, £35 in stereo. Short-lived band The Fairies were in the same mould as The Kinks and have very collectable singles. The 1964 *Don't Think Twice* is £75, 1965 *Don't Mind* £75, and *Get Yourself Home* ★ £140, also '65.

> *Chart Surprise – Manfred Mann's third single 5-4-3-2-1 (£7) became the theme music for the '60s TV show* Ready Steady Go. *After various Pop hits they renamed themselves Manfred Mann's Earth Band to become more serious Prog Rock figures and promptly had a hit with* Blinded by the Light *(£6).*

ABBA were masters of Pop, and their earlier material can be found on vinyl. Their single *Ring Ring* is £45, the LP *Voulez Vous* £70 in picture-disc form, and their limited 26-single *Anniversary Boxed Set* ★, which is in blue vinyl and numbered to 2,000, now fetches £350 (unnumbered sets are £100). Despite their stage status, The Who were never big record sellers but the 1968 single *My Generation* ★ is £125 in export picture-sleeve form and the 1970 US single *Young Man* ★ is $500 if picture sleeved. A withdrawn mail-order-only LP *Who Did It* ★ is worth £350. The Everly Brothers were a classic singles group who offered valuable gems like the 1957 *Wake up Little Susie* ★ ($250 with picture sleeve) and *Keep A Lovin' Me* ★ ($600 with maroon label). The promo sampler LP *It's Everly Time!* ★, issued when they joined Warner Bros, is now $600. Queen also created great Pop singles – for further details on the group *see* Glam Rock (page 87).

The Who *I Can't Explain / My Generation ★ / Young Man ★*

LPs

ABBA *Voulez Vous*

Everly Brothers *Songs our Daddy Taught Us ★ / It's Everly Time! ★*

The Kinks *God save The Kinks ★ / The Kinks are the Village Green Preservation Society ★ / The Kinks Kontroversy ★*

The Rolling Stones *Beggars Banquet ★ / Let It Bleed ★ / Their Satanic Majesties Request ★*

The Who *Who Did It ★ / The Who Sell Out ★*

EPs

The Kinks *The Kinks ★*

HIDDEN TALENTS

Singles

The Birds *Leaving Here / No Good Without you Baby / You're on my Mind*

The Bo Street Runners *Bo Street Runners / Tell Me What You're Gonna Do*

Steve Bret and The Mavericks *Sugar Shack / Wishing*

Sean Buckley and The Breadcrumbs *It Hurts Me When I Cry*

The Cheynes *Going to the River / Respectable*

Neil Christian and The Crusaders *A Little Bit of Something Else*

Episode Six *Morning Dew / Put Yourself in My Place*

Micky Finn *Garden of my Mind / Reelin' & Rockin' / The Sporting Life*

Bobby Graham *Skin Deep / Zoom Widge and Wag*

The High Numbers *I'm the Face ★ / Zoot Suit ★*

Hidden Talents

With just a little knowledge of the forerunners to big groups you can discover some great collectable challenges. Group members moved around too, which polarized collector's values wherever future key figures came to rest. More tantalizing still is the apparent surge in unknown record values, often due to star session musicians.

> *Dads – Julian Lennon and Kim Wilde followed in their talented parents' footsteps, and in 1966 John Lennon's father Freddie reversed the trend, issuing the single* That's my Life *(£40). Elvis Costello's dad Ross McManus braved the ambitious LP ...* Sings Elvis Presley's Golden Hits *(£12).*

You may think that £1,000 is a lot for a 1964 self-titled EP *Bo Street Runners* ★ – until you discover it included Mick Fleetwood (as do The Cheynes' singles). Ronnie Wood's touch elevates The Birds' 1960s singles *You're on my Mind* (£75) and *No Good Without you Baby* (£65), while you'll need £200 to hear Ian Hunter's work on the '60s EP *Apex Rhythm & Blues All Stars* ★. Slade elements feature on The In-Betweens' 1966 single *You Better Run* ★ (£225), and The High Numbers' 1964 singles *I'm the Face* (£350) and *Zoot Suit* ★ (£300) appear outrageous until you discover this music was an embryonic The Who. John's Children singles *The Love I Thought I'd Found* ★ (£250 with picture sleeve) and *Midsummer Night's Scene* ★ (£2,000 as it was withdrawn) seem to fetch silly money until Marc Bolan's involvement is revealed. Davy Jones was in fact David Bowie, so the following single by Jones fetches a lot today – *You've Got a Habit of Leaving* ★, now £325. *You Stole My Love*, £90, by The Mockingbirds involves early 10cc elements, as does The Whirlwinds' *Look at Me* (£50). Episode Six link with Deep Purple, Mike Sheridan and The Night Riders are paired with E.L.O. and The Move, while Rory Storm and The Hurricanes often featured the drumming talents of Ringo Starr.

Jimmy Page

One of the UK's most-used guitarists, Jimmy Page would go on to feature in The Yardbirds and then Led Zeppelin. However, in the 1960s he appeared on many hopefuls' singles, blessing them today with great collecting value.

• Some of the hopefuls he worked with included Sean Buckley and The Breadcrumbs – the single *It Hurts Me When I Cry* ★ is worth £70 or $100. Northampton-based group

The In-Betweens
You Better Run ★

John's Children *Desdemona /
The Love I Thought I'd Found* ★ /
Midsummer Night's Scene ★

Davy Jones *You've Got a Habit
of Leaving* ★

The Mockingbirds *That's How
It's Gonna Stay/You Stole My Love*

The Pickwicks *Apple Blossom
Time / Little by Little*

The Primitives *Help Me* ★ /
You Said ★

Mike Sheridan and The Night
Riders *It's Only The Dogg /
Love Me Right Now* ★

Rory Storm and The
Hurricanes *I Can't Tell*

The Whirlwinds *Look at Me*

LPs

Mike Sheridan & The Night
Riders *Birmingham Beat*

EPs

Apex Rhythm and Blues All
Stars *Apex Rhythm & Blues
All Stars* ★

The Bo Street Runners
Bo Street Runners ★

BUBBLEGUM

Singles

The Archies *Bang-Shang-
a-Lang / Sugar Sugar*

The Banana Splits
Pretty Painted Carousel

David Cassidy *Get It Up For
Love / I think I Love You*

Dawn *Knock Three Times /
Tie a Yellow Ribbon*

Crazy Elephant *Gimme
Gimme Good Lovin / Land Rover*

The Cuff Links *Tracy*

Daddy Dewdrop *Chick-A-Boom*

DeFranco Family
*Heartbeat – It's a Lovebeat /
We Belong Together*

The Primitives' *You Said* ★ and *Help Me* ★ (on Pye) have also seen the Page touch raise their values to £180 and £165.

• Page also worked with Brian Auger, Blue Rondos, Neil Christian, Fifth Avenue, Micky Finn, Billy Fury, Wayne Gibson, Bobby Graham, Tom Jones, The Kinks, P.J. Proby, The Recaps, The Sneekers, Screaming Lord Sutch, The Talisman, Them, The Untamed, The Who, and The Zephyrs.

Bubblegum

The child of Rock & Roll, Bubblegum was created to entertain the second Pop music generation. These were the young teens that were brought up on Pop but naturally lacked enthusiasm for the then-fashionable protest songs and psychedelia.

Two forces united to forge this style, which spanned the mid-'60s until the early '70s. The first was the music industry's newfound profitability that had appeared via Rock, and this created a thirst to stretch trading. Secondly, it was noted that the younger market didn't go clubbing, rather they sat in front of the television – in their millions. The results were predictable: American entertainment executive Don Kirshner placed adverts casting for a musical TV series inspired by The Beatles' *Hard Day's Night*. The Monkees were born – their 1966 single *Last Train to Clarksville* is worth $30 with picture sleeve, and the LP *The Birds, The Bees and The Monkees* ★ is $100 in mono. Scorn poured from Rock's elite because they didn't record their own records, but that fact didn't bother the young market at all. The Partridge Family joined the youth assault – their single *I Think I Love You!* is $5 and the 1973 album *Bulletin Board* is $50.

> *Disinterested – Despite being greeted by 8,000 fans at
> Heathrow, and cute singles like* Long Haired Lover *from*
> Liverpool *($5) and* Young Love *(£4), The Osmonds failed to
> ignite collectors – most records are now in single figures.*

Lighthearted Bubblegum carried well with youth TV, on AM radio, and also in the music charts. It became further refined through TV animation. Various series also produced records, such as *The Banana Splits* with the 1969 *Pretty Painted Carousel* ($25 with picture sleeve) and the album *We're the Banana Splits* ★ ($200). The Archies' No.1 single *Sugar Sugar* is $10 and their 1969 promo set *Everything's Archie Box* ★, including an LP, photos, a press kit, and a lapel button, is $100.

The Jackson Five *Big Boy ★ / You Don't Have to be Over Twenty-One (to Fall in Love) ★*

The Jacksons *Blame It on the Boogie*

Tommy James and The Shondells *Crimson and Clover / Hanky Panky*

The Monkees *I'm a Believer / Last Train to Clarksville*

Ohio Express *Yummy Yummy Yummy*

The Osmonds *Long Haired Lover from Liverpool / Young Love*

The Partridge Family *I Think I Love You!*

Pipkins *Gimme Dat Ding*

Tommy Roe *Caveman ★ / Dance with Me / Dizzy / Sheila ★*

Bobby Sherman *Cold Girl*

Steam *Na Na Hey Hey Kiss Him Goodbye*

LPs

The Archies *Everything's Archie Box ★*

The Banana Splits *We're The Banana Splits ★*

David Cassidy *The Higher They Climb ★*

The Cufflinks *The Cufflinks*

Daddy Dewdrop *Daddy Dewdrop*

The Jackson Five *ABC*

The Jacksons *Victory*

Tommy James and The Shondells *Something Special*

The Monkees *The Birds, The Bees and The Monkees ★ / Head*

1910 Fruitgum Co. *Hard Ride / Simon Says*

Ohio Express *Beg, Borrow and Steel*

The Osmonds *New Sounds of The Brothers*

Tommy Roe *Phantasy / Sheila*

The Archies were masterminded by the songwriting hothouse of the Brill Building (*see* page 193) while two producers at Buddah Records saw the obvious advantages of quick, clean recordings with hired session men. The latter created the leading Bubblegum hit act The Ohio Express, as well as the successful 1910 Fruitgum Co. Inevitably, there were many one-hit wonders, such as Steam's *Na Na Hey Hey Kiss Him Goodbye* ($8 on Fontana in 1969 and $20 on Mercury in '76 with picture sleeve). The Cufflinks used an Archies singer for their 1969 hit *Tracy* ($25 with three-piece sleeve) and 1970 LP *The Cufflinks* ($20). Other shortlived acts include Pipkins, with the single *Gimme Dat Ding* ($6), Daddy Dewdrop, with *Chick-A-Boom* and their 1971 LP *Daddy Dewdrop* ($20), and Crazy Elephant's 1969 hit *Gimme Gimme Good Lovin'* ($8).

Some artists managed to supply the young market as well as retaining a long-term career. For example, Tommy Roe had hits with the 1969 singles *Dizzy* ($10) and *Jam up Jelly Tight* ($12 with picture sleeve), but his full list includes the earlier singles *Caveman* ★ ($100) and *Sheila* ★ ($150), and the LPs *Sheila* (£40) and *Phantasy* ($40). Tommy James and The Shondells scored 11 hits in '68, including *Hanky Panky* ($40) and the grown-up sounds of the classic hit *Crimson and Clover* ($15).

> *Inspiration – The Partridge Family were based on The Cowsills – a real-life family who had major hits like the US No.2* The Rain, The Park and Other Things *($12). Initially just four kids, The Cowsills grew to be six siblings and their mother, but they disbanded as Partridge was launched.*

Another cluster of artists appealed to the same young fans and were mini-idols, even though they were not strictly frivolous enough for Bubblegum. David Cassidy's involvement in The Partridge Family catapulted his record sales – for example, the single *I think I Love You!* sold a staggering five million. But young fans move on quickly and by 1985 his records struggled to tempt at all. *Romance (Let Your Heart Go)* includes a picture disc and pin-up of model Sam Fox, and an instrumental mix on the B-side, but is still worth just £8. In 1968 The Jackson Five pitched in with the singles *You Don't Have to be Over Twenty One (to Fall in Love)* ★ and *Big Boy* ★ (each worth $100), but *Blame it on the Boogie* from a decade later (when they had become The Jacksons) values at just £10. Britain's hugely successful band The Bay City Rollers contributed to this genre too (for further details *see* page 87).

Instrumentals

A now largely forgotten corner of Pop, instrumental music once was a normal part of the music charts. During the '50s pianists like Mrs Mills and Winifred Atwell had hits, as well as trumpet players like Eddie Calvert, and guitarists such as Bert Weedon. Then there was an entire raft of Trad Jazz hits, but what followed them? The benchmark modern instrumental was borne of an LA quintet of session musicians and a record executive on guitar – The Champs' classic 1958 track *Tequila* was initially the B-side to *Nowhere To Run.* It soared to the US No.1 spot and, despite other efforts, it proved to be their only hit. *Tequila* the single is $20, *Tequila* ★ the EP $150. One copy is known to exist of the *Tequila* ★ single in blue vinyl and this is worth $600, while the 1958 album *Go Champs Go* ★ is a breathtaking $2,400 if in blue vinyl, or just $250 if in black!

> *Act of God – Link Wray's key single* The Rumble *(£25) is the most important guitar record ever made – it literally gave birth to Rock's power chords. Pete Townshend spoke for everyone when he called Wray "The King", while Wray himself felt he had help from above.*

The dominant figure within instrumentals was guitarist Duane Eddy. He sold over 25 million records and had more UK chart success than anyone other than The Beatles. He was eventually pushed from power by the Liverpool band – as Beatlemania raged, Eddy released four singles and four LPs in a single year without impact. Now he is a major collectable: most of his singles, like *Yep* and *The Lonely One*, are worth around $50, while the 1957 single *Ramrod* ★ (by Duane Eddy and His Rock-A-Billies) is worth $1,500. Watch out for the 1958 LP *Have "Twangy" Guitar – Will Travel* ★, as it is $400 if Duane is sitting with his guitar case, but less if he's standing. Other instrumentalists of importance include The Tornados – their EP *The Sounds of The Tornados* ★ is worth $200 and the 1963 LP *Telstar* ★ $200. The Ventures' classic EP *Walk – Don't Run* is worth $80, while the $600 single *The Real McCoy* ★ was credited as being by Scott Douglas and The Venture Quintet. Johnny and The Hurricanes' 1959 hit *Red River Rock* is worth $50, while *Green Onions* by Booker T. and the M.G.'s is £40. There are two drum hits to look out for – Sandy Nelson's 1959 *Drum Party* (£50 as a 78') and Cozy Cole's *Topsy* ($200 in LP format).

Regional Pop *"MUSICAL POSTCARDS"*

MERSEYBEAT

Singles

The Dakotas *Cruel Sea / I Can't Break the News to Myself*

The Escorts *Dizzy Miss Lizzy*

Faron's Flamingos *Shake Sherry*

Gerry and The Pacemakers *How Do You Do It? / I Like It*

Billy J Kramer and The Dakotas *Do You Want to Know a Secret? / Little Children*

Tommy Quickly and The Remo Four *Tip of My Tongue*

The Searchers *Kinky Kathy / Sweets for my Sweet*

Freddie Starr and The Midnighters *Never Cry on Someone's Shoulder*

Rory Storm and The Hurricanes *Dr Feelgood*

The Swinging Blue Jeans *Do You Know*

Kingsize Taylor and The Dominoes *Hippy Hippy Shake*

LPs

The Escorts *Head to Toe*

Billy J Kramer and The Dakotas *Billy J*

The Merseybeats *The Merseybeats*

Regional Pop

Regional music provided individuality and today examples of such music make ideal collecting bases. For example, you may choose to collect Philly Sound, Nashville, or the more recent Ibiza sound signature. Here we look at two of the most popular: Liverpool's Mersey sounds and the American West Coast music of '60s California.

Merseybeat

There were around 300 bands active in the Liverpool area in the '60s (apart from The Beatles), developing a happy, upbeat guitar sound borne out of Skiffle fashions. Kingsize Taylor and The Dominoes are claimed by some to be the first Beat Group. Their 1963 EP *Twist & Shake* ★ is £100 and the 1964 single *Hippy Hippy Shake* £18. A local collaboration with a Hamburg Club provided vital stage experience for Mersey bands like Gerry and The Pacemakers, who had three consecutive No.1s in 1963, including *How Do You Do It?* (£6), and The Searchers – their hit *Sweets for my Sweet* is £6 and a rare 1962 privately pressed LP *The Searchers* ★ is £150+. Sharpened stage skills fuelled these bands, and this in turn led to the Merseybeat chart invasion. Triggered by The Beatles' 1963 *Please Please Me* (£60 with red labels), Merseybeat would dominate – at one point in 1963, six of the UK Top 10 singles were by Merseybeat bands.

> *Dream Night – Liverpool tug man Billy Fury was a fan of Marty Wilde. He went early to a show offering his songs and was invited to perform that evening. His stage name was invented, he did the whole tour, and within four months one of the songs from the tour had charted.*

Long forgotten now, The Escorts were voted ninth most popular Liverpool band in 1963 – their *Dizzy Miss Lizzy* single is £18 and the LP *Head to Toe* £25. Entrepreneur Brian Epstein couldn't break Tommy Quickly and The Remo Four but today their single *Tip of My Tongue* is worth a respectable £30. The band The Merseybeats enjoyed hits – their 1964 LP *The Merseybeats* is £85 today and the EP *On Stage* £30. Other leading figures include The Swinging Blue Jeans (their single *Do You Know* is £10 and the 1964 LP *Jeans A' Swinging* is

The Searchers *The Searchers ★*

The Swinging Blue Jeans *Blue Jeans A' Swinging*

Kingsize Taylor and The Dominoes *Teen Beat 2 ★*

CALIFORNIA SOUNDS

Singles

The Astronauts *Competition Coupe / Hot Doggin'*

The Beach Boys *Fun, Fun, Fun / Good Vibrations / Surfin'/Luau ★*

The Challengers *Hot Rod Show / Moondawg*

The Chantays *Pipeline*

The Crossfires *Fiberglass Jungle / Limbo Rock*

Dick Dale *King of the Surf*

The Hondells *Little Honda / You Meet the Nicest People on a Honda*

Jan and Dean *Baby Talk / Gee ★ / There's a Girl ★*

The Rip Chords *Here I Stand / Three Window Coupe*

Ronny and The Daytonas *Beach Boy / G.T.O.*

The Surfaris *A Christmas Surfer's List / Wipe Out ★*

The Trashmen *Bird '65 / Surfin' Bird ★ / Whoa Dad ★*

LPs

The Beach Boys *The Beach Boys' Christmas Album / Pet Sounds / Surf's Up ★*

The Challengers *Surfbeat ★*

The Chantays *Pipeline ★*

Dick Dale *King of the Surf Guitar ★ / Silver Sounds of Surf ★ / Summer Surf ★*

The Hondells *The Hondells*

Jan and Dean *Jan and Dean Take Linda Surfin' / Save for a Rainy Day ★*

The Rip Chords *Hey Little Cobra*

The Surfaris *Fun City USA*

£75), Freddie Starr and The Midnighters (the single *Never Cry on Someone's Shoulder* is £35), and Billy J Kramer and The Dakotas (*Do You Want to Know a Secret* is £5, while the export-only LP, *Billy J*, fetches £40). The Dakotas made solo records, such as the single *I Can't Break the News to Myself* (£55), but Kramer was unsuccessful as a solo artist.

Californian Sounds

This is a fascinating musical niche, albeit quite small. The "movement" lasted for just four or five years, but it has gone on to influence songwriters and musicians around the world. Not all those involved even came from California, but the music acted like an audio postcard of that state's sunshine and good life. As a potential collector you could concentrate either on the tiny handful of key figures, or open up a much wider hunt for many of the one-hit Surfin' groups.

Two influential names fuelled Surf music. The first was Dick Dale and it is his late 1961 hit-single *Let's Go Trippin'* that is generally acknowledged as being the first important Surf disc. His trademark distorted guitar set the style for everyone and his LPs are valuable. For example, *Summer Surf ★* is $120 and *Silver Sounds of Surf ★* $200. The Chantays' hit LP *Pipeline ★* ($350 on Downey) used this guitar sound, as did The Surfaris for their 1963 single *Wipe Out ★* ($3,000 on DFS, $400 on Princess, but just $5 on Dot).

The other core influence was, inevitably, The Beach Boys. The group wrote *Surfin'* for their brother Dennis, who was an avid surfer. The record went out on their local Candix label, it became a minor hit, and they thought that that was the end. However, their airy sounds, magnificent harmonies, and trademark guitar sound caught on and "California Sound" reached round the world. Today their 1961 single *Surfin'/Luau ★* is $1,000 on X label, the single *Fun, Fun, Fun* is £40, and the seminal LP *Pet Sounds* £25. The 1967 album *Smile ★* didn't go ahead, but some covers were made for it and these are worth $1,000! The group endured a complex relationship – at one point Brian Wilson didn't want to release a record that had just cost them $16,000 to produce – *Good Vibrations* (£20) – which became their first million-seller.

Fellow Californians Jan and Dean had a hit single with *Surf City* ($40), and made the 1963 LP *Jan and Dean Take Linda Surfin'* ($80), and the 1967 LP *Save for a Rainy Day ★* ($4,000). They followed in The Beach Boys' footsteps, although they had started recording earlier than them, and also continued after the Surfin' era with singles like *Batman* ($25).

The Godfathers *"FASCINATING MINI PORTFOLIOS"*

PHIL SPECTOR

Singles

Checkmates Ltd. *I Can Hear the Rain / Proud Mary*

The Crystals *Da Doo Ron Ron / There's No Other Like My Baby* ★

The Righteous Brothers *You've Lost That Lovin' Feeling*

The Ronettes *Be my Baby / Born to be Together* ★

Bob B. Soxx and The Blue Jeans *Why Do Lovers Break Each Other's Heart*

The Teddy Bears *I Don't Need You Anymore / You Said Goodbye*

Ike and Tina Turner *River Deep, Mountain High*

LPs

The Beatles *Let it Be* ★

Checkmates Limited *Live at Caesar's Palace / Love is All I Have to Give*

The Crystals *Twist Uptown* ★

George Harrison *All Things Must Pass*

John Lennon *Imagine*

Bob B. Soxx and The Blue Jeans *Zip-a-Dee-Doo-Dah* ★

The Teddy Bears *The Teddy Bears Sing* ★

With such a worldwide music industry it's hard now to comprehend the power of the commercial Pop pioneers. The individuals who set the production and star-making patterns that others followed were effectively self taught, using purely their instincts and love for the music. These figures built up and groomed in-house talent to experiment with their ideas and collectors have now spotted that these Godfathers' portfolios represent exciting challenges.

Phil Spector

Born in the heart of New York's Bronx district, Phil Spector moved with his family to Los Angeles. At the age of 13 he enjoyed his first hit as a member of The Teddy Bears – a group of school friends at Fairfax High. His song *To Know Him Is To Love Him* (£15 as 78'), inspired by the engraving on his father's tombstone, brought a network TV appearance on Dick Clark's show, a major record contract, a gold disc, and eventually two-and-a-half million sales. The 1959 album *The Teddy Bears Sing* ★ is extremely rare and is now worth £175 in the UK, and up to $1,200 in the USA.

Phil Spector went on to form his own Philles label packaging quality songs and girl groups with enormous success. These groups include The Crystals – their 1962 LP *Twist Uptown* ★ is worth $600, or $1,200 if it is the Capitol Record Club Edition. The Ronettes' 1965 single *Born to be Together* ★ is $150, and hit-single *Be my Baby* £6, while Bob B. Soxx and The Blue Jeans' 1963 LP *Zip-a-Dee-Doo-Dah* ★ is $100–500.

Spector evolved a signature "wall of sound", creating great dynamics but reputedly using up to 300 musicians on Checkmates Ltd.'s *Proud Mary* (£5), which actually undermined profitability. Later he created the definitive Pop songs – *You've Lost That Lovin' Feeling*, with The Righteous Brothers, and Ike and Tina Turner's glorious *River Deep, Mountain High*. He also worked on the final bittersweet LP by The Beatles, *Let it Be* ★ (the original 1970 UK boxed version

Using the Law – When Spector and his label partner were separating he was due to divide royalties on the next Crystals' single, so he recorded with them the song The Screw ★, using his lawyer to chant the title line. Ironically, the few records pressed are now worth $6,000!

JOE MEEK

Singles

Deke Arlon and The Off Beats
I'm Just a Boy

Cliff Bennett and The Rebel
Rousers *Poor Joe*

Mike Berry *Tribute to Buddy
Holly / Will You Love Me
Tomorrow*

The Chaps *Poppin' Medley*

The Fabulous Flee-Rakkers
Green Jeans

Heinz *Just Like Eddie*

Kenny Hollywood *Magic Star*

The Honeycombs *Don't Love
You no More* ★

David John and Mood
Bring it to Jerome ★ / *Diggin'
for Gold* ★

John Leyton *The Girl on
the Floor Above / Tell Laura
I Love Her*

Valerie Masters
Christmas Calling

The Moontrekkers
Night of the Vampire

Jenny Moss *Hobbies*

The Sharades *Dumb Head*

Freddy Starr and The
Midnighters *Who Told You*

Screaming Lord Sutch
*Dracula's Daughter / Jack the
Ripper / That Train Kept Rollin'*

The Syndicats *On the Horizon* ★

The Tornados *Granada /
Pop-Art Goes Mozart / Is That
a Ship I Hear*

Toby Ventura *If My Heart
Were a Storybook*

Roger LaVern and The
Microns *Christmas Stockings*

Rick Wayne and The
Fabulous Flee-Rakkers
Hot Chick A-Roo

fetches £225, and the original export ones are £1,500), George Harrison's moving triple album *All Things Must Pass* (£30), and the classic LP by John Lennon – *Imagine* (£60).

Joe Meek

Joe Meek was Britain's pioneering Rock & Roll producer, and was trading as an independent record maker even before Spector. A love of electronics led him to work as engineer on the 1956 Frankie Vaughan No.2 hit *Green Door,* on which he experimented with sound and echo techniques, before co-founding Lansdowne Road Studios. At that location he produced Lonnie Donegan, Acker Bilk, and Chris Barber. An erratic temperament saw him quit and form Triumph Records, which gained him his first hit – the 1960 Michael Cox Top 10 *Angela Jones* (£12). He then set up RGM Studios and began an eclectic list of recordings, frequently with highly compressed sounds and eerie, terrestrial background sounds.

His position as a leading force in music was confirmed with two hits for actor John Leyton – *Johnny Remember Me* (£6) and *Wild Wind* (£7). He created tribute hits such as Mike Berry's *Tribute to Buddy Holly* (£12) and Heinz's *Just like Eddie* (£5). He also had an international hit in 1964 with The Honeycombs' *Have I the Right* (£5). Screaming Lord Sutch appealed to his more macabre side, for whom he produced *Jack the Ripper* (£15) and *Dracula's Daughter* (£40). He also added members to the core of Johnny Kidd's old band to create the Tornados and the first British US Rock & Roll No.1 – *Telstar*. He then turned an ex-Skiffle group into The Blue Men and produced an EP/LP project of extraterrestrial life – *I Hear a New World Pt 1* ★ EP is worth £375 (Pt 2 sleeves only fetch £80). The LP only ever got to the white-label demo stage, and copies are now worth £1,100.

> *Fatal Spiral – Joe Meek lost touch with the fashion of the music world; depressed and short of money, he shot his landlady and then himself in 1967. Police first charged a Meek employee with the crime, and then Heinz; the latter's fingerprints covered the gun, but he had left it in the studio.*

Mickie Most

Thought by some purely to be a judge on TV's *New Faces* series, Mickie Most is probably the UKs most successful record producer. Passionate about music, he befriended Terry Dene and Wee Willie Harris at London's fabled 2i's coffee bar.

LPs

The Blue Men
I Hear a New World ★

EPs

The Blue Men
I Hear a New World ★

MICKIE MOST

Singles

The Animals *Baby Let Me Take You Home / Don't Let Me Be Misunderstood / House of the Rising Sun*

Jeff Beck *Hi-Ho Silver Lining / Love is Blue*

Donovan *Mellow Yellow / Sunshine Superman*

Herman's Hermits *Hold On / I'm Henry the Eight I Am / I'm Into Something Good / Silhouettes*

Brenda Lee *Is it True?*

Mickie Most and Gear *Mr. Porter / Sea Cruise*

Mickie Most and The Playboys *Johnny B. Goode / Rave On*

The Most Brothers *Whistle Bait / Whole Lotta Woman*

LPs

The Animals *Animalism* ★ / *The Animals* ★

Jeff Beck *Beck-Ola / Truth*

Donovan *Sunshine Superman*

Herman's Hermits *Herman's Hermits*

Lulu *The Boat that I Row*

The Nashville Teens *Tobacco Road* ★

EPs

The Animals *The Animals is Here*

Herman's Hermits *Hermania / Mrs Brown You've Got a Lovely Daughter*

Nashville Teens *Nashville Teens*

He formed The Most Brothers before marrying a South African and emigrating. However, he continued to produce – creating Mickie Most and The Playboys, who achieved 11 consecutive No.1s with covers of hits such as *Johnny B. Goode* and *Rave On*. In 1962 he returned to the UK, formed Mickie Most and Gear, and gained a minor hit with *Mr Porter* (£15). He then hunted round for an artist to produce and found The Animals in a Newcastle pub gig. He chose their material, recorded them, and delivered an international No.1 with *House of the Rising Sun* (the American picture-bagged version is $30, while US yellow-labelled DJ promo versions of the LPs *Animalism* ★ and *The Animals* ★ are now $100 each).

Meek also found The Nashville Teens and produced their 1964 Top 10 hit *Tobacco Road* ($15), then delivered Herman's Hermits' string of UK/US hits, starting with the No.1 *I'm Into Something Good* (£5). (Watch out for that group's 1966 *Hold On* ★ promo-only picture-sleeved version – it's worth $250.) He made singles with Lulu, Brenda Lee, and hugely successful hits for Donovan. He also surprised the industry by creating hit singles for gifted rock guitarist Jeff Beck, such as *Hi-Ho Silver Lining* (£10). At a time in his career when many others would relax, he formed RAK Records in 1969 and got talented writers Nicky Chinn and Mike Chapman on board. The raft of chart hits that followed included Suzi Quatro, The Sweet, Mud, Kim Wilde, Steve Harley, Chris Spedding, and Smokie. He also steered the British Funk band Hot Chocolate to huge sales.

> *Rare Species – Look out for the 1963 version of* I Just Wanna Make Love to You ★ *as a 12" EP. It's one-sided, and just 99 private pressings were made with blank white labels. The typed information on it might read "Alan Price Rhythm & Blues" or "The Animals" – these EPs are valued at £375.*

Larry Parnes

To complete this era's power base there was Larry Parnes – Britain's first major Rock & Roll manager – who, like Joe Meek, built up a stable of highly collectable talent. A shopkeeper with '50s club interest, he began his success story with Tommy Hicks, whom he renamed Tommy Steele. Steele perfectly fitted Parnes' criterion of all-round entertainers, capable of records, films, or concerts (though naturally the main quality required was image). With Presley capturing

LARRY PARNES

Singles

Joe Brown
People Gonna Talk Jellied Eels

Vince Eager *Five Days, Five Nights / Makin' Love*

Billy Fury *Maybe Tomorrow ★*

Johnny Gentle *Milk from the Coconut / Wendy*

Duffy Power *Dream Lover / Starry-Eyed*

Dickie Pride *Slippin' & Slidin'*

Tommy Steele *Rock with the Caveman / Tallahassee Lassie / Singing the Blues*

Marty Wilde *Honeycomb / Sing, Boy Sing*

EPs

Joe Brown *A Picture of Joe Brown*

Vince Eager *Vince Eager and The Vagabonds No. 1*

Billy Fury *Am I Blue*

Johnny Gentle *The Gentle Touch*

Dickie Pride *Sheik of Shake ★*

Tommy Steele
Tommy the Toreador

Marty Wilde
Presenting Marty Wilde

the youth markets, Parnes made sure his charges gained their fair share of at least the UK market. Steele had No.1s like *Singing the Blues* (£18), as well as movies such as *Tommy the Toreador* (EP £10). Others in the famed stable include Joe Brown – his 1962 EP *A Picture of Joe Brown* is £18, major UK star Billy Fury – his *Maybe Tomorrow ★* is now £100 as a 78' (£25 as a 45'), and Duffy Power – the single *Starry-Eyed* is £30 as a 78' (£10 as a 45'). Other stars included Johnny Gentle – *The Gentle Touch* (EP £50), Marty Wilde – the 1957 single *Honeycomb* (£45), Vince Eager – the 1958 EP *Vince Eager & The Vagabonds No.1* (£80), and Dickie Pride – *Sheik of Shake ★* (EP £200). By far the most unfortunate thing that Parnes ever did was to pass on The Beatles a year and a half before Brian Epstein signed them.

Playing Safe – Larry Parnes always ensured his key stars developed a second strand of talent as a safety net. And, despite being the UK's top manager he also developed a second business, as a promoter. For example, he even hired The Beatles to back Johnny Gentle on his tour.

Pop Composers *"COLLECTOR'S MECCA"*

Suggested Strands

Singer-Songwriters
The Beatles

Average Record Cost

Singer-Songwriters ☆☆☆
The Beatles ☆☆☆☆☆

Rising Stars

Neil Sedaka
The Beatles

SINGER-SONGWRITERS

Singles

Joan Armatrading
Lonely Lady / Love and Affection

Jackson Browne
Running on Empty

Billy Joel
The Ballad of Billy the Kid

Elton John *Club at the End of the Street ★ / It's Me That You Need / Lady Samantha ★*

Carole King *Going Wild ★ / It Might as Well Rain until September ★ / Oh Neil ★*

Randy Newman
Golden Gridiron Boy

Harry Nilsson
Do You Wanna

Neil Sedaka *Breaking up is Hard to Do / Calendar Girl / Oh Carol ★ / Ring-a-Rockin' ★ / Run Samson Run ★ / Stairway to Heaven ★*

Bob Seger
The Horizontal Bop ★

Paul Simon *Hey Schoolgirl / I'm Lonely ★ / True or False ★*

Bruce Springsteen *Blinded by the Light ★ / Born to Run ★ / Spirit of the Night ★*

Singer-Songwriters

Singer-Songwriter is an exacting definition. Performers had been writing their own material for decades but most legitimate singer-songwriters emerged after the pioneering work of Bob Dylan. A largely American phenomenon, it's produced fascinating and highly personal records that by and large remain affordable. It is a style represented by crafted albums – although occasionally a hit single is achieved.

Anything Counts – Bob Dylan is covered in the Folk section, but as he was the architect to modern singer-songwriters even the artwork to any never-released albums of his are like gold dust. For example, the cover for the 1965 Bob Dylan in Concert *★ is worth $4,000.*

There are a healthy number of women in this category, with the leading figure being Carole King who initially worked with college friend Gerry Goffin. She wrote many classics hits for other people, such as *Take Good Care of my Baby* for Bobby Vee (£25 as export version), *Up on the Roof* for The Drifters (£7), *Will You Love Me Tomorrow* for The Shirelles (£10), and *Goin' Back* for Dusty Springfield (£5). Neil Sedaka dedicated *Oh Carol ★* to her (£175 as a 78') and she responded with the 1959 single *Oh! Neil* ($700). Most of her work was for Don Kirshner at the Brill Building. Then she recorded her own single *It Might as Well Rain Until September ★* ($300 on Champion label), and after her move to LA she eventually wrote and released the magnificent 15-million-selling album, *Tapestry*, which is filled with haunting moods and many songs that others would cover, such as *You've Got a Friend* (sung by James Taylor) and *Natural Woman* (covered by Aretha Franklin).

Joni Mitchell offered a more sophisticated and reflective mood, having little care for singles. Each LP was like a personal sketchpad of her visions on life and her relationships. This resulted in less cover versions than Carole King, although Judy Collins did record *Both Sides Now*. Mitchell's albums eloquently trace her journey from Folk to Rock to Jazz fringes using lyrics that would grace a poetry anthology. Prices for her records aren't high – for example, two later LPs in audiophile form, *Court and Spark* and *The Hissing of Summer Lawns*, are worth $50 and £15 respectively. Less venerable but

James Taylor *Carolina in My Mind* ★ / *Sweet Baby Jane*

LPs

Joan Armatrading
Whatever's For Us

Jackson Browne
Jackson Browne's First Album ★

Tim Buckley *Blue Afternoon / Goodbye and Hello / Happy Sad / Tim Buckley*

Philip Goodhand-Tait
Philip Goodhand-Tait / I Think I'll Write a Song

Billy Joel *Songs in the Attic / Souvenir*

Elton John *Captain Fantastic and the Dirt Cowboy* ★

Carole King *Tapestry / Writer – Carole King*

Joni Mitchell *Court and Spark / The Hissing of Summer Lawns*

Randy Newman *Randy Newman / 12 Songs*

Harry Nilsson *Scatalogue* ★ / *The True One* ★ box set

Lou Reed *The Blue Mask / Metal Machine Music* ★

Neil Sedaka *Neil Sedaka* ★

Bob Seger *Brand New Morning* ★ / *Noah*

Simon & Garfunkel
Wednesday Morning 3.0 AM

James Taylor *James Taylor*

equally gifted was the largely forgotten '70s singer-songwriter Joan Armatrading. Her initial Folk-tinged LP *Whatever's for Us* was followed by the fine 1976 LP *Joan Armatrading*, which featured the hits *Down to Zero* and *Love and Affection*. She currently has no American collectors' lists and £10 would buy you any one of her UK records.

Carole King's friend and admirer Neil Sedaka also worked out of the Brill publishing building. He co-wrote (with Howard Greenfield) *Stupid Cupid* for Connie Francis ($8) and *Love Will Keep Us Together* for The Captain & Tennille ($6), along with his own interpretations of *Calendar Girl* ($25), *I Go Ape* (£65 as a 78'), *Breaking Up is Hard to Do* ($25), and *The Tra La Days are Over*. A 78' single of the 1958 *Ring-a-Rockin'* ★ is worth £100 today, while the 1960 singles *Run Samson Run* ★ and *Stairway to Heaven* ★ are each worth £175.

Paul Simon's skills took a while to be appreciated – a failed New York LP *Wednesday Morning 3 A.M.* ($30) by Simon and Garfunkel led a depressed Simon to play the London Folk clubs. Art joined him on his holiday and performed a live acoustic version of *Sounds of Silence*. This triggered the extraordinary success of *Mrs Robinson*, which was a No.1 US single. *The Graduate*, *Bookends* (mono white label $30), and *Parsley, Sage, Rosemary & Thyme* ($20) were US No.1, 2, and 3 LPs respectively; even *Wednesday Morning 3 A.M.* made No.163.

Not What You Think – A single, Hey Schoolgirl *($50), was put out on Big Records by college friends Jerry Landis (Paul Simon) and Tom Graph (Art Garfunkel). It reached the US Top 40 and sold 100,00 copies. Unfortunately, the label credit reads "Tom & Jerry"!*

Despite his writing talent, over-exposure has so far inhibited collectors from choosing Elton John, although his 1969 single *It's Me That You Need* is £80 with picture sleeve, *Lady Samantha* ★ DJ singles are $100, and a withdrawn picture-sleeved *Club at the End of the Street* ★ is worth £500. There are excellent homeland narratives – particularly LP tracks – from Rock songwriters such as Bruce Springsteen. His singles include the 1973 *Spirit of the Night* ★ ($1,500 with picture sleeve) and the 1975 *Born to Run* ★ ($1,200 as DJ test pressing with text in script writing, mailing envelope, letter from CBS and patch). Bob Seger's LP *Brand New Morning* ★ is worth $100 and the single *The Horizontal Bop* ★ fetches $100 with the picture sleeve but a paltry $5 without.

The Beatles

The mythology surrounding The Beatles makes objectivity difficult. They certainly changed the face of the music industry but they were also lucky to evolve such carefree music at the very time the UK had full employment, felt good about itself, and had a teenage surplus due to the immediate post-war birth bulge. The Beatles are the world's number one for collectors by an enormous margin, helped somewhat by a relatively mediocre early career.

Early German recordings in which they backed the more established Tony Sheridan (as well as some solo tracks) drew the attention of their future manager Brian Epstein, and these songs eventually also impacted the American market. The two best tracks became a German single, *My Bonnie/The Saints* * (value $15,000), by Tony Sheridan and The Beat Brothers (they were known by this name as "Beatles" was uncomfortably close to the German for genitalia). The record gained a UK release days before their ill-fated unsuccessful Decca audition, and six months then passed before a UK deal materialized.

Once Beatlemania struck, the Germans sold recording licenses to a variety of US labels, including MGM, Atco, Metro, Clarion, and Savage, creating heaven for collectors. The most complex to collect now is Vee-Jay, as they have hugely desirable records but critical detailing. The label produced oval, bracketed, and blocked logos, yellow labels with green print, blue print, purple print, and even upper and lowercase styles. As Capitol had rejected the group four times, Vee-Jay benefited enormously until the group stormed the USA and Capitol issued numerous lawsuits to try suppressing Vee-Jay. Vee-Jay squeezed every conceivable release out of their limited catalogue – the LP *Introducing The Beatles* * had 17 subtle variations alone for collectors – and hosts of counterfeit examples (the main difference between these and other versions were that Capitol's final victory forced the replacement of two disputed songs).

UK records had up to seven pressing editions, re-pressings, and export versions – all with detail and value changes – giving LP prices from the high hundreds up to £2,000. At the extreme

> *Beatles Power – After the relative flop of UK's initial release,* Love Me Do, *every single release for six years would reach No.1 or No.2, and million-sales were accrued within the initial weeks. In the USA in 1964 they sold 2.6 million records in just one month.*

end of the market, the 1968 Apple LP *The Beatles* ★, grades from £8,000+ for those numbered to 10, down to £120 for above 10,000. However, despite the world's most expensive rarities (*see* below) more down-to-earth collectables are very reasonable due to the fact that so many were sold initially.

After Hours – American pressing plant subcontractor Savoy made just two unofficial translucent yellow copies of Can't Buy Me Love ★, *two half-yellow/half-black ones, and around a dozen red vinyl copies of* I Want to Hold your Hand. *A pure yellow one is now valued at just under £20,000.*

EXAMPLES OF BEATLES RARITIES

• *Can't Buy Me Love* single from 1964. The unofficial yellow pressing Capitol 5150 is worth $30,000.

• *Yesterday and Today* 1966 LP. In its first state it was known as "The Butchers Cover", as it featured the group as butchers with cutting tools and portions of toy dolls. This was issued only to media, then recalled, but many kept hold of them. Initial replacements pasted over the cover and then the third state version was slightly smaller overall. Capitol ST-2553 is worth $25,000.

• *Hear The Beatles Tell All* LP. Running out of ideas with their limited Beatles tracks, in 1964 Vee-Jay issued a John Lennon and group interview, which did sell to the public. (Label number Pro-202 $10,000). Two known white-label copies with blue print are valued at $18,000.

• *My Bonnie/The Saints* single by Tony Sheridan and The Beat Brothers. The 1962 US Rainbow label design, with silver printing Decca 31382, is $15,000. It was reissued on MGM K 13213 as The Beatles with Tony Sheridan, and this is worth £90, while in the UK a Polydor NH 66833 version was released from 1962 to '68, and this is now worth £50.

• *Introducing The Beatles* LP. The most valuable examples of these are those with 25 mini Vee-Jay artist adverts on the back, hiding the fact that the two disputed tracks were included.

After Capitol's success a second media pressing had blank back covers again to hide *Love Me Do* and *P.S. I Love You,* but commercial copies did list the tracks and Capitol sued. Later versions used *Please Please Me* and *Ask Me Why* instead. Seventeen distinct collectable versions exist, of which the best is worth $15,000. There are lots of counterfeit versions – the real ones have "Stereo" on the label.

• *Anna/Ask Me Why* single. This was a Vee-Jay 1964 promo pressing for American DJs, and there are thought to be only five copies in existence (DJ-8) – worth $15,000.

• *The Beatles & Frank Ifield on Stage* LP. This was a cash-in pairing of two Vee-Jay acts – not a concert but rather a re-use of four existing Beatles' recordings. The first pressing was actually called *Jolly What!,* and featured a very British gent on the front cover. It's the handful of late re-pressings done in 1964 (VJLP 1085) that are worth $12,000 today.

• *A Hard Day's Night* single. This one-off unofficial employee-pressing in pink on United Artists, UAS 6366, from 1964, is in stereo and worth $12,000.

• *The Beatles Again* LP. Regular copies have no title on the cover, and "Hey Jude" on the spine. Desirable prototypes have "Beatles Again" on the cover. It was never released, so it is the covers that hold the value. The Apple SO-385 version is worth $8,000.

SOUL

Stevie Wonder *Hotter Than July* By the early '80s the purity of Soul had been lost in the commercial interests of both stars and record companies.

Soul emerged from R&B at the beginning of the 1960s and was centred within major American urbanizations – each colouring it slightly differently. For example, the Memphis Stax sound is strong and brassy, Detroit's Motown has a lighter Pop feel, while early R&B has southern influences, and New York has smoother vocal-dominated productions. This diversity struggled into the 1970s with Blue-Eyed Soul, which was made up of white talents mixing Pop and Soul into prime A.O.R. radio fodder. The talent included Average White Band, Hall and Oates, Boz Scaggs, and Robert Palmer, and this is currently a very cheap collectable strand. Here we leave aside Soul Jazz and Soul Blues and concentrate on the prime centres of '60s Soul music.

It's hard to escape the importance of Motown – or indeed the value of founder Berry Gordy's support from family and friends. The songwriter Smokey Robinson, along with the in-house writers Holland-Dozier-Holland, were the architects of so many classic records. Dozens of small supporting labels, complex funding, and distribution deals with major record companies make collecting complete sets of artists quite a challenge. For example, a US company like Motown might have a variety of UK licensing deals, and collectors are concerned with such details. For instance, the 1962 Mary Wells album *The One Who Really Loves You* is worth $140, but only if the label address is positioned above the record's central hole – if it's lower down then the record is worth just $40. Like misspellings and sleeve alterations, these tiny distinctions actually denote the precise age of a particular pressing.

Another aspect to consider is Northern Soul. This is a journalistic term for Britain's northern cities' clubland taste, but it is not a specific musical sound. The qualifications are simple: the record must sound conspicuously American and be very obscure. Because it was dance-floor driven, fashions (and therefore values) fluctuate freely, but it is estimated there are 30,000 forgotten '60s danceable singles. This means that great opportunities exist for collecting.

Highs and Lows – The Isley Brothers endured mixed fortunes. They had a string of hits, including the fabled single Shout, *and toured relentlessly, employing an unknown Jimi Hendrix whose guitar they had to rescue from a pawn shop. Later two of the brothers fell out, one died of heart failure, another had both legs amputated, and one became a minister.*

Soul *"A DECADE OF CHOICE"*

Suggested Strands

Leading Lights
Philadelphia
Memphis
Detroit

Average Record Cost

☆☆☆☆

Rising Stars

Martha Reeves and
The Vandellas
Jackie Wilson

LEADING LIGHTS

Singles

Ray Charles *Georgia on My Mind* ★ / *Midnight Hour* ★ / *The Sun's Gonna Shine Again* ★

The Chi-Lites (Hi-Lites) *Have You Seen Her* / *I'm so Jealous* ★ / *One by One* ★ / *Pretty Girl* ★

Sam Cooke *Only Sixteen* / *You Send Me*

Fontella Bass *Rescue Me*

Al Green *Back Up Train* / *Let's Stay Together*

The Isley Brothers *Angels Cried* ★ / *I Hear a Symphony* ★ / *Shout* ★

Etta James *Tell Mama* / *I'd Rather Go Blind*

Jackie Wilson *Talk that Talk*

LPs

Ray Charles *Genius + Soul = Jazz* / *Soul Brothers*

Sam Cooke *Sam Cooke* ★ / *The Soul Stirrers Featuring Sam Cooke* / *The Wonderful World of Sam Cooke* ★

Al Green *Back Up Train*

The crudest definition of commercial Soul is of a transitional form rising from R&B in the early 1960s and splintering off a decade later into styles such as Funk. This means that a band like Sly and The Family Stone qualifies to be within Soul as well as in Funk, Rock, and R&B. To collect Soul vinyl it is therefore easier to approach it from one of its epicentres, such as the label or production house.

Leading Lights

Pioneering figures of Soul were Sam Cooke and Ray Charles. Cooke was previously in the gospel group Soul Stirrers, before he topped the US Pop charts with his first solo single in 1957, *You Send Me* (£30). His LPs include *The Wonderful World of Sam Cooke* ★ ($350) and *Sam Cooke* ★ ($200). Ray Charles' talent stretches from Hoagy Carmichael's single *Georgia on my Mind* ★ (£100 as a UK 78') to the LP *Soul Brothers* with Jazz master Milt Jackson (£25). His own early singles *Roll with Me Baby* ★ from 1952 and *The Sun's Gonna Shine Again* ★ from 1953 are both very valuable – $500 and $400 respectively.

Other luminaries include Jackie Wilson – his 1959 LP *Lonely Teardrops* ★ is $150, and the single *Talk that Talk* £80 as a UK 78' or $60 for a US-pictured sleeved version. The Isley Brothers' 1957 single *Angels Cried* ★ is $800, their classic hit *Shout* ★ £200 as a UK 78', and the LP *Shout* ★ is $120 in mono if it has "Long Play" on its label, but $200 with "Living Stereo" labels. A V.I.P. labelled 1965 single *I Hear a Symphony* ★ is also worth $800. The Chi-Lites' famed 1971 single is *Have You Seen Her* ($8), but early Daren label singles use the name The Hi-Lites for *One by One* ★ and *I'm So Jealous* ★ (each $100). Chess offered Etta James' great single – *I'd Rather Go Blind/Tell Mama* (£12) and the Fontella Bass classic hit *Rescue Me* (£20).

Philadelphia International

Philadelphia was the third child of producers Gamble and Huff – the first was Excel Records, which was renamed Gamble, and the second was Neptune Records. Gamble and Huff had written many hits to build the Neptune roster, including The Three Degrees' single *Reflections of Yesterday* ($6), Billy Paul's single *Mrs Robinson* ($10), and the O'Jays 1969 LPs *The O'Jays in Philadelphia* ($30) and *Back Stabbers* (£12). P.I.R. linked up with C.B.S. to sell millions of records that had

The Isley Brothers
Shout ★ / This Old Heart of Mine

Etta James *Miss Etta James ★*

Jackie Wilson *Body and Soul /
Lonely Teardrops ★ / So Much ★*

PHILADELPHIA INTERNATIONAL

Singles

The O'Jays *Love Train*

Harold Melvin and
The Blue Notes *If You Don't
Know Me By Now*

Billy Paul *Mrs Robinson*

The Stylistics
*Betcha by Golly Wow /
You Make Me Feel Brand New*

The Three Degrees
Reflections of Yesterday

MEMPHIS STAX

Singles

Isaac Hayes *Walk on By*

Wilson Pickett *If You Need Me /
Let Me be Your Boy*

Otis Redding *Respect / (Sittin'
on) The Dock of the Bay*

Sam and Dave *Hold on I'm
Comin' / Soul Man*

LPs

Isaac Hayes *Hot Buttered
Soul / Presenting Isaac Hayes*

Wilson Pickett
In the Midnight Hour

Otis Redding *The Great Otis
Redding Sings Soul Ballads ★ /
Otis Blue / Pain in my Heart ★*

Sam and Dave *Double Dynamite*

DETROIT MOTOWN

Singles

The Four Tops *Reach Out
(I'll Be There) / Standing in the
Shadows of Love*

previously been on the Neptune roster, as well as their fresh signings such as Harold Marvin and Thelma Houston. They also enjoyed the later success of The Stylistics, who had 12 straight Top 10 hits in the USA, including *Betcha by Golly Wow* and *You Make Me Feel Brand New* (each $5). Harold Melvin was more romantic with his single *If You Don't Know Me By Now* (£5). His self-taught drummer Teddy Pendergrass had been in groups since his teens and eventually turned to a solo career creating strings of platinum and gold records, as well as his fabled "Ladies Only" concert events.

Memphis – Stax Records

The Memphis company Stax Records was run from a local theatre by Jim Stewart and his sister Estelle Axton after a faltering start under a disputed trade name, Satellite Records. Stewart, an ex-bank employee, built up an important stable, including Sam and Dave (their single *Hold on I'm Comin'* is $15 and the LP *Double Dynamite* $40), Booker T. and the M.G.'s, and Isaac Hayes (the 1969 LP *Hot Buttered Soul* is $20 and the single *Feel Like Makin' Love* $5). Their one-time

> *Mixed Family Fortunes – The brother and sister fused
> their names to christen STAX Records – STewart & AXtone.
> From rundown premises they built a powerful company
> that captured Otis Redding's contract. However Otis'
> death, termination of deals, and bankruptcy followed.*

parking valet, Otis Redding, managed to audition for them and two unplanned tracks cut with the available house band included his first release *Hey, Hey, Baby*. His contract with their side label, Volt, went on to generate classic singles such as *Pain in My Heart* (£18) and the posthumous US No.1 (*Sittin' on) The Dock of the Bay* (£5), plus the timeless 1966 LP *Otis Blue* ($50). Numerous posthumous hits and two Grammy awards would also act as memorials to Redding, but by the '70s the company had become discredited and was declared bankrupt.

Detroit – Motown

Established with an $800 family loan by ex-boxer and record shop-owner Berry Gordy, Motown was conceived as a small inner-city label, but its distinctive commercial blending of smooth R&B and Pop became the worldwide hallmark of an organization so polished in music production that at one time it achieved a 75 per cent success ratio with single releases.

The Jackson Five *ABC*

Marv Johnson *Why Do You Want Me to Let You Go / You Got What it Takes* ★

Gladys Knight and The Pips *Midnight Train to Georgia*

The Marvelettes *Locking up My Heart* ★ */ Please Mr Postman* ★

Martha Reeves and The Vandellas *Dancing in the Street* ★ */ I'll Have to Let Him Go* ★

Smokey Robinson and The Miracles *Everybody's Gotta Pay Some Dues* ★ */ Tears of a Clown / What's So Good About Goodbye* ★ */ You've Really Got a Hold on Me*

The Supremes *Baby Love / Stop! In the Name of Love*

The Temptations *My Girl* ★ */ Papa was a Rollin' Stone / Since I Lost My Baby*

Mary Wells *My Guy / The One Who Really Loves You / You Beat Me to the Punch* ★

Stevie Wonder *For Once in My Life / I was Made to Love Her*

LPs

The Four Tops *The Four Tops*

Marvin Gaye *Marvin Gaye* ★ */ Moods of Marvin Gaye / That Stubborn Kinda' Fella* ★

Marv Johnson *Marvellous Marv Johnson* ★

Gladys Knight and The Pips *Gladys Knight and The Pips* ★

The Marvelettes *The Marvelous Marvelettes* ★

Martha Reeves and The Vandellas *Come and Get These Memories* ★ */ Heatwave* ★

The Supremes *Meet The Supremes* ★

The Temptations *Meet The Temptations* ★

Stevie Wonder *The Twelve Year Old Genius – Live*

Gordy built up a fine catalogue of talents for his Tamla, Motown, and Gordy labels, leasing United Artists' Marv Johnson's singles *You Got What it Takes* ★ (£100 as a UK 78') and *I Love the Way You Love* (£18), the former reaching No.7 in the UK charts. Their first US Motown No.1 was Mary Wells' *My Guy* in 1964 ($20). Others included the Four Tops' *Reach Out (I'll Be There)* ($80 with picture sleeve) and Martha Reeves and The Vandellas' 1963 LP *Come and Get These Memories* ★ ($800), *Heatwave* ★ ($400 stereo), and *Dancing in the Street* ★ ($120 with picture sleeve).

The Supremes were their biggest group. Their hits included the 1965 *Stop! In the Name of Love* ($30 with picture sleeve) and the LP *Meet the Supremes* ★ ($900 if the group is pictured sitting on stools but $40 for faces only). Also under the Motown umbrella were The Temptations, whose 1965 single *My Girl* ★ is now worth $120, and their LP *Meet The Temptations* ★ £100, and Gladys Knight and The Pips – their big singles are cheap but the group's 1960s album *Gladys Knight and The Pips* ★ is currently $200. Stevie Wonder also created many fine hits for Gordy – *For Once in My Life* typically is valued at just £5, but rare copies of a cancelled 1963 album, *Workout Stevie, Workout* ★, command $1,000. Marvin Gaye has two valuable LPs – *That Stubborn Kinda Fella* ★ from 1963, worth $600, and 1964's *Marvin Gaye* ★, which costs £140. Of the many records by The Jackson Five, their single *ABC* is worth the most, at £50.

It was a glorious house of talent, built upon the solid foundations of powerful songwriters and producers. At one time Motown was the largest black-owned corporation in the USA, but in 1967 accounting disputes with their critically important writer/producer team of Brian Holland, Lamont Dozier, and Eddie Holland led to the trio's departure, a corporate move to Los Angeles, and the loss of major artists such as Diana Ross. The name Motown survived but the trademark "Motown Sound" had been lost forever.

Perfect Gift – To promote Marvin Gaye, DJs were sent a special pressing of Masquerade is Over *stamped with "single not available – extracted from album TM-221". If his name is misspelled as "Gay" on it, the pressing is now worth $600.*

As the world's most collectable band, there is breathtaking variation in the details and values of The Beatles' many releases, from £8,000 plus for a first Apple pressing of *The Beatles* to £10 an LP for a 1970s re-pressing.

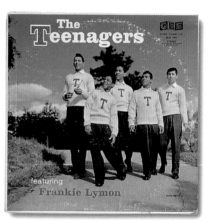

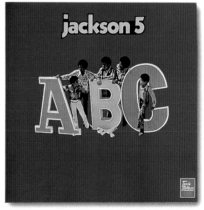

There are thousands of Classic American Pop Groups, from landmark recordings such as The Beach Boys' *Pet Sounds* to a 1950s LP by The Teenagers (£500).

Classic Euro Pop groups are all rising in value but the real
gems are among the less familiar – a 1965 Honeycombs LP,
All Systems Go, is worth £75 – twice any of these illustrated.

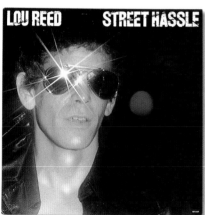

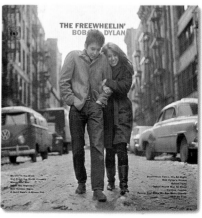

Singer-Songwriters is a niche collecting area of high-quality talent that generally commands around £15–25 a record, but a rare copy of Bob Dylan's *The Freewheelin'* can fetch £15,000 or more.

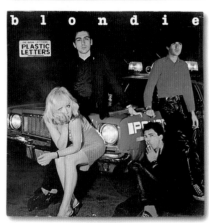

These images illustrate the dramatically changing face
of female Pop over just two decades, yet values are
remarkably comparable, being £12–20 across the board.

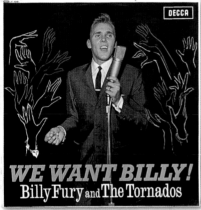

Success collecting Pop stars is in the detail, age, rarity, and occasional special editions. Billy Fury's *Christmas Prayer* single is £35, £70 with a tri-centre, £300+ as a 78'.

Instrumental recordings stretch from Jazz and Movies
to lighthearted tour-de-forces of 1950s Pop and Rock
musicians, the prices adjusting with each genre.

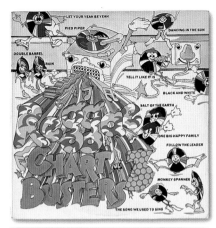

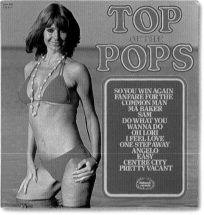

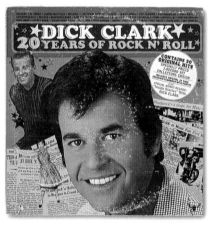

Compilations are a neglected area – cheap to buy and astonishingly diverse. This 1973 Dick Clark double LP, complete with booklet and extra cardboard 7", is just $20.

COMPILATIONS

The underlining theme throughout this guide is the importance of researching your chosen topic. You need to understand the key artists or figures, the specialist record companies, and the important timelines. However, without the necessary knowledge it's hard to know where to start. The world of compilations is a currently unfashionable area of vinyl that will, nevertheless, get you into the swing of collecting, as well as educate you in the basic artists, recordings, and labels involved in your particular area of interest.

Compilations are probably the last remaining strand of vinyl that can still be found in abundance in secondhand shops and scattered across the fields of car boot sales. Unloved, frequently with good reason, thousands of releases are still audio scrapbooks of a year, a fashion, and a style of music and, as such, are perfect basic research materials. Compilations are generally associated with rock-bottom prices and garish assortments of old chart singles. As you will discover, there is actually a lot more than that on offer, and occasionally values compete directly with major music strands. For example, a party record fetches $3,000, internal non-consumer record company pressings command $2,000, and promo-compilations that showcase work to radio DJs are also valuable – in one case a staggering $7,500 (the 1960s *Phil Spector Spectacular – see* p214).

Where compilations can start to become fascinating collectables in their own right is within a specific style. Choose a theme like Reggae and you will quickly be presented with an intricate progression of style names, artists, and even production techniques. However, just a handful of Reggae compilations will immediately give you an insight into the differing sounds, the artists, and the differences. These include the 1969 *Sounds like Ska* on Joy (£12), the 1967 *Ska to Rocksteady* on Studio One (£80), and the 1968 *Explosive Rocksteady* on Amal (£45). If you add to this collection a Dub record and one or two general hits collections such as Island's 1973 *This is Reggae Music Island* (£12) or Trojan's 1970 *Hot Shots of Reggae* (£20), then you will get a feel for the movements and perhaps also gain an appetite to collect a single artist or style. Those particular examples are fairly desirable, so are more valuable than usual.

Beyond the obvious themes of Pop, Rock & Roll, Jazz, and Country there is an unexpected collecting challenge in the compilations created by record companies for promotion purposes. Samplers of a new product were often pressed on a regular basis for circulation to radio stations and store owners, and these can be very collectable simply because of their limited pressing numbers.

Extremes of Value – Promo compilation values are frequently linked to the artists that are featured. For example, A & M's regular series of samplers, Foreplay, *range from $10 each, while ABC's double LP version is $12. However, RCA's 1957 EP,* Dealer's Preview **, which featured Eddie Fisher, Perry Como, and their new star Elvis Presley, has a value of $3,000 if it still has its envelope and sleeve.*

Compilations *"GATEWAY TO SO MUCH"*

Suggested Strands
Fads
Young and Old
Specialists
Labels

Average Record Cost
☆☆☆

Rising Stars
Reggae Material
RCA Promo Discs

FADS – all LPS

*At the Cavern / Beach Party ★ /
Big Surf Hits / Bubble Gum /
Greatest Hits / Disco Mania /
Disco Teen / Discotheque in
Astrosound / Everybody's Goin
Surfin' / The First National Skiffle
Contest / Greatest Twist Hits /
Group Beat / Joe Meek Story /
Kent Rocks ★ / Mods Mayday /
Music for Hand-Jiving / My Son
the Surf-Nut / Original Surfin'
Hits / Skiffle / Surfin' in the
Midwest / Surf's Up at Banzai
Pipeline / This is Merseybeat /
Waikiki Surf Battle ★*

YOUNG – all LPs

*The Beat Merchants / Black
Slacks & Bobby Socks ★ / Brum
Beat / Dimension Dolls ★ /
English Freak Beat / Girls, Girls,
Girls Around the World / Music
for the Boyfriend (He Digs Rock
& Roll) ★ / Music for the Girlfriend
(Did Someone Say a Party?) /
Pyjama Party / Party After Hours /
Teen Age Rock ★ / Teen Time ★*

Let's deal with the clichés first. Many compilations use "Oldies" in their titles while others add in "Golden" too. A better-than-average 1960 Decca LP, *Golden Oldies* ($60), includes Buddy Holly, Bobby Darin, and Bill Haley and The Comets, and Carlton's 1960 *One Dozen Goldies* ★ is worth $125. The word "Original" also features – the *Original Toga Party* (2 LPs on the label Adam VIII) is $12, and "Hot", although it is rarely as apt as it is for Capitol's 1963 *Hot Rod Magazine Rally* ★, which includes the Super Stocks and Shutdown Douglas ($100).

Fads

Within compilations there are wonderful niche choices, including *Bubble Gum Greatest Hits* – two volumes on Accord that are each worth $25 – and K-Tel's 1975 *Disco Mania* ($10). Terry Dene, Bob Cort Skiffle, and Tommy Steele appear on *Music for Hand-Jiving* ($50). There is also Atlantic's 1962 *Greatest Twist Hits* ($35), the 1957 10" LP *The First National Skiffle Contest* on Esquire (£50), and the 1979 *Mods Mayday* (£10). Regional collections are also interesting: the 1981 *Kent Rocks* ★, on White Witch, had only 200 pressings (£150), the two volumes of *This is Merseybeat* are each worth £60, and Decca offered *At the Cavern* (£60) and the *Joe Meek Story* (the 2 LPs together are worth £30).

> *Tongue-in-Cheek – Perverse compilations include Rhino's* World's Worst Records *($10), which throws together The Troggs and Killer Pussy. Leapy Lee and Ray Stevens are on K-Tel's* 24 Greatest Dumb Ditties *($12), while the album* 12 Flip Hits ★ *on Flip is worth a serious $250.*

Surfing was a fad that had strong music links. For example, the 1963 *Waikiki Surf Battle* ★ came in two volumes ($100 each), and The *Beach Party* ★ ($100) also appeared in 1963, with Surfair, The Charades, and Surf Bunnies. Capitol offered *My Son the Surf-Nut* ($40), while the surfing craze hit mid-America with *Surfin' in the Midwest* ($10), featuring The Bleach Boys, Little John and The Sherwood Men, and The Slough Boys!

Young and Old

The late '50s opened up new youth markets that were eagerly fed by surging record companies. In 1958 Capitol offered

OLD

LPs

Easy Listening Hits of the '60s & '70s 7 LPs / Enchanted Evenings with Rodgers & Hammerstein / Encores from the '30s (1930–35) / Greatest Hits of the War Years / Mood Music for Dining 10 LPs / Music for Candlelight and Wine / Music to Trim your Tree By / Playboy Music Hall of Fame Winners ★ 3 LPs / Ten for Cocktails / 25 Polka Waltz Greats

EPs

Perfect for Dancing

SPECIALISTS

FOLK – all LPs

All Time Country & Western Hits / Ayrshire Folk / The Best of British Folk / The Best of Scottish Folk / Deep Lancashire – Songs and Ballads of the Industrial North-West / Edinburgh Folk Festival / Firepoint – A Collection of Folk Blues / Folk Nottingham Style ★ / Folk Scene ★ / Folk Singers of Washington Square / The Folk Songs of Britain ★ 10 LPs / Folksongs 'round Harvard Square ★ / Good Folk of Kent / Irish Folk Night / Napton Folk Club / Newport Folk Festival / Newport Folk Festival Evening Concert / A Pinch of Salt – British Sea Songs Old & New / Some Folk in Leicester / Southern Folk Heritage LP series / The World of Contemporary Folk

Teen Age Rock ★ ($100), with Tommy Sands, Sonny James, and Gene Vincent, while Verve had already produced the 1957 Teen Time ★ ($300), with Ricky Nelson and Johnny Rivers. The 1958 LP Black Slacks & Bobby Socks ★ (£200) caught the mood of the day perfectly, while among the girls' albums was Dimension Dolls ★ ($250) featuring Little Eva, Carole King, and The Cookies. Decca's Music for the Boyfriend (He Digs Rock & Roll) ★ ($100) used a painting of an Esquire pin-up girl, which is also found on the cover of Music for the Girl Friend (Did Someone Say a Party?) ($30). The album Pyjama Party ($75) features The Heartbeats, The Valentines, and Frankie Lymon. Aladdin's Party After Hours ★ is $1,000 if it is the 10" black LP, and $3,000 if on red vinyl.

Compilation Power – Ronco's anti-smoking campaign LP, Do It Now, used a Beatles track– yellow-label versions are $20. Otis Redding contributed to the 1967 Stay in School – Don't be a Drop Out ★ ($100), while the 1973 Get Off anti-drug promo had Alice Cooper, Frank Zappa, and The Eagles ($20).

Now we turn to the "older" market. An American release of the UK/US 2-LP compilation Greatest Hits of the War Years featured Vera Lynn, Marlene Dietrich, Gracie Fields, Tommy Dorsey, and Harry James ($15). Enchanted Evenings with Rodgers & Hammerstein is worth $20 (2 RCA LPs), a 7-LP Reader's Digest set Easy Listening Hits of the '60s & '70s is $55, while their 10-LP set Mood Music for Dining, from 1967, is $35. Capitol gave us the Ray Charles Singers, Oscar Peterson, and George Shearing on Music for Candlelight and Wine ($12), and Columbia's Ten for Cocktails has music by Glenn Miller and Percy Faith for $10. RCA has a vast EP series called Perfect for Dancing ($10–20 per EP), each one featuring a single dance tempo such as the Tango, Rumba, or Waltz, while K-Tel offered a 1971 LP 25 Polka Waltz Greats ($12). Playboy issued a 3-LP Playboy Music Hall of Fame Winners, now $200; just as American but more modest was RCA Victor's 1966 festive offering Music to Trim Your Tree By ($10).

Specialists

These are the subjects that can really help you get to grips with a music style – as well as develop an unusual compilation collection. Many can be bought for loose change but here we look at the more desirable material of Folk, Country, Reggae, and Jazz, giving a paragraph to each one.

COUNTRY

LPs

Authentic Cowboys & Their Western Folksongs / Classic Country Music 8 LPs / Country & Western Classics / Country Boy – Country Girl / Country Favourites Vol. 1 / Country Hymns / Country Music Hall of Fame / Country Music in the Modern Era (1940s–1970s) / Grand Ole Opry Spectacular / Hillbilly Hit Parade / Opry Time in Tennessee / 30 Years of No.1s Country Hits 7 LPs

EPs

Great Country & Western Hits ★ 10 EPs / Hayride Medley

REGGAE – all LPs

Club Rock Steady / Derrick Harriott's Rock (Ska) Steady ★ / Duke Reid's Rock Steady ★ / Explosive Rocksteady / Fly Flying Ska ★ / Get Ready Rock Steady ★ / Greatest Jamaican Beat / Jump Jamaica Way ★ / Party Time in Jamaica / Reggae in the Grass / Reggae Time / Ride me Donkey / Ride your Donkey / Rocksteady / Ska-a-Go-Go / Ska at the Jamaica Playboy Club ★ / Ska-Boo-Da-Ba / Ska to Rocksteady / This is Blue Beat ★

The 1960 LP *A Pinch of Salt – British Sea Songs Old & New* (£30) typifies standard Folk visions. Certainly traditional roots are Folk's goldmine – 1965's *The Best of British Folk* on Xtra is £15, *The Best of Scottish Folk* from 1967, again on Xtra, is £12, and the 1976 *A Feast of Irish Folk* on Polydor is also £12. Compilations allow further regional definition, such as the 1969 *Deep Lancashire – Songs and Ballads of the Industrial North-West* on Topic (£12), the 1971 100 private pressings of *Napton Folk Club* on Eden (£35), or *Good Folk of Kent* on Eron (£40). In the USA the *Southern Folk Heritage* series offers *Sounds of the South* and *Blue Ridge Mountains Music,* each £18. There is also *Folksongs 'round Harvard Square* ★ (the 1960 limited, numbered edition including Joan Baez fetches $200) and 1962 *Folk Singers of Washington Square* on Continental ($20). Festival compilations are good collectables – *Edinburgh Folk Festival* on Decca is £25, *Folk Nottingham Style* ★ from Nottingham Festival is £100, and many '60s Vanguard LPs featured Newport festivals ($10–30).

The American Country collector's price bible from Osborne's actually issued its own 1984 promo EP, *Hayride Medley* ($10), featuring Jim Reeves and Loretta Lynn. The more general releases include *Opry Time in Tennessee Stateside* (£15), *The Stars of the Grand Ole Opry* (2 LPs on CBS, £15), and the impressive 12-volume London Records set *Country Music Hall of Fame* (each £12). Another collection is RCA's 1956 *Great Country & Western Hits* ★ – the boxed set of 10 EPs is worth $1,000 and features Elvis Presley, Jim Reeves, and Hank Snow. There are lots more specific compilations too, such as *Authentic Cowboys & Their Western Folksongs* on RCA (£12) and the 1957 *Hillbilly Hit Parade* on Mercury ($40).

Authentic early Reggae compilation material is looking very collectable today with the 1966 *Ska at the Jamaica Playboy Club* ★ fetching £200, 1967's *Derrick Harriott's Rock (Ska) Steady* ★ £150 on Island, and *Ska-a-Go-Go* on Coxsone and *Ska-Boo-Da-Ba* on Doctor Bird, each £90. Another valuable Island record was the 1964 *This is Blue Beat* ★ – it was never released but in white label form it fetches £200+. A tricky find is the 1969 *Tighten Up*. It actually has three volumes – Vols. 1 and 2 are on Trojan (orange labels) and are each worth £18 but the rarer Vol. 3 is on Island (pink labels) and fetches £40. Rocksteady is much prized: *Duke Reid's Rock Steady* ★, again on Island, is £140, *Club Rock Steady* on W.I.R.L is £50, and *Get Ready Rock Steady* ★ on Coxsone £100. Plenty of general collections exist, such as the 1970 *Greatest Jamaican Beat* on Trojan (£90), *Jump Jamaica Way* ★ on R&B (£175), and *Ride Me Donkey*, on Coxsone (£90).

Recorded Histories These three 1970s retrospective double LPs come complete with printed company histories. Decca's outlet for classic American R&B and Rock & Roll – London Records – is perfectly reflected; so desirable are this label's singles that some collectors attempt to gather all the company's releases, up to number 10,000.

JAZZ – all LPs

Great Big Bands 10 LPs / *Great Jazz of All Time* 10 LPs / *Kansas City Jazz / Jazz Composer's Workshop / Jazz Men / Jazz West Coast / Jazz in Britain 68–69 / Ragtime Piano Roll / Riverboat Jazz / Slipstream – the Best of British Jazz Funk / Southside Chicago / Swing Easy / Third British Festival of Jazz / Traditional Jazz at The Royal Festival Hall / Winners All! Downbeat Jazz Poll / Winners of the Downbeat's International Critics Poll for 1960*

Jazz is notoriously complex to master and ideal samplers are the American Downbeat winner's LPs – *Winners All! Downbeat Jazz Poll* on Verve ($25) and *Winners of the Downbeat's International Critics Poll for '60* on Philips (£12). More general examples include the 1962 *Great Jazz of All Time* 10-LP set on Pickwick ($50), and *Great Big Bands* – 10 LPs from Reader's Digest ($40). There are also plenty of more precise style compilations like *Swing Easy* on Coxsone (£90), *Riverboat Jazz* (a 10" LP on Vogue, £15), *Ragtime Piano Roll*, again a 10", this time in four separate volumes on London (each £20), *Southside Chicago* on Python (£35) – only 99 copies pressed – and the 1956 *Jazz West Coast* on Vogue (£12). UK material is relatively cheap to buy – for example, the 1955 *Traditional Jazz at the Royal Festival Hall* on Decca is £20, *Slipstream – the Best of British Jazz Funk* 2 LPs on Beggars Banquet is £15, 1972 *Jazz in Britain 68–69* on Decca £25, and the 1957 *Third British Festival of Jazz* on Tempo just £12.

Value for Money – Northern Soul makes natural compilations. The LP Record Collector, *on Destiny, is £25,* The Northern Soul Story *provides 16 double LPs, but, best of all,* Sound of the Grapevine *contains over £3,500 worth of desirable singles material for only £20!*

Labels

The record labels themselves also have important histories and products. The *Best from Buddah* ($15) featured Ohio Express and The 1910 Fruitgum Co., and mirrored its phenomenal 1967 launch with these artists by achieving $5.8 million in its first year. *The Deram Golden Pops* ★ 1968 sampler is £100, but more successful was EMI's progressive label Harvest (home of Pink Floyd) – it released a 1971 *Harvest Bag* (£12) and earlier 1969 promo-only *Harvest Sampler of the Initial 4 June Releases* (£80). Other promo-only samplers include George Harrison's 1976 *Dark Horse Records* (£40), the 1959 *Del-Fi Album Sampler* ★ ($100 in green vinyl), which includes Richie Valens, and *ABC Album Release Sampler* – made up of 2 LPs that feature Don Everly, B.B. King, and Dionne Warwick ($12).

Sue Records was founded in 1957 as a home for R&B. Most famously it attracted Ike and Tina Turner, but its full history is covered on *The Sue Story* (four 1960s compilation records worth approximately £50 each). A 1965 *Sue Sampler* ★ record that was meant for clubs and has no sleeve, type labels, or data sheet now fetches £100. The famed UK Indie label Stiff Records traded in compilations such as *Stiffs Love Stiffs* (£12), *A Bunch of Stiff Records* (£12), and the 1978 *Be Stiff* tour LP (£12). Phil Spector's 1981 9-LP box set *Wall of Sound* is worth £45, but his 1960s *Phil Spector Spectacular* ★ promo-only compilation for DJs, on Philles, which included a signed letter, today fetches a stunning $7,500 (this drops to $6,000 without the letter).

Regular promotion compilations were issued by labels in order to generate professional interest. For example, a March 1957 *Capitol New Album Preview* ★ 2-LP set is $100 and this includes Gene Vincent, Les Baxter, and, for some reason, The Glasgow Police Pipe Band. There are several hundred Capitol promo releases (each worth $20 on average), and many RCA ones – the *RCA No. 4 – untitled* ★ features Elvis Presley and Tommy Dorsey, and is $1,500, while the No.10 is $1,200. Some of these are EPs, but if they include Elvis then they still fetch $1,000 each today

Leadership Trophies – An 8-EP promo box set called RCA Sound of Leadership *is now worth $2,200; to celebrate an RCA executive, 50 copies of* Robert W. Sarnoff – 25 years of RCA Leadership * were made, featuring John F. Kennedy, Toscanini, Bowie, and Presley (worth $2,000 today).*

COUNTRY

If you have a collector's spirit then this could be just the challenge for you. The high-profile Country names such as Glen Campbell, Johnny Cash, Faith Hill, and Garth Brooks should be avoided as they are the modern popularists whose work is more Pop than Folk. This means they have sold far too many to be attractive to collectors and have also appeared frequently on CD.

If you look into any of the areas of Country that are more suitable for collectors, then you will automatically be plunged into American social history. With roots in travelling minstrels and Folk, Country echoed real-life sentiments – at least up until the '70s explosion of white middle-class Country with the likes of Kenny Rogers or John Denver. The USA correctly celebrates the old traditional music roots and, rather than sweeping them away as being old-fashioned, they are being perpetually revitalized by traditionalists from each generation. Ironically, it is in fact Europe that most respects Country talent – in Germany there are many "American"-style Country bands, such as Truck Stop, that have even replicated US Country-style LP covers. So Country records aren't restricted to American shores, and the vast majority of the material is highly affordable. With so many decades and styles you are spoilt for choice with collecting themes. At its extreme there are, for instance, 50 differing copies out there of Vernon Dalhart singing just one hit for various different labels.

Western Swing is fascinating, having many parallels with Jazz because it was driven by the same public urge for escapism and entertainment, and it also evolved into dance music. Western Swing would be performed at county fairs and dance halls that featured great varieties of dance styles. Again, as within Jazz, the band leader sold the show to the audience while secondary singers supported the material. Because it was very regional, bands frequently linked themselves to local radio, so there was a real camaraderie between musicians and their audiences and many of the artists' compositions relived familiar events or local people.

Modern crossover Country drifts comfortably into A.O.R. and soft-Rock formats, as well as Easy Listening. For this reason, and because it is a relatively new genre, prices of artists such as Linda Ronstadt or Larry Gatlin remain extremely low – for some far-sighted collectors this is highly attractive. Whatever strand tempts you, always remember that as a genre authenticity is paramount, and the more diluted the music style becomes the more likely it is to remain in the wings of this traditional music stage.

Small Country – During the 1980s there was a huge number of tiny Nashville labels issuing singles that rarely got noticed. Door Knob, for instance, had 100 singles that just crept into the lower chart positions. Rarity value alone will launch many such records into higher values. This is, therefore, a good collector's theme – and a sound investment.

Country *"VINYL HISTORY OF AMERICA"*

Suggested Strands

Pioneers
String Bands
Western Swing
Bluegrass
Popular

Average Record Cost

☆☆☆

Rising Stars

The Carter Family
Jimmie Rogers
Uncle Dave Macon

This is a subject of such authenticity and developments that it really deserves its own guide book. This style of music prompted a million-seller as early as 1924, and still boasts artists that achieve this regularly three quarters of a century later. If you enjoy tunes and lyrics from the heart (and taken from real life experiences), then there can be no greater choice of collecting route than Country.

Pioneers

Fiddles, banjos, mandolins, and harmonicas were the sounds of early Country, but the practitioners were far more varied. The Carter Family were hugely popular, using Folk lyrics along with skilful Country musicianship. Their early '30s singles include *On the Sea of Galilee* ★ ($200) and *Gold Watch & Chain* ★ ($150). Eccentric John Hartford, who wrote Glen Campbell's smash hit *Gently on My Mind*, threatened popularists with *They're Gonna Tear Down the Grand Ole Opry* on his 1971 LP *Aero-Plain* ($12). Eck Robertson is claimed to have made the first Country releases – six songs for Victor Records.

PIONEERS

Singles

The Carter Family *Gold Watch & Chain* ★ / *On the Sea of Galilee* ★

Vernon Dalhart *The Mississippi Flood* ★ / *Papa's Billy Goat*

The Delmore Brothers *Got the Kansas City Blues* ★

Eck Robertson *Brown Kelly Waltz* / *Great Big Taters*

LPs

The Delmore Brothers *Songs by the Delmore Brothers* ★

John Hartford *Aero-Plain*

Popularity Stakes – Vernon Dalhart had the first Country hit, The Prisoner's Song, *which in 1924 became a million-seller. The most popular US singer pre-Bing Crosby, Dalhart recorded 3,000 sides for most of the Country labels, under a variety of names.*

String Bands

Emerging out of old time music were String Bands. They were almost Jazz-like in their musical interplay, and paved the way for Bluegrass. The band names are almost reason enough to collect this area: Gid Tanner & The Skillet Lickers made *McMichen's Breakdown* ($80), while Uncle Dave Macon's band (sometimes called The Fruit Jar Drinkers) created *Don't Get Weary Children* ★ ($150) and *Save my Mother's Picture From that Sale* ($30). Do not confuse the latter with The Fruit Jar Guzzlers – their *Black Sheep of the Family* is worth $50.

STRING BANDS – all singles

The Fruit Jar Guzzlers *Cripple Creek* / *Black Sheep of the Family*

Al Hopkins and The Hill Billies *Bug in the Taters*

Uncle Dave Macon's Band (The Fruit Jar Drinkers) *Save My Mother's Picture From that Sale* ★

Gid Tanner and The Skillet Lickers *Bully of the Town No.2* / *Miss McLeod's Reel*

Bluegrass

In the 1940s Country mutated into Pop, so string band traditionalists, under the influence of Bill Monroe, developed Bluegrass. This was faster, more technical, and used

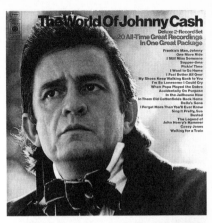

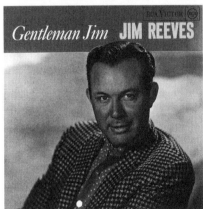

BLUEGRASS

Singles

The Fendermen
Mule Skinner Blues ★

Bill Monroe *Blue Moon of
Kentucky/Mother's Only Sleeping*

Earl Scruggs and Lester Flat
Over the Hills to the Poorhouse

LPs

The Country Gentlemen
*Bluegrass at Carnegie Hall /
Songs of the Pioneers*

Bill Monroe
Knee Deep in Bluegrass

Earl Scruggs and Lester Flat
Country Music

A permanent tussle between the traditionalists and the soft-Rock elements within Country divides both the industry and collectors; quintessentially American, it's cheap to collect in Britain.

legitimate Country sounds. Monroe's daring Bluegrass version of Elvis' *Blue Moon of Kentucky* ($20) caused the most impact, and so his backing group, The Blue Grass Boys, provided the name for this new type of music. Ex-Monroe sidemen Earl Scruggs and Lester Flat also joined in – their 1950 single *It's Too Late Now* is $30 and *Country Music* LP $40. The Fendermen's one hit *Mule Skinner Blues* ★ ($200) is the perfect union of Bluegrass and Rockabilly.

Western Swing

From the 1930s right into the '50s pre-Rock & Roll days came Western Swing – danceable and entertaining – even early Bill Haley and The Comets' records qualify. The term was reputedly coined by Spade Cooley, who was proclaimed "King of Western

WESTERN SWING

Singles

Milton Brown and His Brownies
Ida Sweet as Apple Cider

The Light Crust Doughboys
El Rancho Grande / Nancy Jane

LPs

Bob Wills and His Texas
Playboys *Old Time Favorites ★ /
Ranch House Favorites ★*

Spade Cooley and His
Orchestra *Dance-O-Rama ★*

COWBOY

Singles

Gene Autry *Bear Cat Papa ★*

Johnny Cash *I Walk the Line ★*

Tex Ritter *Jailhouse Lament*

Marty Robbins *Big Iron / El Paso*

Roy Rogers *Hi-Ho Silver*

LPs

Johnny Cash *Johnny Cash
with his Hot & Blue Guitar ★*

Marty Robbins
The Songs of Robbins ★

Hank Snow *Just Keep A-Movin ★*

POPULAR

Singles

Glen Campbell
By the Time I Get to Phoenix

Jimmie Rogers *Blue Yodel
No.12 ★ / Hobo's Meditation ★*

Kenny Rogers *That Crazy
Feeling ★ / Jole Blon ★*

LPs

Willie Nelson *Texas in my
Soul ★ / Willie Nelson ★*

Dolly Parton
Just Because I'm a Woman ★

Ricky Skaggs *Second
Generation Bluegrass*

Randy Travis *Live at the
Nashville Palace ★ / Storms of Life*

Swing". He had got film work via Roy Rogers, formed a band, and then captured a 10-year TV show. However, he suspected his second wife and Rogers of having an affair, murdered his wife, and died in prison. His records include the 1949 *Texas* single *Playboy Rag* on green vinyl ($40), and the LP *Dance-O-Rama ★* ($300). There is a huge affordable list for the equally colourful Bob Wills and His Texas Playboys. Wills had five wives, 600 musicians, 3,600 songs in his repertoire, and 20 million sales. Some of the rare records are *Old Time Favorites ★* ($500) and *Ranch House Favorites ★* ($300) from the 1950s. Popular artist Milton Brown influenced bands by introducing the electrified pedal steel guitar and the lap steel guitar.

> *Western Revival – Cowboy songs had virtually died when Hollywood revived them by using actor/singers like Roy Rogers, Tex Ritter, and Gene Autry. There were 25 cowboy chart entries in 1944–51, the biggest being Autry's* Mail Call Today, *which reached No.1 in the USA.*

Popular

The first to popularize Country was Jimmie Rogers back in the '30s . His *Blue Yodel* ($30) was a global bestseller and prompted a strange set of *Blue Yodel* releases that were numbered up to 13. *Blue Yodel No.12 ★* is a particularly rare 78' picture record that is worth $1,500. He made 100 recordings in six years and his singles include *The Southern Cannon Ball ★* ($200) and *Hobo's Meditation ★* ($100). Willie Nelson personifies a modern traditionalist – his 1957 single *No Place for Me ★* is $300, and *Texas in My Soul ★* LP $100. Watch out for *As Time Goes By* – a picture-sleeved single of Nelson and Julio Iglesias ($25); it was immediately withdrawn, so prices will rise in the future.

The talented Dolly Parton has turned Country into big business, but her early records are worth hunting out. The 1959 single *Puppy Love ★* fetches $600, and *It's Sure Gonna Hurt ★* is worth $300. There are also new traditionalists, such as Ricky Skaggs – his *Second Generation Bluegrass* with Keith Whitley is $20. He also did a version of Bill Monroe's *Uncle Pen* ($4), which suggests that Country traditions remain safe.

NEW AGE

The spirit of New Age was not an '80s fad but was born way back in 1964 with a clarinetist from New Jersey – Tony Scott. He made an LP called *Music for Zen Meditation* that delicately fused the sounds of Eastern and Western music. It survived as a kind of oddball Jazz item until marketing departments in the 1980s discovered the "New Age" phenomenon. The disillusioned Scott had long gone to Italy, but similar blends of gentle instrumental sounds and different ethnic colours would briefly become fashionable.

While Windham Hill and Private Music were the primary homes for the 1980s output of impressive solo New Age instrumental performances, there was another influential figure. After decades of natural-world film making, Dan Gibson started releasing mood-music soundtracks called *Solitudes* – a series of LPs and CDs. Healing recordings were mainly made up of standard New Age instrumental records, but were dressed and marketed to evoke faith in their impact. Meditation records also appeared that deliberately lacked any pronounced tempo or melody that might distract the listener.

Within the strictly instrumental area, all manner of tiny subgroups exist, such as Ambient, which used lots of echo and special effects. Ethnic Fusion blended any two or more musical styles, while Neo-classical contained Classical pieces that were revisited by late 20th-century thinking. Other subgroups include Electronic, Techno-Tribal, and even Minimalism.

It is virtually impossible to provide benchmark values for New Age records simply because no one wants to collect them at the moment, and most can be picked up for small change. Who knows, this could be just the moment to collect, ahead of a rise in interest. Certainly the existence of many ignored records with inevitably low pressing-runs is in keeping with collectable tastes. Another adage about what makes certain records more collectable relates to the appeal of the record sleeves: certain Windham Hill LP releases are truly worthy of hanging on the wall, and could therefore become collectables of the future.

Second Home – Many New Age albums lack profile as the music is intended to soothe not impose. However, there has been a windfall to their philosophy – movie music – as directors appreciate skilful mood-setting without intrusion. Brian Eno, Vangelis, Tangerine Dream, and even Mike Oldfield, have all written for this market.

New Age *"SO CHEAP, PRICES AREN'T LISTED"*

Suggested Strands
Calming
Virtuoso
Electronic

Average Record Cost
☆

A journalistic phrase for anything of a reflective nature to come out of the 1980s, "New Age" was tarnished by many ungifted opportunists who viewed simple, sparse recordings as short-cuts to stardom. At the moment this is an unfashionable, and therefore cheap, area of vinyl collecting.

Calming

Clannad fed popularist New Age ideals with TV's *Theme From Harry's Game* single and the LP *Sirius*. Enya left the band and delivered the solo hit-single *Orinoco Flow* and the 1987 album *Enya*. Little-known Claire Hamill's LP *Voices* uses layered voices instead of instruments, while Scottish Christian band Iona creates positive yet ethereal moods – the 1978 LP *Iona* is now £35. Haunting textured dreamscapes feature on Lucia Hwong's LPs – the first, *House of the Sleeping Beauties*, is the best. Ancient Future combine contemporary and ancient music styles.

Virtuoso

William Ackerman founded Windham Hill in 1976 and it was the first and leading New Age label. His initial LP, *In Search of the Turtle's Navel,* was privately funded, while label mates included George Winston who made a seasonal trilogy, with *Autumn* giving Windham Hill its first bestseller. Mark Isham came from Jazz to record nine Windham Hill LPs.

Electronic

Andreas Vollenweider redesigned the harp to create Grammy-winning records such as *Behind the Gardens ... Behind the Wall*. Peter Baumann left Tangerine Dream and founded a New Age label, Private Music, which created abstract electronic LPs like the 1973 *Atem* (£15). He signed friend Patrick O'Hearn, who made the LP *Ancient Dreams*, while Yanni's romantic compilation *Reflections of Passion* sold over a million copies. Jean-Michel Jarre offered undemanding compositions but excessive stage shows.

CALMING

Singles

Clannad
Theme From Harry's Game

Enya *Orinoco Flow*

LPs

Ancient Future *Dreamchaser / Natural Rhythms / Quiet Fire*

Clannad *Magical Ring / Sirius*

Enya *Enya / Watermark*

Claire Hamill
Touch Paper / Voices

Lucia Hwong *Secret Luminescence*

Iona *Beyond These Shores*

VIRTUOSO – all LPs

William Ackerman *Imaginary Roads / Past Light*

Mark Isham *Tibet / We Begin*

George Winston *December / Winter into Spring*

ELECTRONIC – all LPs

Jerry Goodman *Ariel / On the Future of Aviation*

Jean-Michel Jarre *Rendezvous*

Patrick O'Hearn *Ancient Dreams*

Tangerine Dream *Alpha Centauri / Atem / Zeit 2 LPs*

Andreas Vollenweider
Caverna Magica / Down to the Moon / White Winds

Yanni *Reflections of Passion*

Bridging Styles – Japanese hi-tech ace Tomita fused New Age and Cassical for his award-winning electronic treatments, such as 1975's The Firebird Suite, *the 1976* Holst: The Planets, *and multi-Grammy-nominated* Snowflakes Are Dancing. *His success led to gigs for up to 80,000 fans.*

STAGE MUSICALS

Contemporary stage musicals may appear to many people to be a succession of expensively marketed exercises draped in a single memorable song, but it has not always been so. During the heyday of the musical, song after song in a show would be popular – in fact between 1945's *Song of Norway* and 1964's *Hello Dolly* no less than 12 musical albums reached the very top of America's album chart. These lavish productions were prime showcases for composers, and each song would be recorded time and time again by major artists. The fame of each production grew further with Hollywood's film interpretations.

With industry switches from 78's to 45's, and from LPs to CDs, masters with minority sales often got dropped from production, which places many musical records in an increasingly rarified status. However, the collector's market is currently very flat. To the newcomer being faced with dozens of records that have the same title is extremely confusing. It's important to understand that "Original Cast" recordings are normally (not always) stage, and may be audience inclusive, while "Studio Cast" LPs are frequently dressed to look like the former but are really standard studio output. There are also quantities of albums that showcase a musical but add in rival shows' standard songs to make them different. However, prices are generally the same throughout. In the case of the 1927 production of *Show Boat,* the current collector's listings reveal three "Original Cast" LPs, 17 "Soundtrack" versions, nine "Original Revival Cast" LPs, 14 "Studio Cast" LPs, and a "London Studio Cast" LP. They come as EPs, boxed sets of EPs, 78' albums, mixed compilations, as part of a series called *Ed Sullivan Presents Songs and Music of …* , plus Jazz interpretations, and three-LP sets including the rejected "London Cast" – basically a 30-year release span that is anything from $8 to $30 in value. If your love affair is with a single major musical, then an entire collection awaits you. One of the most interesting strands to collect revolves around the output of the great composers, such as Cole Porter, George Gershwin, Rodgers and Hart, or Rodgers and Hammerstein.

Phoney Sound – Most records are similarly priced, but "Rechanneled Stereo" versions are cheaper. These were electronically simulated mono recordings that offered a "stereo" effect. Some like them, but many scorn them, and prices tend to support their unfavoured status. When S.E. is used in parentheses ahead of catalogue numbers it means "Stereo is Electronic".

Stage Musicals *"AFFORDABLE ESCAPISM"*

Suggested Strands
Landmark Shows
Long Runs
Most Expensive

Average Record Cost
☆☆

Rising Stars
Jeeves London Cast
The Pajama Game
Original Cast

LANDMARK SHOWS

LPs
Man of La Mancha Studio
Cast, Buena Vista

My Fair Lady Modern Jazz
Performances, Contemporary

Of Thee I Sing Original Revival
Cast, Capitol, boxed set of 78's

Oklahoma! Original Cast
Vol.1 & 2, Decca, 8 78's

Porgy and Bess Jazz
Renditions, Bethlehem

Show Boat Original Cast,
RCA Victor

EPs
Of Thee I Sing Original Revival
Cast, Capitol

West Side Story Original Cast,
4 EPs, Columbia

LONG RUNS

LPs
Cabaret Original London
Cast, CBS

Damn Yankees Original
Cast, RCA

Fiddler on the Roof Original
London Cast, CBS

Guys and Dolls
London Cast, Brunswick

Stage Musicals represent a different kind of vinyl collecting, as it is possible to concentrate on one single classic show yet still be hunting down more than 50 separate records. The classic composers also make a good collecting theme, as do the central show stars and even a specific theatre's output. With long-running shows there are sometimes key cast changes, which prompt further record releases, and classic songs naturally attract other stars to make studio recordings of the material.

Landmark Shows
This really is too big a topic to cover extensively but any important list of shows that helped mould the stage musical would have to start with *Show Boat*, which opened at New York's Ziegfeld Theatre in December 1927. This introduced interpretation and artistry into what had previously been simple stage-music entertainment. There are 44 recordings of this show listed – the most expensive is a 10" LP shared with the *Cat and the Fiddle* production ($25). The next significant landmark was *Of Thee I Sing* – George and Ira Gershwin's anti-political satire that opened on Broadway in 1931 and won the first musical Pulitzer Prize. A 1952 boxed set of 78's of the Original Revival Cast is worth $45. Folk opera *Porgy and Bess* was savaged by critics when it opened in 1935, and it closed

> *Consolation Prize – Child star Julie Andrews went on to conquer Broadway with* My Fair Lady *but a nervous Warner's chose Audrey Hepburn for the movie – substituting her voice with Marni Nixon's. Although disappointed, Andrews went on to star in* Mary Poppins *and* The Sound of Music.

after 142 performances, but cast recordings crusaded the music and the 1942 revival was a massive hit. There are now over 74 different recordings, each worth around $10. The classic *Oklahoma!* redefined stagecraft but was actually based on a failed play. Richard Rodgers teamed up with the older, unsuccessful Oscar Hammerstein II and eventually delivered $100 million to the investors. There are 75 recorded versions of the stage and movie versions – the best is the 1943 Original Decca Cast Vol.1, which includes six 78's ($20). Volume 2 has just two 78's but features tracks not on the normal recordings ($45). Other musical milestones include *My Fair Lady*; there are over 100 separate recordings of this, including Italian and

Hair Original Cast, RCA Victor

Hello Dolly Original London Cast, RCA Victor

How to Succeed in Business Original London Cast, RCA Victor

The King and I Original London Cast, Philips

The Music Man Original London Cast, RCA

The Pajama Game Original London Cast, RCA

EPs

Annie Get Your Gun Original cast, Decca

South Pacific Original London Cast, Columbia

MOST EXPENSIVE – all LPs

Athenian Touch ★ Original Cast, Broadway East – Mercury

Be My Guest ★ X.C.T.V.

Body in the Seine ★ Private Label – Alden-Shaw

Breakfast at Tiffany's ★ Original Cast, S.P.M.

Clownaround★ Original Cast, RCA Victor

Cradle will Rock ★ Original Cast, American Legacy

Dancing Years ★ Original London Cast, RCA Victor

Jeeves ★ Original London Cast, M.C.A.

Parade ★ Original Cast, Kapp

Paris '90 ★ Original Cast, Columbia

Mrs. Patterson ★ Original Cast, RCA Victor

Top Banana ★ Original Cast, Columbia

WAA-MU Show ★ RCA Victor

Wedding in Paris ★ Original London Cast, Parlophone

Spanish shows. The Original London Cast version on CBS is $30 and the *Modern Jazz Performances of ... with André Previn* is $60. Leonard Bernstein's Jazz-influenced classic *West Side Story* has a huge selection of recordings all under $15, although the Original Cast 1958 version, on four boxed EPs, is $20. *Man of La Mancha* included the classic song *Impossible Dream*; the Buena Vista version had a bound booklet ($30), another had cut-outs ($20–40 depending on condition), and there is even a Mexican Cast version on Decca ($20).

Long Runs

At the height of musical records' popularity, sales closely depended on long-running shows for promotion. In the late '70s *Fiddler on the Roof* was top with over 3,000 performances (Original London Cast, $35), then *Hello Dolly* with 2,844 (Original London Cast, £20). Others who later dominated include *South Pacific* (Original London Cast EP with Mary Martin singing $55), *Hair* ($12, or Original Japanese Cast LP $25), Barbra Streisand's Cast LP of *Funny Girl* ($30), Yul Brynner in *The King and I* (Original Cast LP $85), *Guys and Dolls* (1950 London Cast LP on Brunswick $25 – US has differing artwork), and Judi Dench in *Cabaret* (1968 CBS release $65 – same year reissue on Embassy just $25).

Most Expensive

Shows that survived on local audience catchments naturally highlight UK/US taste differences, which makes standardized pricing complex. However, certain shows do command reasonable money. *Athenian Touch* ★ by the 1964 Original Cast on Broadway East is $160. A much earlier show from the same production team was *Body in the Seine* ★; on a private label it never got staged, but the 1955 LP is worth $400. Other recordings to look for include The Lloyd Webber/Alan Ayckbourn show *Jeeves* ★ (Original London Cast $250 but £50 in the UK), Eartha Kitt in *Mrs. Patterson* ★ (1954 Original Cast LP, RCA Victor is $150), and *Breakfast at Tiffany's* ★ (Original Cast, S.M.P. label [The Society for Preservation of Musicals] with Mary Tyler Moore and Richard Chamberlain is $150).

> *Extra Value – A background dancer in a 1960 Northwestern University WAA-MU Show ★ on RCA Victor was in fact the future Ann-Margret (Olsen), which makes it $150. The year before* Be My Guest ★ *by New Trier High School on X.C.T.V. featured Ann-Margret singing* Heat Wave – *worth $200.*

GLOSSARY

Acetate A soft lacquered reference-pressing, usually cut at recording studios.

A.O.R. Abbreviation for Adult-Orientated Rock – a non-threatening variant of Rock.

Audiophile Disc A limited run of a record pressing using high-grade materials.

Avant-Garde A semi-free form of Jazz.

Bebop The 1940s beginnings of modern Jazz.

Big Band Jazz Large Jazz line-ups that used disciplined arrangements.

Blaxploitation A form of Funk, a bass-heavy post-Soul style.

Bluegrass Fast, technical, form of Country music.

Blues Associated with various music styles but the lyrics always express struggles with life.

Boogie-Woogie A 1930s popular Jazz form that has characteristic piano driving rhythms.

Bootleg Illegal or counterfeit records of material, frequently live concerts, not sanctioned for public sale – at their most dangerous when passed off as highly collectable singles.

Brit Invasion The substantial influx of British Beat groups that led up to The Beatles' impact on the USA.

British R&B The 1950s UK absorption of Chicago R&B styles.

Coloured Vinyl Colouring vinyl was used as a spur to sales from the 1950s; includes single colours through to valuable, unofficial multi-coloured factory one-offs.

Company Sleeves Paper singles covers that display a company ID.

Cool Jazz Soft, melodic, American West Coast Jazz form.

Country Umbrella term for a rural music style, later infused into Rock.

Cover Recordings Generally refers to secondary recordings of a successful chart record by lesser acts. However, in the 1950s UK stars such as Marty Wilde launched careers by covering existing American hits.

Deep Groove A circular manufacturing indent beneath a record's label, particularly valued on Blue Note records.

Demo See DJ records. Also used as a name for basic recordings showcasing new material.

Disco Short, fashionable 1970s dance-based repetitive music.

DJ Records Advanced copies of records that are about to go on release to the public. Generally higher-grade pressings, they often have different labels with "Promo copy – not for sale" or an enlarged "A" (for Advance copy) to denote the important side. Sometimes they even feature just one song on both sides.

D.M.M. Abbreviation for Direct Metal Master, from which the vinyl is pressed.

Doo Wop Infectious, close-harmony singing style.

Dub Caribbean re-mixing of music that removes the vocals and accentuates the rhythm tracks.

Elevator Music Smooth, background music.

Exotica Adventurous, ethnic-tinged form of Easy Listening.

Flip-Backs 1960s LP covers with glued flaps on the rear.

Folk Rock A '60s fusion of traditional Folk music and the emerging Rock style.

Fusion A blending of music styles, most frequently within Jazz.

Gatefold Generally, LP sleeves that fold out and sometimes house two LPs.

Half-speed Mastering A final pre-pressing stage of fine-tuning the sound, which is performed at a slower speed to gain maximum quality.

Inserts Photos, press releases, and give away postcards found within record sleeves.

Laminated Covers Covers that have a thin clear film, which creates a gloss effect.

Lounge Largely American-style Easy Listening.

Matrix number A company product ID in mixed numbers and letters found on a label and printed or scratched into the run-off area of the vinyl disc.

New Age An introspective style of music, usually calming and based on nature.

Northern Soul The UK nightclub adoption of early American Dance music.

Picture Disc Laminated images sandwiched within clear vinyl records. First used by RCA Victor in the 1930s, they were highly fashionable in the '80s.

Picture Sleeves Paper record covers with images printed on them, as though they are mini-LPs; generally used for 45's and a few 12" singles; they can add significant value.

Prog Rock Mid-'60's to mid-'70s exploratory Rock form.

Promo Records See DJ Records.

Psychedelic Used to be linked to US West Coast hippy cultures but also used to refer to some now largely forgotten British bands.

Punk An overused umbrella term for the many and varied non-conformist '70s Rock bands.

Ragtime Infectious, popular, southern Jazz music.

Reprocessed Stereo Cosmetic stereo electronically processed from mono.

Rhythm & Blues Important transitional style from Jazz to Rock & Roll.

Ska The '60s precursor to Reggae.

Skiffle A style that merged into Pop after its own brief fashion, and used primitive home instrumentation.

Soul 1970s US popular club-based music movement.

Surf 1960s American West Coast Pop that had a distinctive guitar sound.

Test Pressings Factory-generated trial-run records with plain white labels. These can be valuable, particularly if the commercial pressing didn't proceed.

Trad Jazz Highly commercial '60s UK Jazz derivative.

Tri-centres Prized triangular push-out centres found on 1950s 7" records.

Western Swing A mix of Jazz, Country, and Blues .

White Label Generally a slightly more limited, and therefore exclusive, DJ pre-release.

RECORD CARE

Records that hold memories are beyond monetary value, but because so many discs are increasing in worth, some to huge figures, it is still important to treat all the records you own with considerable care. With vulnerable inserts like paper posters or lyric sheets, and ancient cardboard sleeves perhaps covered with wafer-thin laminates, it's a case of maximum care is best.

Handling and storing records

You should always handle vinyl either on its outer edge or by the labels, and ensure you have clean hands as the body's oils only add to the problems. Records should always be stored vertically and you should also keep them well away from direct heat, sunlight, or areas with high humidity or potential damp, as fungi can easily attack the packaging or even the vinyl itself.

There are a number of choices of new, dirt-free sleeves, and frequently collectors store this freshly sleeved disc alongside the original cover, sleeve, and inserts, all within a protective PVC outer sleeve, therefore retiring the original packaging from its operational use. Naturally, equal care should be taken when playing vinyl, and the age and condition of the record player's stylus is paramount – they have limited lifespan so if you are in any doubt as to the age of yours, talk to your local audio store about a replacement.

Cleaning and restoring records

Restoration of old records is really limited to cleaning, and on this subject you will discover divergences of opinion. Commercial cleaning agents tend only to marginally improve dirty records and are almost better used if the tried and proven handwashing has failed. Most post-1950s records are made of polyvinyl, and opinions are strongly split on the use of diluted alcohol. However, a brief and gentle wash, or soft brushing, in a much-diluted lukewarm premium washing-up liquid is widely recognized as being the best course of action. Always use a clean, soft cloth, rinse it out frequently, and wipe it along the path of the grooves, keeping away from the labels. Dry records quickly and thoroughly in the same manner with a fresh cloth and stack on a dish-drying rack to finish them off. However, don't expect complete success as, ironically, many 78's are more resilient to this treatment than modern vinyl, except for early, very thick Edison examples, which do not respond well.

Nothing exists to mend a scratched or cracked disc, so all commercial or practical value will have disappeared. The one repair that can be attempted concerns warping. It is sometimes possible to "straighten" warped 78's using heat. Even though it may sound extremely radical, you can heat your oven up to 200°F and place the damaged record inside on a perfectly flat surface such as a baking tray (the record mustn't overhang it at all). Then check the record after about two and a half minutes – if it has become flat, withdraw it quickly and slide it, without touching or prodding it, onto another flat surface to cool. If it isn't flat enough you can try again, but be careful because if you heat it up too much then the game's over! A less radical way requires decent sunlight. You can sandwich the troubled 78' between thick sheets of glass, then place it in the sunlight and monitor it until it flattens. Again, a natural cooling time is required. These techniques can sometimes be applied to modern vinyl but the success rate is not as high.

UNDERSTANDING THE SUBJECT

Strangely, there are parallels between collecting recorded music and wine appreciation. The amount you get out of both has a direct correlation to the knowledge you have of a particular example's environment and lineage. A love of music in whatever form is a likely precursor to starting a collection, and I strongly recommend you take time to research your favoured area or artist before building up the collection. We have already discussed the possibilities for beginning research on the Internet, but it is always a good idea to purchase some good books on your chosen subject too. Suddenly, you'll discover that the particular type of music you've enjoyed sits like a piece of a jigsaw among a variety of subtly different styles. Reading around a subject will help you particularly with the multi-stranded genres of music such as Jazz, Rock, and Reggae, as well as with transitional ones like Soul and R&B, where the genre effectively fades in and out of existence among other similarly styled relations.

There clearly isn't the space here to attempt to recommend suitable reading for every style of music covered in the book. Instead, the list that follows reflects the sources that have been used in preparing this guide. Clearly each one contains useful material, while some are long out-of-print editions that have been sourced via the Internet. The allmusic.com website, although not a collector's site, offers a fabulous quick reference source for histories of artists and the styles under which they fall, while collectors' magazines constantly expand your knowledge through their feature material – though you may have to wait your turn for insight into your particular topic.

TOP MAGAZINE AND PRICE GUIDE REFERENCES

UK – Magazine
Record Collector Magazine, Parker Meade (Monthly)

UK – Book
Record Collector Rare Record Price Guide, Parker Meade (Annual)

USA – Magazines
Goldmine Magazine, Krause Publications (Monthly)
Discoveries Magazine, Krause Publications (Monthly)

USA – Books
Neely, Tim, *Goldmine Price Guide to 45rpm Records*, Krause Publications, 2001
Neely, Tim, *Goldmine Record Album Price Guide*, Krause Publications, 1999

Bibliography

Barrow, Steve & Dalton, Peter, *Reggae,*
Rough Guides, reprint 1998

Berendt, Joachim, *The Joachim Berendt Jazz Book*, Paladin Press, 1976

Brown, Mark, Conner, Thomas & Wooley, John,
Forever Lounge, Antique Trader Books, 1999

Brown, Tony, Kutner, Jon, & Warwick, Neil, *Complete Book of British Charts*, Omnibus Press, 2000

Buckley, Jonathan, Duane, Orla, Ellingham, Mark, & Spicer, Al, *Rock*, Rough Guides, 1999

Carr, Ian, Faithweather, Digby, & Priestley, Brian,
Jazz, Rough Guides, 2000

Carr, Roy, Case, Brian, & Deller, Fred,
The Hip, Faber and Faber, 1986

Clemente, John, *Girl Groups,*
Krause Publications, 2000

Cliffe, Peter, *Fascinating Rhythm,*
Egon Publishing, 1990

Cox, Perry & Lindsay, Joe *Official Price Guide to The Beatles Records*, House of Collectables, 1995

Docks, Les, *American Premium Record Guide 1900–1965*, Krause Publications, 1997

Feather, Leonard, *Encyclopaedia of Jazz in the Sixties*, Quartet Books, 1978

Feather, Leonard & Gitler, Ira, *Encyclopaedia of Jazz in the Seventies*, Horizon Press, 1976

Finis, Rob and Logan, Nick, *The NME Book of Rock*, Star Books, 1975

Gillett, Charlie *Rock File Vols.*, Panther Rock, 1972, 1974, 1975

Gribin, Dr. Anthony J. & Schiff, Dr. Matthew M., *Complete Book of Doo-Wop*, Krause Publications, 2000

Hardy, Phil, *The Faber Companion to 20th Century Popular Music*, Faber & Faber, revised 2001

Heggeness, Fred, *Goldmine Promo Record & CD Price Guide*, Krause Publications, 1998

Jackson, Arthur, *The Best Musicals*, Crown Publishers, 1977

Lanza, Joseph, *Elevator Music*, Picador USA, 1995

Larkin, Colin, *The Guinness Who's Who of Blues*, Guinness Publishing, 1993

Larkin, Colin, *The Virgin Encyclopedia of Dance Music*, Virgin, 1998

Larkin, Colin, *The Virgin Encyclopaedia of Eighties Music*, Virgin, 1997

Lofman, Ron, *Goldmine Celebrity Vocals*, Krause Publications, 1994

McKnight-Trontz, Jennifer, *Exotiquarium*, St Martin's Griffin, 1999

McRae, Barry, *The Jazz Handbook*, Longman Group, 1987

Murrells, Joseph, *The Daily Mail Book of Golden Discs*, McWhirter Twins, 1966

Neely, Tim, *Goldmine Country & Western Record Price Guide*, Krause Publications, 2001

Neely, Tim, *Goldmine Jazz Album Price Guide*, Krause Publications, 2000

Neely, Tim & Thompson, Dave, *Goldmine British Invasion Record Price Guide*, Krause Publications, 1997

Ogg, Alex, *Top Ten – The Irreverent Guide to Music*, Channel 4 Books, 2001

Osborne, Jerry, *Official Guide to The Money Records*, House of Collectables, 1998

Osborne, Jerry, *Official Price Guide to Elvis Presley Records*, House of Collectables, 1998

Osborne, Jerry, *Official Price Guide to Movie/TV Soundtracks/Cast Albums*, House of Collectables, 1997

Osborne, Jerry, *Various Artists Compilations*, Osborne Enterprises, 2000

Pascall Jeremy (ed.), *Story of Pop*, Phoebus Publishing, 1973

Smith, Ronald L., *Goldmine Comedy Record Price Guide*, Krause Publications, 1996

Southall, Brian, *A–Z of Record Labels*, Sanctuary Publishing, 2000

Szabla, Charles, *45rpm Picture Sleeve Price Guide*, Krause Publications, 1998

Talevski, Nick, *The Encyclopaedia of Rock Obituaries*, Omnibus Press, 1999

Unterbereger, Richie, *Music USA*, Rough Guides, 1999

Vale, V. & Juno, Andrea (ed.), *Incredibly Strange Music Vols. 1 & 2*, Re/Search Publications, 1993–94

Useful Websites

www.legends.gemm.com general vinyl site

http://picsleeves.virtualave.net/elvis.html good Elvis site

www.allmusic.com excellent record source/database

www.bigboppa.co.uk helpful early Rock & Roll and singles covers site

www.birdpages.co.uk big directory of record dealers

www.cadencebuilding.com source for Jazz and Blues, including a huge Jazz discography

www.coolandstrange.com gateway to Exotica and Lounge sites

www.ebay.com premier US auction house

www.8trackheaven.com includes a history of the format, and where to buy hardware and tapes

www.helsinki.fi/~tuschano/records huge gateway site

www.inprint.co.uk source of out-of-print books

www.intoxica.demon.co.uk dealer in Surf, Blues, 1960s music, 1970s music, and Exotica

www.jerryosborne.com publisher of US vinyl price guides

www.krause.com publisher of US vinyl price guides

www.lcv.ne.jp Bay City Rollers' fan site

www.moremusic.co.uk excellent gateway into many reference and dealer sites

www.nfo.net good Big Band database

www.recordfinders.com vinyl hunting and auctions

www.researchpubs.com good Exotica/Lounge book site

www.showandtellmusic.com vinyl and cover art

www.tracks.co.uk predominantly Beatles vinyl site

www.vinylrecords.co.uk good vinyl shop site

www.vip-24.com UK record fair site and vinyl links

www.weirdomusic.freeservers.com Exotica, Lounge, and Easy Listening news, reviews, and books

RECORD COMPANIES

The following list represents some of the leading labels favoured by vinyl collectors, with the dates they were established and some of the major artists on each label. Acquisitions, mergers, and overseas licensing scatter the key artists freely, and sometimes they feature on small satellite labels that belong to the named companies. Those starred are particularly interesting to collect because of artist rosters or the number of releases. (Artists and labels from the later CD era are not embraced.)

A&M Records 1962 *Bryan Adams, The Carpenters, The Police, Supertramp*

ABC-Dunhill 1955 *Paul Anka, Ray Charles, Steely Dan, The Mamas and Papas, Tommy Roe, The Tams, Three Dog Night*

Apple ★ 1968 *Badfinger, The Beatles, Hot Chocolate, Mary Hopkins, Billy Preston*

Arista 1975 *Aretha Franklin, Whitney Houston, The Kinks, Barry Manilow, The Alan Parson Project*

Asylum 1971 *Jackson Browne, The Byrds, The Eagles, Joni Mitchell, Linda Ronstadt*

Atco 1957 *The Bee Gees, Acker Bilk, Eric Clapton, Bobby Darin, Sonny and Cher, Yes*

Atlantic ★ 1947 *Abba, Ray Charles, The Coasters, John Coltrane, Crosby, Stills, Nash, & Young, Charlie Mingus, The Drifters, Foreigner, Genesis, Led Zeppelin, Wilson Pickett, The Rolling Stones, Sam and Dave*

Bell 1960 *The Bay City Rollers, David Cassidy, Gary Glitter, Barry Manilow, The Partridge Family, Del Shannon, Showaddywaddy*

Blue Note ★ 1939 *John Coltrane, Miles Davis, Herbie Hancock, Thelonious Monk*

Brunswick 1916 *The Andrew Sisters, The Crickets, Bing Crosby, Bill Haley, Harry James, Al Jolson, Brenda Lee, The Who, Jackie Wilson*

Buddah 1967 *Lou Christy, The Lemon Pipers, Melanie, 1910 Fruitgum Co., Ohio Express, Sha Na Na*

Cameo-Parkway 1956 *Chubby Checker, Charlie Grace, Bobby Rydell, The Tymes*

Capitol 1942 *The Beach Boys, The Beatles, Glen Campbell, Nat King Cole, Peggy Lee, Dean Martin, Tex Ritter, Frank Sinatra, Tina Turner*

Casablanca 1973 *Captain and Tennille, Kiss, Parliament, Donna Summer, The Village People*

Charisma 1969 *Genesis, Lindisfarne, Monty Python's Flying Circus, The Nice, Van der Graaf Generator*

Chess ★ 1947 *Chuck Berry, The Dells, Bo Diddley, Fontella Bass, Howlin' Wolf, Jimmie Rogers, Muddy Waters*

Chrysalis 1969 *Pat Benatar, Blondie, Billy Idol, Jethro Tull, Ten Years After, Ultravox*

Columbia 1887 *Count Basie, The Clash, Doris Day, Bob Dylan, Duke Ellington, Benny Goodman, Johnny Ray, Guy Mitchell, Simon and Garfunkel, Frank Sinatra,*

Bruce Springsteen, Barbra Streisand, Andy Williams

Coral ★ 1949 *Teresa Brewer, Buddy Holly, Debbie Reynolds, Jackie Wilson*

Decca 1929 *Louis Armstrong, Bing Crosby, The Everly Brothers, Ella Fitzgerald, Billy Fury, Jack Hylton, Al Jolson, Tom Jones, Little Richard, Vera Lynn, The Moody Blues, Roy Orbison, The Rolling Stones, The Ronettes, Tommy Steele*

Deram 1969 *Amen Corner, Honeybus, The Moody Blues, Procol Harum, Cat Stevens*

DJM 1969 *Elton John*

Dot 1951 *Pat Boone, The Chanteys, Tab Hunter, The Surfaris*

Elekra 1950 *Bread, Judy Collins, The Doors, Phil Ochs, Tom Paxton, Carly Simon*

EMI 1900 *The Animals, Kate Bush, Russ Conway, Duran Duran, Gerry and The Pacemakers, Herman's Hermits, Iron Maiden, Ruby Murray, Olivia Newton-John, Pink Floyd, Queen, Cliff Richard, Cliff Richard & The Shadows, The Rolling Stones, The Sex Pistols, T. Rex*

EMI-America 1978 *David Bowie, Kim Carnes, Sheena Easton, J Geils Band, John Waite*

Epic 1953 *Jeff Beck, The Hollies, Michael Jackson, Ozzy Osbourne, R.E.O. Speedwagon, Charlie Rich, Sly and The Family Stone, Bobby Vinton, Yardbirds*

Fontana 1960s *Joan Baez, Spencer Davis, Manfred Mann*

Geffen 1980 *Aerosmith, Cher, Elton John, John Lennon, Donna Summer*

Harvest ★ 1969 *Deep Purple, E.L.O., Barclay James Harvest, Pink Floyd, Soft Machine*

HMV 1890 *Sarah Brightman, Alma Cogan, Johnny Kidd and The Pirates, Julian Lloyd Webber, Elvis Presley, The Swinging Blue Jeans*

Immediate 1963 *Chris Farlowe, Fleetwood Mac, Humble Pie, Nico, The Small Faces.*

Invictus 1968 *Chairman of The Board, Freda Payne*

Island ★ 1962 *E.L.P., Fairport Convention, Free, Jethro Tull, Grace Jones, King Crimson, Bob Marley and The Wailers, Robert Palmer, Roxy Music, Toots and The Maytals, Traffic, U2, Stevie Winwood*

Kapp 1955 *Louis Armstrong, Cher, Brian Hyland, Jane Morgan, Roger Williams*

King 1943 *James Brown, Otis Redding, Otis Williams*

Liberty 1955 *Teressa Brewer, The Chipmunks, Eddie Cochran, Fats Domino, Jan and Dean, Ricky Nelson, Bobby Vee*

London ★ 1947 *Chuck Berry, Del Shannon, The Everly Brothers, Little Richard, Roy Orbison, The Rolling Stones, The Tornados*

MCA 1962 *Neil Diamond, Elton John, Meat Loaf, Tom Petty, Olivia Newton-John*

Mercury 1947 *The Big Bopper, Bruce Channel, The Platters, Rod Stewart, Tears for Fears, 10cc*

MGM 1946 *The Animals, Connie Francis, Herman's Hermits, The Osmonds, Conway Twitty*

Modern 1945 *Etta James, John Lee Hooker, Lightnin' Hopkins*

Monument 1958 *Kris Kristofferson, Willie Nelson, Roy Orbison, Dolly Parton*

Motown ★ 1959 *The Four Tops, Marvin Gaye, Martha Reeves, Smokey Robinson, The Supremes, Mary Wells, Stevie Wonder*

Ode 1967 *Carole King, Scott McKenzie*

Okeh 1918 *Louis Armstrong, The Dorsey Brothers, Major Lance, Johnny Ray, Larry Williams*

Oriele 1950s *Maureen Evans, Chas McDevitt, Nancy Wilson*

Pablo 1973 *Count Basie, John Coltrane, Ella Fitzgerald, Dizzy Gillespie, Oscar Peterson, Sarah Vaughan*

Parlophone 1920s *Louis Armstrong, The Beatles, Cilla Black, Johnny Dankworth, Charlie Drake, Duran Duran, Duke Ellington, The Fourmosts, Gerry and The Pacemakers, Nat Gonella, The Hollies, Billy J. Kramer, The Pet Shop Boys, Peter Sellers, Victor Sylvester*

Philadelphia International 1971 *Thelma Houston, Harold Marvin and The Blue Notes, Wilson Pickett, Dusty Springfield*

Philips 1950 *Doris Day, The Four Seasons, Johnny Ray*

Philles ★ 1961 *The Crystals, The Righteous Brothers, The Ronettes, Ike and Tina Turner*

Polydor 1924 *James Brown, Gloria Gaynor, Jimi Hendrix, James Last, The New Seekers, The Osmonds, Slade, Vangelis*

Pye 1953 *Kenny Ball, Chris Barber, Brotherhood of Man, Max Bygraves, Petula Clark, Lonnie Donegan, Val Doonican, Emile Ford and The Checkmates, The Kinks, Jimmy Young*

Qwest 1982 *Patti Austin, James Ingram, Quincy Jones*

Rak 1969 *Hot Chocolate, Suzi Quatro, Smokey Robinson, Kim Wilde*

RCA 1929 *David Bowie, Perry Como, Sam Cooke, John Denver, Tommy Dorsey, Benny Goodman, Hall and Oates, Mario Lanza, Glenn Miller, Elvis Presley, Lou Reed, Jim Reeves, Neil Sedaka, Fats Waller*

Reprise 1960 *The Beach Boys, Freddy Cannon, Petula Clarke, Sammy Davis, The Kinks, Dean Martin, Joni Mitchell, Frank Sinatra, Nancy Sinatra*

Rocket 1976 *Blue, Kiki Dee, Elton John, Cliff Richard, Neil Sedaka*

RSO 1970s *The Bee Gees, Eric Clapton, Yvonne Elliman, Frankie Valli, Film soundtracks of* Saturday Night Fever *and* Grease

Savoy ★ 1942 *Big Maybelle, Coleman Hawkins, Johnny Otis, Ester Phillips*

Shire 1966 *Madonna, The Pretenders, The Ramones, The Seachers, The Smiths, Talking Heads*

Speciality ★ 1946 *Roy Milton, Little Richard, Lloyd Price, The Soul Stirrers*

Stax ★ 1961 *Booker T. & The M.G.'s, Isaac Hayes, Wilson Pickett, Otis Redding, Sam and Dave*

Stiff 1976 *Elvis Costello, Ian Dury, Dave Edmunds, Nick Lowe, Madness, Graham Parker, Rachel Sweet*

Sugar Hill 1974 *Grandmaster Flash, Sequence, The Sugarhill Gang*

Sun ★ 1952 *Johnny Cash, Jerry Lee Lewis, Roy Orbison, Junior Parker, Carl Perkins, Elvis Presley, Rufus Thomas*

Swan Song 1975 *Bad Company, Maggie Bell, Led Zeppelin, The Pretty Things*

Top Rank late 1950s *Craig Douglas, Freddy Cannon, John Leyton, Sandy Nelson, Bert Weedon*

Track Records 1980s *The Crazy World of Arthur Brown, Jimi Hendrix, The Who*

Transatlantic 1965 *Billy Connolly, Ralph McTell, Pentangle, Gerry Rafferty*

Trojan 1968 *Ken Boothe, Jimmy Cliff, Dave and Ansell Collins, The Pioneers*

UK Records 1972 *Jonathan King, 10cc*

United Artists 1919 *Paul Anka, Shirley Bassey, Bobby Goldsboro, Don McLean, Gerry Rafferty, Soundtracks for James Bond and The Beatles'* Hard Days Night

Vanguard 1950 *Louis Armstrong, Joan Baez, Tom Paxton, The Rooftop Singers, Pete Seeger, The Weavers*

Vee Jay 1953 *The Beatles, The Dells, The Four Seasons, John Lee Hooker, Frank Ifield, The Impressions, The Staple Singers*

Vertigo late 1960s *Black Sabbath, Colosseum, Status Quo, Thin Lizzy*

Verve ★ 1957 *Count Basie, Ella Fitzgerald, Stan Getz, Dizzy Gillespie, Richie Havens, Mothers of Invention, Lauro Nyro, Charlie Parker, Oscar Peterson, The Righteous Brothers, Jimmy Smith*

Virgin 1972 *Culture Club, Peter Gabriel, Genesis, The Human League, Mike Oldfield, The Sex Pistols, Tangerine Dream*

Warner Bros 1958 *America, The Doobie Brothers, The Everly Brothers, Fleetwood Mac, The Grateful Dead, Bob Newhart, Henry Mancini, Alan Sherman, Paul Simon, Frank Sinatra, Connie Stevens, James Taylor, Van Halen*

Windham Hill 1976 *William Ackerman, Peabo Bryson, Barry White, George Winston*

INDEX

240 ACKNOWLEDGMENTS

Such a distillation of detail represents months of work for the whole team. Apart from thanking Jane Aspden and Anna Sanderson for the opportunity to create this book, I particularly wish to thank my Project Editor, Emily Anderson, for her unfailing enthusiasm, care, and good humour, the editor Claire Musters for helping to bring it all together, and Sue Farr for undertaking the huge index. My gratitude also to Executive Art Editor Rhonda Fisher, designers Colin Goody and Vicky Bevan, and photographer Steve Tanner for dressing my text in such fine style. My unreserved thanks to all those experts whose work I've absorbed (see pages 226–227), and to Ruth Edge and Greg Burge who graciously opened up the wonderful EMI Archives to provide rare sleeves, as did Keith Skues, Moss Taylor, and Alan Murchison. I have much appreciated general advice from expert Doug Price, whose Bigboppa website is listed (see p227). The publishers would also like to thank Simon Anderson for his valuable contribution. All record covers reproduced in the book are the sole copyright of the record company. Photography by Steve Tanner, copyright of Octopus Publishing Ltd, unless stated otherwise.

Half-Title: Old Grey Whistle Test Badge/JS; **2:** Hulton Archive/Corbis; **6:** *Tommy*/Ode/JS, *Mahler's Song of the Earth*/Columbia/JS; **10:** *Lovable*/London/JS, *To Know Him, Is To Love Him*/London/JS; **11:** *Sacred Songs*/Philips/JS; **12:** Red Light Zone/Jive/JS, *Welcome to L.A.*/Stork/JS; **13:** *Hear the Beatles Tell All*/Vee-Jay/JS, *Godbluff*/Charisma/JS; **13:** *Since You've Been Gone* x4: Cherie & Marie Currie/Capitol/JS; Rainbow/Polydor/JS, Clout/Carrere/JS, Russ Ballard/Abbey Road Studios/JS; **20:** *Smokey*/EMI Studios/JS, *No More the Fool*/Abbey Road Studios/JS; **22:** Record 1: Side 1/JS, Test Pressing/JS; **24:** *Sail Away*/EMI/JS, *Liar*/Date/JS, *Winning*/Columbia/JS, *Sneakin' Sally*/Island/JS; **30:** *Night of the Quarter Moon*/Capitol/JS; **58:** *Lowrider*/United Artists/JS; **60:** *Black & White Minstrel Show*/HMV/JS; **65:** 15 singles sleeves/Various/JS; **66:** *Down to Earth*/Polydor/JS, *Love is a Game*/Jet/JS, *Empty Words*/EMI/JS, *Rage to Love*/MCA/JS, *Loving the Alien*/EMI America/JS; **67:** *Wild Guitars*/Capitol/EMI Archives, *The Best of Martin Denny*/Liberty/EMI/EMI Archives, *Whipped Cream and Other Delights*/A&M/JS, *Uniquely Mancini*/RCA Victor/KS, *Down Drury Lane*/Pye/Golden Guinea/JS, *Peace in the Valley*/RCA/JS; **68:** *Tenderly*/London/JS, *Wee Small Hours*/Capitol/JS, *Showcase of Hits*/ Philips/KS, *Greatest Hits*/CBS/KS, *Movin' 'n' Groovin'*/London/KS, *Connie Francis Sings Italian Favorites*/ MGM/EMI Archives; **69:** *Here I Go Again*/Mercury/JS, *The Blue Angel*/HMV/AM; *Samantha Fox*/Jive/JS, *Marilyn*/20th Century/ EMI/EMI Archives, *Make Love to Me*/London/KS, *And God Created Woman*/Stemra/ JS; **70:** *Keynsham*/Sunset/United Artists/JS, *Just Folks … A Firesign Chat*/Butterfly/JS, *At the Drop of a Hat*/Angel/JS, *Bob Newhart*/Warner Bros/MT, *Meet The Rutles*/Warner Bros/KS, The Best of Sellers/Parlophone/EMI Archives; **71:** *Hey You!*/BBC/JS, *Top TV Themes*/EMI/JS, *Six-Five Special*/ Parlophone/EMI Archives, *Thunderbirds Are Go*/United Artists/EMI Archives, *Dr Who – The Music*/BBC/EMI Archives, *Dick Emery Sings*/Pye/JS; **72:** *Saturday Night Fever*/RSO/JS, *The Magic of Boney M*/Atlantic/JS, *Cruisin'*/Mercury/JS, *Star Wars Disco*/ Splash/JS; **74:** *Halfway to Paradise*/Decca/KS; **75:** *The Beginning of Doves*/Receiver/KS; **76:** *Air Conditioning*/Warner Bros/JS; **77:** *Still & Under the Sky*/Manticore Records & Boydell Press/JS, *The Alan Parsons Project*/Arista/JS; **100:** *Free Me*/Polydor UK/JS, *Free Me*/ Polydor USA/JS, *McVicar*/Polydor/JS; **105:** Eddie Cochran/Liberty/JS, *Elvis' Golden Records*/RCA/KS, *In the Spotlight*/Pye Int./KS, *Live in London*/Antic/WEA/JS, *The Explosive Little Richard*/Columbia/EMI Archive, *Rhythm & Blues*/OPG/Ian Booth photography/Memory Lane; **106:** *Led Zeppelin*/Atlantic/JS, *Sticky Fingers*/Rolling Stones/JS, *Goodbye*/Polydor/JS, *1984*/Warner Bros/JS, *Highway to Hell*/ Atlantic/JS, *Burn*/EMI/JS; **107:** *Fleetwood Mac*/Reprise/JS, *Candy-O*/Electra/JS, *Buckingham-Nicks*/Polydor/JS, *Hotel California*/ Asylum/JS, *Escape*/CBS/JS, *Buffalo Springfield*/Atco/JS; **108:** *Genesis Collection Volumes 1 & 2*/Charisma/B&C/JS, *The Piper at the Gates of Dawn*/EMI/EMI Archives, *Brain Salad Surgery*/Manticore/WEA/JS, *Tales of Topographical Oceans*/Atlantic/JS, *War of the Worlds*/CBS/JS; **109:** *Rebel Yell*/Chrysalis/JS, *The B-52's*/Island/JS, *Grip-London Lady*/UA/EMI Archives, *Neat Neat Neat*/Stiff/Island/ EMI Archives, *New Hope for the Wretched*/Stiff/JS, *Easter*/Aristra/JS, *Making Plans for Nigel*/Virgin/JS; **110:** *G.I. Blues*/RCA/JS, *James Bond 007 Themes*/Liberty/Capitol/JS, *Rocky Horror Show*/A&M/Ode/JS, *The Glenn Miller Story*/Decca/JS, *Oklahoma!*/Capitol/JS, *Lawrence of Arabia*/Colpix/Pye/JS; **111:** *From Mighty Oaks*/Decca/JS, *Missing Persons*/Komos Productions/JS; **112:** Ace Frehley/ Casablanca/JS, *Agnetha Faltskog*/Polar/Epic/JS; **115:** *Elvis Presley Story*/Watermark Inc/JS; **119:** *Burnin'*/Island/JS; **124:** *Still Trad*/ Columbia/JS, 2.19 Skiffle Group/Esquire/JS; **148:** *Chords of Fame*/A&M/JS; **155:** *Liege & Lief*/Island/JS, *Joan Baez*/Fontana/JS, *The London Muddy Waters Sessions*/Chess/JS, *The Turning Point*/Polydor/JS, *Historically Speaking, The Duke*/Parlophone/ EMI Archives, *Poll Results*/Fontana/JS, *The Fabric of Jazz*/Oriole/JS, *Preservation Hall*/Columbia/JS, *Getz/Gilberto #2*/Verve/EMI Archives, *Workin' with Miles Davis Quintet*/Prestige/JS, *The Benny Goodman Album*/HMV/EMI Archives; **162:** *Past Light*/Windham Hill/JS, *Piano Solos*/Windham Hill/JS, *Voices*/Coda/JS, *Tideline*/Windham Hill/JS; **163:** *Billy*/CBS/JS, *Salad Days*/CBS/JS, *A Little Night Music*/CBS/JS, *Cabaret*/CBS/JS, *Jesus Christ Superstar*/MCA/JS, *Annie*/CBS/JS; **164:** *Careful*/Capitol/Cover: Duggie Fields/JS, *Arc of a Diver*/Island/Cover: Tony Wright/JS, *Listen*/Chrysalis/Cover: Alexander Vethers/JS, *Rio*/EMI/Cover: Nagel/JS, *Voyage of the Acolyte*/Phonogram/Cover: Kim Poor/JS, *Silk Torpedo*/Atlantic/Cover: Hipgnosis/JS, *Bundles*/EMI/Cover: Reg Cartwright/JS; **165:** *Once A Rebel*/Abbey Road Studios/EMI/JS, *Stigwood Music*/Gibb Publishing – RSO Music/Chappell/JS, *Imagine*/Apple/JS; **166:** *God Save the Queen*/A&M/Beanos, *God Save the Sex Pistols*/UK/JS, *Shoulder to Shoulder*/Safari/JS, *I Will Be There*/Food for Thought/JS; **167:** *The Starlit Hour*/Brunswick/JS, *Love Vigilantes*/Cooking Vinyl/JS, *Quintessence*/Island/JS; **168:** *Woman's Hour*/ BBC/JS, *History of Offshore Radio*/I.B.S./JS, *The Sounds of Time*/Oriole/JS, *Disasters*/BBC/JS, *Pirate Radio*/K-Tel/KS, *Wakey Wakey*/ Columbia/KS; **170:** *The Place I Love*/A&M/JS; **197:** *Hotter than July*/Motown/EMI/JS; **201:** *Revolver*/Parlophone/JS, *Hard Day's Night*/Parlophone/JS, *Yellow Submarine*/Apple/EMI/JS, *Oldies*/Parlophone/EMI/JS, *Help*/Parlophone/JS, *Sgt Pepper*/Parlophone/JS, *Abbey Road*/Apple/EMI/JS, *Let It Be*/Apple/EMI/JS, *Rubber Soul*/Parlophone/JS, *Please, Please Me*/Parlophone/JS, *Beatles For Sale*/Parlophone/JS; **202:** *Complete Buddy Holly Story*/MCA/JS, *Everly Brothers' Original Greatest Hits*/CBS/JS, 24 Original Hits/ Bell/Atlantic/JS, *The Teenagers*/Gee/Roulette/JS, *Pet Sounds*/Capitol/AM, *ABC*/Tamla Motown/EMI/EMI Archives; **203:** *Autumn '66*/ Fontana/JS, *Go Now*/London/JS, *The Singles*/Epic/JS, *Animalisms*/Decca/JS, *The Kink Kontroversy*/Pye/JS, *The Shadows*/Columbia/JS, *Outlandos d'Amour*/A&M/JS, *The Miracle*/Parlophone/JS, *It's The Searchers*/Pye Popular/JS; **204:** *Fantasy*/Ode/A&M/JS, *Court and Spark*/Asylum/WEA/JS, *Street Hassle*/Arista/JS, *Honky Chateau*/DJM/JS, *Born to Run*/CBS/JS, *The Freewheelin'*/CBS/AM; **205:** *Cilla Sings a Rainbow*/Parlophone/JS, *Ev'rythings Coming up Dusty*/Philips/JS, *Music Makes My Day*/Pye/JS, *Plastic Letters*/ Chrysalis/JS, *Like a Virgin*/Sire/JS, *Crimes of Passion*/Chrysalis/JS; **206:** *Thriller*/Epic/JS, *Atlantic Crossing*/Warner Bros/JS, *We Want Billy*/Decca/EMI Archives, *Aladdin Sane*/RCA Victor/JS, *Cliff's Hit Album*/Columbia/JS, *Roger Daltrey*/Track/JS; **207:** *Zebop*/ Columbia/JS, 461 Ocean Boulevard/RSC/JS, *Tubular Bells*/Virgin/JS, *Equinoxe*/Polydor/JS, *Heaven and Hell*/RCA/JS, *Chartbusters*/ Fontana/KS, *Blow By Blow*/Epic/JS; **208:** *Polka Party*/Starr/JS, *Reggae Chart Busters*/Trojan/JS, 30 Smash Hits of the War Years/ Crest/JS, *Top of the Pops*/Hallmark/Pickwick/JS, *Juke Box Jive*/K-Tel/JS, *Dick Clark*/Buddah/JS; **213:** *The American Dream*/ London/JS; **213:** *Spirit*/RCA/JS, *The World of Johnny Cash*/CBS/JS, *Gentleman Jim*/RCA Victor/JS, *High Time*/Monument/JS

Key to Sources: JS: John Stanley Collection; KS: Keith Skues Collection; AM: Alan Murchison Collection; MT: Moss Taylor Collection